OPEN LETTERS
TO THE
INTIMATE THEATER

AUGUST STRINDBERG

Translations and Introductions by

WALTER JOHNSON

UNIVERSITY OF WASHINGTON PRESS

SEATTLE AND LONDON

Open Letters to the Intimate Theater

HISTORICAL PLAYS OF AUGUST STRINDBERG
Translations and Introductions by Walter Johnson

Queen Christina, Charles XII, Gustav III
The Last of the Knights, The Regent, Earl Birger of Bjälbo
Gustav Adolf
The Vasa Trilogy: Master Olof, Gustav Vasa, Erik XIV
The Saga of the Folkungs, Engelbrekt

Strindberg and the Historical Drama by Walter Johnson

To Ruth Ingeborg

PREFACE

When August Strindberg's works have been as thoroughly studied for their own sake as they have been as revelations of the details of his stormy life, it will probably be clear that he is unique, at least among Scandinavian writers, in having revealed in astounding detail the secrets of his whole creative activity. It is already certain that no other Scandinavian writer has more fully put into black and white the author's intentions with his various works, his procedure in assembling his raw material, his use of the material, and his own assessment of what he created.

Although he contributed significantly to almost every kind of literature and wrote a great deal that can under no circumstances be called literature in the sense of belles-lettres, the area in which by general consensus he made his greatest contribution and on which future evaluation of him as a writer is likely to rest is drama. His importance to the drama and consequently to the theater of his own time and ours is so overwhelming that anything he wrote about drama and theater deserves serious consideration by anyone who hopes to understand modern theater. Developments during the twentieth century in both areas cannot be understood and explained if Strindberg's works are disregarded. That is a generalization that every serious student of the drama and the theater must accept.

What Strindberg wrote about drama and theater is so extensive that there is no possibility of including all of it in one volume. It is scattered throughout his letters (published and unpublished), his numerous autobiographical volumes such as all four volumes of *The Son of a Servant* (*Tjänstekvinnans son*), and many of his other works, some of which in fragment and note form have never been printed. Fortunately, a few of the most important are available in English translation — his essay on modern drama, his profoundly important preface to *Lady Julie* (or, as some translators have it, *Miss Julie*), and his preliminary note to *A Dream Play*. What appears in the letters (and he was one of the world's most industrious letter writers) and many of his other literary works, aside from the first two volumes of *The Son of a Servant*, will probably for some time be unavailable to anyone who does not read Swedish.

Strindberg's most extensive writing about drama and theater appeared in 1907 and 1908 in a series of brochures directed mainly toward the realization of one of his fondest dreams — a theater in his native Stockholm devoted exclusively to the production of his plays. The so-called open letters to the Intimate Theater were published by Björck & Börjesson and were republished in 1919 under the title *Öppna brev till Intima teatern* (*Open Letters to the Intimate Theater*) as Volume 50 of John Landquist's fifty-five-volume *Strindbergs Samlade Skrifter* (*Strindberg's Collected Works*).

The importance of this volume does not lie in the literary quality of the various parts. When Strindberg wrote the letters, his primary purpose was to teach the members of the company at the Intimate Theater the sort of things that he found it extremely difficult if not impossible to teach them orally as director or adviser. In other words, he was not producing literary art when he wrote these letters. Their importance lies in the insight they provide the reader into Strindberg as an instructor, as a man of the theater, as a dramatist in theory and practice, as a student of Shakespeare, and as a student of problems that face the creative artist within a vital area of human activity.

In presenting this American translation, I have provided an introduction to each of the five letters and supplied at the end of the book brief notes on primarily Swedish and other Scandinavian details, the explanation of which may not be readily available to those who do not read Swedish. The introductions are obviously not designed to be, for example, exhaustive studies of Strindberg as a man of the theater or of Strindberg's debt to Shakespeare.

I appreciate the help of the Swedish Institute and the Royal Library in securing illustrations.

CONTENTS

ILLUSTRATIONS

Open Letters to the Intimate Theater

FIRST LETTER

Introduction

MUCH has been made of Strindberg's lack of practical experience in
the theater before 1907, particularly by Martin Lamm [1] and some of
his disciples. They point invariably to three sets of experiences, all
three of which Strindberg discusses in some detail, the first two in his
autobiographical novel *The Son of a Servant*, and the third in various letters. Strindberg did fail when he tried out as an actor at the
Royal Theater as a youngster; his efforts at Göteborg a few years
later were futile; his attempt at founding an experimental theater in
Copenhagen, as we shall see, was unsuccessful.

But, slight as these "practical" experiences were, they were perhaps
more important than their very brevity would suggest. For Strindberg had certain qualities — a remarkable memory, a gift for acute
observation, a knack for sharp and penetrating analysis, a rich imagination that permitted him to visualize quickly and vividly, and a
great deal of common sense — that probably more than compensated
for his lack of years of painstaking labor in the theater itself. His
willingness to investigate and to learn, his eagerness to experiment,
his sense for what would go or at least might go on stage (given able
personnel and favorable conditions), and his ambition to see his own
plays presented help account for a phenomenon that has startled

3

Swedish producers and Swedish actors time and again. Strindberg plays when read have seemed to many members of both groups absolutely unsuited for the stage; when the plays have actually been tested, actors and directors have found to their amazement that Strindberg had a truly uncanny sense for theater. He wrote his plays for presentation on the stage; he was keenly aware of the limitations of the theater, but he was just as keenly aware of the fact that the theater had far greater possibilities than most theater people understood.

In 1889, after years of rarely alleviated frustration because of the failure of theater directors to read his plays with understanding and to accept them for production, Strindberg tried to do something about the matter himself. Contemplating the founding of an experimental Scandinavian theater in Copenhagen,[2] he wrote three one-act plays — *Pariah*, *The Stronger*, and *Samum* — all of them designed to meet the limitations imposed by limited resources. The director was his wife, Siri von Essen, with whom he was then barely on speaking terms, and the supporting actors were little more than amateurs. The net result can hardly be labeled anything but a fiasco — there were only two performances and a private performance of *Lady Julie* at the Student Society — not to mention Strindberg's own inner suffering and open conflict with his "troupe."

As late as 1892, Strindberg was still dreaming of establishing an experimental theater, this time in Stockholm's fashionable suburb Djursholm. No theater materialized, but Strindberg fortunately wrote a number of one-act plays in preparation, one of which is a remarkably good drama — *The Bond*. The others — *Debit and Credit*, *The First Warning*, *Facing Death*, and *Mother Love* — are not among his better plays. The failure of his effort in Denmark did not make Strindberg give up the idea of having a theater of his own. At various times in the decade or so that followed, the seemingly futile dream flared up in terms of a theater in, successively, Berlin, London, Paris, and Djurgården in Stockholm.

It was not until 1906 that Strindberg could seriously hope to see

a Strindberg theater established, and then only because a young man
in many ways remarkably like able young theater people in the
United States in our day appeared at Strindberg's door in Stockholm.
The young caller was August Falck (1882–1938),[3] a Stockholmer,
who not only was dedicated to theater but who also had some five
years of practical experience behind him. The son of a house manager at the Royal Dramatic Theater, August Falck had been a pupil
at the private Swedish Theater in Stockholm in 1901, was a member
of a touring company in Sweden in 1901 and 1902, and had been an
actor and financial manager at the Swedish Theater in Helsingfors
during the seasons 1902–3 and 1903–4. As important as his practical
experience as actor, director, and producer and his knowledge of
and enthusiasm for drama and the theater were his profound faith
in the excellence of Strindberg's dramas, his conviction that they
should be produced, and his ambition to be the one Swede who at
long last would see justice done to Strindberg and his plays. Besides,
August Falck had demonstrated all these qualities with his own
touring company in 1906 when, with Strindberg's blessing, he had
given *Lady Julie* its Swedish première in Lund on September 18,
then brought the play north in equally successful performances, and
finally, in spite of misgivings on Strindberg's part, produced the play
in Stockholm starting on December 13 at the Folk Theater. It was
a triumph for the young director-actor, and it was a vindication of
sorts for Strindberg himself.

The initial meeting between Falck and Strindberg was to shape
Falck's whole future and to give Strindberg his one chance to realize a persistent dream. All the evidence available — and there is a
great deal — indicates that the two men were equally enthusiastic
about a Strindberg theater and that the younger man had the common sense and tact to deal with the frequently difficult Strindberg
so that the project did not die at the planning stage or collapse
before the project had been realized and made its impression on
Swedish theater life.

Neither of the men had any illusion about either getting a large theater or duplicating the setup in any of the existing Stockholm theaters. Strindberg's orientation lay in the little experimental theaters of Paris[4] and Berlin, theaters in which *The Father, Lady Julie,* and *Creditors* had been successfully produced some fourteen years before; Strindberg, who had read widely in the theater journals, knew quite well what was going on in the little theaters on the continent. Falck had been very much impressed by the preface to *Lady Julie,* had taken his stand against the artificiality of acting then dominant in the Swedish theaters, and was quite convinced that he could help make Swedish theater exciting and alive. Unfortunately, neither Strindberg nor Falck was wealthy: Strindberg was not a businessman, and Falck was only twenty-five.

The search for a theater ended on June 27, 1907, when a contract was signed by Falck and guaranteed by Strindberg for the rental of a building at Norra Bantorget, a structure never intended for a theater. In spite of difficulties, foreseen and unforeseen, that involved rebuilding and providing, for example, the sort of ventilation that the city code required, the Intimate Theater opened on November 26, 1907, with *The Pelican,* the sequel to *Dance of Death,* II. What the audience saw as the visible results of Falck's planning and labor and of Strindberg's enthusiastic and varied suggestions must have been an attractive little theater with a décor in subdued green and yellow, soft dark green wall-to-wall carpeting, 150 seats covered in brownish green, and a copy by Carl Kylberg of Arnold Böcklin's painting *The Island of Life and Death* [*Toten-Insel*][5] on either side of the proscenium. There were, moreover, an attractive ladies' foyer, a lounge, and several small dressing rooms, which must have pleased the cast tremendously.

Falck and Strindberg had good reasons for being both hopeful and worried about the theater. Strindberg knew that few critics would be inclined to be friendly to the production of a series of Strindberg plays, and, even though he was not financially practical, he knew that bills have to be met, loans financed, and personnel paid. Falck knew he had a marvelous idea, worth fighting for, but Falck knew about the economic hazards of operating a theater, too.

Nevertheless there were causes for hope: a great playwright still in the full vigor of creative activity; a young director, dedicated and determined; and a small but promising group of young actors.

Seldom if ever in his life had Strindberg entered so enthusiastically into a venture that involved working with other people, but this was his first real chance to participate in theatrical activity. Moreover, he could look forward to the presentation of one of his plays after another under the direction of a young man who believed in them and him. From the time they agreed that the idea was sound, the two men were in almost daily contact—at suppers in Strindberg's apartment, during long discussions that began in the evening and often lasted until three or four o'clock in the morning, on walks, and through Strindberg's notes and letters to Falck, many of which are extant.

Examining the material about this remarkable partnership, one finds increasing evidence for the conclusion that it was the young hero-worshiper and not the aging hero who had to make the greater effort to keep the venture going. Not only did Falck manage to keep his faith in Strindberg and his plays, but he learned quickly what he had to do to keep the partnership from quickly foundering. Years later Falck made this revealing but undoubtedly justified comment: "It was as always with Strindberg: glowing enthusiasm—overwhelming gratitude—suspicion and irritation—and then breaking off. Many tried to help him, but they soon quit. He was easily irritated when he felt that he was not the primary force in the venture." [6] The evidence suggests, however, that Strindberg managed to control his irritation and suspicion to an unusual extent—for him —for some three years, and the theater kept going, in spite of financial handicaps, from December 5, 1907, to December 11, 1910.

In later years Falck could look back with satisfaction to the fact that the Intimate Theater had produced twenty-four of Strindberg's plays, most of them successfully. Some, particularly such chamber plays as *Storm* (*Oväder*), *The Burned House* (*Brända tomten*), and *The Ghost Sonata*, were written for initial production at the Intimate. Falck could also take some of the credit for the development in Sweden of appreciably new concepts of acting, drama, and theater.

Perhaps Falck's greatest achievement lay in giving Strindberg the chance to participate in theatrical activity directly with due regard to the facts of his temperament and habits. Strindberg's failure as an actor may very well have had much to do with his dread of public speaking, which was to last as long as he lived. At first Strindberg attended only dress rehearsals, although that did not mean that he was neglecting either Falck or the Intimate Theater. But what Strindberg had to say to Falck came largely through suggestions, either orally or in writing. Strindberg was interested in the minutest details of interpretation, acting, and staging, and he freely shared his ideas with Falck. Not only that, but he was very much interested in stage properties and, to Falck's occasional dismay, often picked up "bargains" on his walks or lent "appropriate" objects from his home.

In the summer of 1908 Strindberg was persuaded to take an even more active part in the Intimate Theater. He agreed to direct the production of *The Father* — and it is largely a result of that decision that the letters in this volume were written. But now as before Strindberg could not force himself to speak out in the presence of the whole cast. He remained silent during rehearsals, interrupted no one, but sent practically everyone notes containing both praise and criticism. Take, for example, this brief note to one actress, after her performance as Alice in *The Dance of Death*:

September 8, 1909

Anna Flygare:

Brilliant, charming; your technique like nature itself . . . But, a little criticism of great importance. Keep your attractive, highly effective glissando, *but* phrase [your speeches] better (stress) = speak more distinctly, because the house is larger than you think; and yesterday some of your lines couldn't be heard.

De Verdier [the actor who played Kurt] must not embrace you so roughly you lose your hat, but you're to keep your hat on, for it's becoming and provides variety.

Aside from this: Nothing! only praise = A plus (*Laudatur*), the first prize with a gold medal.

Yours

SNG.[7]

What Strindberg had to say is worth considering, for his letters reveal an understanding of actors and the institution in which they worked, a grasp of the practical facts of theater life, and an idealism about the art that proved inspiring to Falck and the other actors. During most of the period, Strindberg was at his best in terms of human relations: it was perhaps the most extended time in which he could and did work with other people who were on his side. Enthusiastic and helpful, he helped them analyze whole plays as well as individual roles and cooperated with Falck and his personnel in arriving at new standards not only of acting but of producing and staging. For the goal of the Intimate Theater was high. New values within drama and theater were to be achieved; the Swedish audiences were to be given a series of theater experiences unlike any they had had before. When the history of that remarkable phenomenon, the flourishing modern Swedish theater, is written, a goodly measure of credit will have to be given to the Intimate Theater, and Strindberg's open letters as well as his other letters and notes will be major evidence in establishing the nature and the degree of that contribution.

In the intensely human documents, the open letters, Strindberg reveals more clearly than elsewhere his concept of the theater. He believed that this concept cannot be fixed once and for all, for he knew that the theater is an institution at the mercy of the whims of the public and that it consequently must constantly adjust itself to the public and the times. But he also knew that, while the theater is designed for entertainment, it can also be a force in educating its public. If good taste and good judgment are accepted as key points of departure, he believed that the theater can provide the public with meaningful experiences. Using the very simple but basic idea that the drama is a work of art to be played before and for an audience, Strindberg was convinced that neither drama nor theater need be confined to what has been done — he believed that infinite possibilities remained to be exploited. In the Intimate Theater he wanted both old and new plays of his to be produced. But in both the already accepted and in the experimental what had to be avoided were such stilted, affected, and "theatrical" matters as unjustified, calculated effects, places for applause, roles for individual stars, and solo numbers. Such matters had had their day, he thought, and did not belong in the modern theater.

In the individual theater, the director is obviously the key person. Strindberg has some very sensible things to say about the ideal director: he must be a person who knows drama and theater; he must be able to work with other people. Specifically, he must know thoroughly each play to be produced; he must understand his actors; he must be able to listen to his artists, weigh their points of view, and give the individual actor as much freedom as possible. If the director does not know his job; is not able to adjust to the artists, the public, and the times; is not practical; and does not have the final word, the goals of the theater cannot be achieved.

Few dramatists have had as much respect as Strindberg had for acting as a profession and for the dedicated actor as an artist. Since he knew that actors were ultimately the artists who brought a drama alive, he felt it was important that no one should enter the profession for frivolous reasons or because of false notions. It is an interesting and sensible list of qualifications and prerequisites that he lists and discusses for the potentially talented young person who contemplates entering the profession: willingness to work hard, willingness to sacrifice many of the pleasures of life, the capacity to endure the vicarious emotional suffering implicit in the creation of roles, the ability to cooperate with both one's fellows and the director, and dedication to the art and the capacity to grow as a creative artist.

"Our acting must be simple, but not common; easy, but not slovenly." In a way that statement summarizes Strindberg's philosophy of acting but in the open letters he develops his thinking about acting in some detail. If acting is to be a creative art, Strindberg believed that actors must strive for honesty and naturalness of voice, movement, gesture, and expression. Above all, the actor must have respect for the spoken word; honest regard for the rich nuances of his native language could and should be expressed by clear-cut enunciation and natural but careful phrasing so that he could be heard and understood throughout the theater. Movements should be natural and easy, the positions on stage determined by the hints given in the role and the situations themselves. Good acting, Strindberg believed, is acting where there is absolute avoidance of mannerisms, artificial devices, and tricks. Acting, he felt, can really approach greatness only if all these matters are observed and if the acting is cooperative, since no role is an isolated segment but rather an integral part of ensemble playing. Thus the actor must not only act well when he is speaking but act cooperatively when someone else is speaking.

It cannot be emphasized too much that Strindberg, unlike a great many people in his own and other times, did not regard the dedicated and talented actor as a member of an inferior social caste. He knew that actors are human and have their human problems; he deals with these in detail throughout the open letters. But he also believed that the genuine actor is a creative artist who can and should be an individual capable of creative activity—hence, within the limits of a cooperative project, the actor should be allowed to create and, if and when needed, improvise. Such a thinking, feeling being has both responsibility to assume and work to do. He should learn his role at home; have the role take shape and pick up ensemble playing, the mood, and intimacy at rehearsals. He must always keep the role fresh, never allowing it to become mere mechanical repetition of lines. If he does all this, he will "create a character, and not a caricature," and make neither rehearsals nor performances ineffective.

Rehearsals should, Strindberg believed, involve the reading of the whole play for the total effect, not just the acquisition of one's own role. If neither the play nor the roles were analyzed to death, if room were left for individuality and improvisation, and if the whole rehearsal were kept a cooperative project, the performances before audiences could provide the sort of experience that an audience should have; it would have the necessary tone, the consistency of moods, and the appropriate tempo; it would deserve the complete attention of the audience. In short, it would make the Intimate Theater what a theater should be artistically for the group on either side of the footlights. It was, both Strindberg and Falck believed, an ideal worth striving for.

The two partners and the actors as well strove and to a great degree succeeded in approaching the achievement of that ideal, as this table of plays actually produced at the theater suggests:

Title	Number of Performances	
The Outlaw	9	
The Secret of the Guild	26	
Lord Bengt's Wife	48	
The Father	77	
The Comrades	27	
Lady Julie	134	(Besides 7 at the Folk Theater, 2 at the Swedish Theater, and 11 at the People's House in 1912)
Creditors	21	
Paria	53	
The Stronger	3	
The First Warning	8	
Playing with Fire	13	
The Bond	50	
To Damascus	8	
Crimes and Crimes	50	
Easter	182	
Dance of Death, I	85	(After the twenty-second time, I and II were given together)

Total: 24 Strindberg plays; 1,147 performances in three years, besides tours in the provinces and abroad. Since some of the plays were given two in one evening, the total number of performances was 1,025.[8]

It was unfortunate that means were not found for adequate financial support of the Intimate Theater, and that Strindberg's failing health (he was to die of cancer in May, 1912), suspicion, irritability, and lack of sustained enthusiasm were factors Falck had to take into consideration. The details of the financial problems as well as Strindberg's very real personal difficulties do not make cheerful reading, although some of the details that caused the final collapse of the Intimate Theater are not in the least amazing for anyone who knows Strindberg's biography.

Falck took the company on successful guest visits to Copenhagen and Oslo, and he brought the company to various places in Sweden for special and financially rewarding performances. Strindberg did not always approve. Note his furious resentment of the fact that Falck had permitted Anna Norrie to sing songs by the great contemporary poet Gustaf Fröding in connection with an open-air performance of *Swanwhite* at Baron Adelsvärd's estate Adelsnäs in Östergötland in the summer of 1909:

Dear Falck:

If I'm to make arrangements for *The Crown Bride* in Mora [Dalarna], I want guarantees that your café diva won't be roped in on it with Fröding's draftee's ditties. Adelsvärd was unhappy about that [episode], and I most of all! Why do you drag that old vampire into my repertory? Do you have a purpose for doing it? Or is it pure spite?

If you don't intend to put on *The Crown Bride* this summer, tell me; I have others who can do it. Making a promise you don't intend to keep is poor tactics. You'll lose all credit.

June 26, 1909.   STRINDBERG[9]

When Falck had the audacity to propose putting on Maeterlinck's *L'intruse* along with *Creditors*, he got this reaction:

> If I'm to continue my interest in the Intimate Theater, its program has to be realized. . . . First my plays! and nobody else's. I can't afford to sacrifice anything for Maeterlinck, whom I do admire, though!
>
> And my supporters and the friends of the theater are ready to make new sacrifices — for *my* sake, not for foreigners or beginners (They have the Royal Dramatic Theater!) . . .
>
> The Intimate Theater *is* threatened! Divert the attacks by keeping up your ties with me — and don't think I'm dead. For every enemy I get, I get two friends — have got!
>
> Most likely I'll turn down the Anti-Nobel Prize[10] and suggest [setting up] a fund with one reasonable stipulation: that my plays are produced! . . .
>
> September 14, 1910.   STRINDBERG

Strindberg had apparently forgotten that, when the founding of the theater was originally discussed, he had doubted that its repertory could be limited to his plays and had even suggested possible plays by other writers, an idea to which Falck had not then responded. But the inclusion of *L'intruse* was to be the primary cause of the closing of the theater. Strindberg proceeded to attack Falck publicly in print.

Unpleasant as such matters were, there were pleasant matters, too. Falck's generous assessment in later years is undoubtedly sincere:

> The advice and suggestions, which Strindberg gave us young people, have been of inestimable value.
>
> The years of almost daily personal association with Strindberg were for me, and for all of us, so instructive, a time so rich in memories,

happy and unhappy, a time, which we shall never be able to forget, but will always recall with gratitude, when we were granted the privilege of living in contact with and being under the direction of *the great spirit and human being August Strindberg* [Falck's italics].[11]

What is most important, however, is the fact that the Intimate Theater had earned a significant place in the history of the Swedish theater. It had emphasized factors in Swedish acting: the actors' subordination to the play and the demonstration of the value of ensemble playing. It had successfully experimented with simplified but imaginative staging. It had allowed both Strindberg and Falck to go far toward the achievement of new values in the theater. It had put on twenty-four Strindberg plays, among them some of his chamber plays. These were no small achievements. [W.J.]

Memorandums
to
the Members
of
the Intimate Theater
from
the Director

Now that I am entering the regular service of the Intimate Theater, I greet the personnel with these written speeches, because I cannot make any speeches orally.

I call them memorandums, because I am not saying anything particularly new, but simply pulling together what I have already given you in the form of suggestions, comments, encouragement, warnings, and advice in brief notes after dress rehearsals.

We shall soon have worked together a year; we have put up with difficulties which it would be good to forget, even if our memory counsels us to consider them. You have been criticized, sometimes unjustly, sometimes justly, but you have been praised as well. You have taken the bad days with the good; you have worked, sometimes without pay, sometimes with pay; you have not disdained to take part in the humblest activities which are not included in your contracts. Your willingness to sacrifice and your love of your work have made my burden light, and the thought of how much beauty and talent I have seen at your performances and the good will you have shown in receiving my criticism fill me with the greatest hope, now that I shall from this time on appear as

THE DIRECTOR OF THE INTIMATE THEATER

The Idea of Intimate Theater. When anyone in the 1860's and 1870's submitted a full-length play to the Royal Theater, he had to observe the following requirements if he were to get it performed. The play should preferably have five acts, each act [should be] approximately twenty-four sheets long or, in all, 5 x 24 = 120 folio pages. The division into scenes was not appreciated and was considered a weakness. Every act should have a beginning, a middle, and an end. The end of an act should be the place for applause, which was aroused by an oratorical figure, and, if the play was in blank verse, the last two lines should rhyme. Within the plays were "numbers" for the actor which were called "scenes"; the soliloquy or monologue was permitted and frequently was the high spot or climax; a longer emotional outburst or a speech of condemnation or an exposure was almost necessary; one could even relate something — a dream, an anecdote, an event.

But roles were required, too — rewarding roles for the stars of the theater.

Such poetics for the drama had, of course, much that was justified and attractive; it stemmed ultimately from Victor Hugo and was in the 1830's a reaction against the antiquated abstractions of Racine and Corneille. But this form of art degenerated like all others when it had run its course, and into the five-act play were forced any and all motifs, even the insignificant *historiette* or anecdote. Practical considerations such as not letting any of the theater's large personnel be unoccupied forced one to include minor characters, who were not, however, to be extras, but roles. The matter of roles was confused with the depiction of character, and we have lately heard the practical Björnson[12] called the great creator of roles.

Along with the fear of the strong motif went the stretching out of bagatelles so that the managers finally had to suggest the elimination of long uninspired passages.

About 1870, when I had written *Blotsven* in five indifferent acts in verse and tried to read it aloud to fellow poets at Uppsala, I found that the whole play was unjustifiably extended and uninspired. I burned it up (and an *Erik XIV*, too). Out of the ashes rose the one-act *The Outlaw [Den fredlöse]*, which along with its great weaknesses has the merits of sticking to the subject and of being brief but complete. I was undoubtedly influenced by Björnson's splendid one-acter: *Between the Blows [Mellem Slagene]*, which, I found, was my model.

The times had, you see, picked up speed; people demanded quick results and had become impatient.

In my first version of *Master Olof*, I tried a compromise, though: I substituted prose for verse, and instead of the opera-like blank verse drama with solo and special numbers, I composed polyphonically, a symphony, in which all the voices were interwoven (major and minor characters were treated equally), and in which no one accompanied the soloist. The attempt succeeded, but since then they have had to cut the play, for it has proved too long for contemporary people. But in the 1880's a new time began to extend its demands for reform even to the theater. Zola attacked the French comedy with its Brussels carpets, lacquered shoes and lacquered motifs, and a dialogue reminiscent of the questions and answers in the catechism. In 1887 Antoine opened the Théâtre Libre [13] in Paris, and [Zola's] *Thérèse Raquin*, although it was only an adaptation of the novel, became the model. The strong motif and the concentrated form were new, although the unity of time still was not observed and the lowering of the curtain remained. Then I wrote *Lady Julie*, *The Father*, and *Creditors*. Antoine put on *Lady Julie*, which got a well-known preface, but not before 1892 (93?) although it had been given in the Student Society in Copenhagen [14] in 1888 (89?). In the spring of 1893, *Creditors* was produced at l'Oeuvre [15] in Paris, and in the fall of the same year *The Father* was put on at the same theater (with Philippe Garnier in the title role). But Freie Bühne [16] had opened in Berlin in 1889, and before 1893 all three of my plays had been presented, *Lady Julie* being preceded by a lecture by Paul Schlenther, now director of the Hofburg in Vienna. Rosa Bertens, Emanuel Reicher, Rittner, and Jarno played the major roles, and under the direction of Sigismund Lautenburg, director of the Residens Theater, *Creditors* was performed one hundred times.

A certain silence then ensued, and the drama resumed fairly old lines until Reinhardt at the beginning of the new century

opened Kleines Theater.[17] I was in on that at the beginning with
the long one-act drama *The Bond*, *Lady Julie* (Eisoldt), and
Crimes and Crimes.

Last year Reinhardt went the whole way by opening the Kam-
marspiel-Haus,[18] which by its very name indicates its real program: the concept of chamber music transferred to drama. The
intimate action, the highly significant motif, the sophisticated
treatment. Last autumn the Hebbel Theater[19] was opened in almost the same spirit, and throughout Germany theaters with
the name Intimate Theater have sprung up.

One of the last days in November, 1907, August Falck opened
the Intimate Theater in Stockholm, and I then got the chance
to follow theatrical activity in all its details more closely. Memories from my forty-year career as a dramatist were awakened,
older observations were checked, old experiments were repeated,
and my newly awakened interest gave me the idea of writing
these memorandums.

*   *   *

If anyone asks what it is an intimate theater wants to achieve
and what is meant by chamber plays, I can answer like this: in
drama we seek the strong, highly significant motif, but with
limitations. We try to avoid in the treatment all frivolity, all calculated effects, places for applause, star roles, solo numbers. No
predetermined form is to limit the author, because the motif de-
termines the form. Consequently: freedom in treatment, which
is limited only by the unity of the concept and the feeling for
style.

When Director Falck avoided the long performances which
end close to midnight, he also broke with the classic tradition
of serving liquor in the theater. That was courageous, for the
sale of liquor usually pays at least half the rent in the large

theaters. But the combination of theater art and alcohol was accompanied by long intermissions, the length of which was determined by the restaurant keeper and the observation of which was controlled by the director.

The drawbacks of letting the audience out to imbibe strong drinks in the middle of the drama are well known. The mood is destroyed by talk, the transported spirit loses its flexibility and becomes conscious of what should remain unconscious; the illusion the drama wanted to give cannot be sustained, but the theatergoer who has been half carried away is awakened to utterly banal reflections, or he reads the evening paper, talks about other things with acquaintances he meets at the bar; he is distracted, the threads in the play are cut, the development of the action is forgotten, and in a completely different mood he returns to his seat to try in vain to pick up what he had left.

That system degenerated to the point where many theatergoers engaged tables before the play started and treated the play as interludes; yes, there were those who missed an act if the shag sofa was really soft and difficult to get out of.

The finances of the Intimate Theater suffered from this break [with tradition], but the theater gained in another way. The attention of the audience was more completely given to the stage, and the members of the audience were compensated by being able after the performance to go comfortably to their suppers to discuss what they had heard and seen.

We looked for a *small* house, because we wanted the voices to be heard in every corner without forcing the actors to shout. There are, you know, theaters so large that the actors must strain their voices so that every utterance becomes false, and where a declaration of love has to be shouted, a confidence revealed as if it were a military order, the secret in one's heart whispered with full voice, and where it sounds as if everyone on the stage were angry or were in a hurry to get offstage.

We got the little house, and, since the voices have been modulated, we have gradually approached the desired goal without yet having fully achieved it.

*　　*　　*

The art of acting is the hardest and the easiest of all arts. But like beauty it is almost impossible to define. *It* is not the art of pretense, for the great artist does not pretend but is honest, true, and natural, while the low comedian does everything to dissimulate through mask and costume. *It* is not imitation, because poor actors most frequently have a fiendish ability to imitate well-known people, while the genuine artist lacks that gift. The actor is not the author's medium except in a certain way and with reservations. In esthetics the art of acting is not considered one of the independent arts but rather one of the dependent ones. It cannot exist, of course, without the author's text. An actor cannot do without an author, but, if necessary, an author can do without the actor. I have never seen Goethe's *Faust* (Part II), Schiller's *Don Carlos*, or Shakespeare's *The Tempest* performed, but I have seen them all the same when I have read them, and there are good plays that should not be performed, that cannot bear to be seen. But there are poor plays that must be played in order to live; they have to be filled out, ennobled, by the art of acting. The dramatist usually knows for what he must thank the actor, and he usually is grateful. So is the superior actor grateful to his author, and I would prefer to see them thank each other, since the obligations are mutual, but they should have the greatest mutual understanding if that unjustified question were never raised. But it is raised by conceited fools and by stars, when they happen to have given life to a play that deserves destruction; and then the author is a necessary evil or someone who writes the text for their role since there has to be some text.

I have never heard this question considered at the Intimate Theater and I hope I never shall. There I have seen [the creation of] roles which were better and more attractive than my originals, and I have admitted that frankly.

*   *   *

The art of acting seems to be the easiest of all arts since every person in everyday life can talk, walk, stand, gesture, and express himself by means of facial expressions. But then he is playing himself, and that is clearly something else again. Because if he gets a role to learn and perform, and is let out on the stage, one soon notices that the wisest, most profound, and strongest person is impossible as an actor, while a quite simple person is at once playing the part. Some people show that they are born with the art of creating; others just do not have it. But it is always hard to judge the beginner, because the gift can be there without being immediately revealed, and great talents have on occasion had a very miserable start. Therefore the director and manager has to be careful in his judgment when the fate of a young person rests in his hands. He has to test and observe, have patience, and postpone judgment to the future.

What makes a person an actor and what qualities are required it is very hard to say, but I shall try to list a few.

First of all, he must be able to attend to the role, to concentrate all his thoughts on it, and not let himself be distracted from it. Anyone who plays an instrument knows what it means when his thoughts begin to stray. Then the notes disappear, the fingers fumble and hit the wrong notes, and he gets confused even if he knows the composition. The second requirement is,

I suspect, having an imagination or the gift of imagining the character and the situation so vividly that they take shape.

I assume that the artist gets into a trance, forgets himself, and finally *becomes* the person he is to play. It reminds me of sleep-walking, but it is most likely not quite that. If he is disturbed in this state or awakened to full consciousness, he becomes confused and lost. That is why I have always hesitated to interrupt a scene during rehearsal: I have seen how the actor is tortured by being awakened; he stands there fully awake and needs time in which to get into the trance again, to recover both the mood and the modulation of voice.

No other form of art is less independent than the actor's; he cannot isolate his artistic creation, display it, and say: It is mine. Because if he does not get resonance from the supporting or opposing actor, if he does not get support from his fellow player, then he is pulled down, lured into false notes, and even if he makes the best of his own role, it does not jell. Actors are at each other's mercy, and I have seen unusually selfish actors, who play down their rival, efface him in order to show themselves off and to be seen alone.

For that reason the spirit at a theater or a good relationship is of the greatest importance if the play is to have its full effect and to go. Above all else the actors must work together, fit themselves into a unit. That is asking much of human beings, especially in an activity in which a justified desire for honor drives every last actor forward to be seen, to win recognition, and to take well-earned prizes with justified means.

*   *   *

If the actor has a thoroughly vivid concept of the character and the scene he is to play, the next thing he must do is to memorize the role. That begins with the spoken word, and I believe the spoken word is the major fact about the art of acting. If the utterance is right, gestures, play of features, bearing, and stance follow of themselves if the actor has a strong imagination. If he lacks that, we see his arms and hands dangling like lifeless things, his body seems dead, and all one can see is a speaking head on a lifeless body. The beginner usually has this difficulty. The *spoken* word has not had the power to penetrate the body and make all the joints in the body function together; there are breaks in the line, but contacts may be established so that muscles that are not pertinent begin to move and jerk; the fingers pick away, the feet constantly try to find new positions without becoming comfortable; the actor is nervous and makes the audience uneasy. For that reason it is not unimportant to keep one's body healthy so that one has control of it.

I am inclined to consider the spoken word most important. You can present a scene in the dark and enjoy it, if only the actors speak effectively!

Speaking effectively!

The first requirement is to speak slowly. The beginner has not the slightest notion how exceedingly slowly he can and ought to speak on the stage. As a young actor-to-be, I imitated our foremost conversational actor, repeating his lines softly. I was amazed, for no one could ever have made me believe that anyone could speak *that* slowly on the stage without making what he had to say sound like a sermon.

Then there is this: the tone is to be set in the larynx, which, along with the vocal chords, is made for this purpose. But the vowels and the consonants are formed with the mouth, the tongue, the lips, and the teeth.

Only when one whispers, does one speak with the mouth alone, and conversation in private is usually a sort of whispering. When two people are talking, they omit consonants particularly, because in intimate situations one almost *sees* by watching the other's mouth what is being said.

It is another matter on the stage; there you are talking to an audience of many people whether you want to or not. There the larynx has to function, and there no sound may be omitted.

If every sound is included, particularly the consonants, and if one phrases correctly, even the weakest voice is heard and understood. Rachel[20] had a very little voice, but she was heard in every corner of the Théâtre Français by the audience.

The most common mistake is to speak too fast, and to slur away the consonants.

For example: *"De gå fö fott!"* instead of *"Det går för fort!"* *Svåt = Svårt; Teaten = Teatern.*[21] The actor does not need to read for anyone, but only take care that from the very beginning he reads his role pedantically slowly, and listens to himself so that he knows how it sounds when all consonants are enunciated. Later the tempo will increase of itself, and when he then glides over the sounds he will sound absolutely natural and not at all pedantic.

But first and last he must take the tone from the larynx in order to form the sounds in his mouth.

People are always happy to listen to the person who speaks well even if he is just a very ordinary actor; he will never fail; he will never spoil the words; he will get roles and can go far. If on the other hand he has a beautiful voice and becomes infatuated with it, then he often stops right there and never gets any farther. That, too, is a danger! So: let's talk on the stage and not chatter! Poor enunciation occurs most frequently in small theaters where the roles are swallowed hastily and carelessly learned, but where there is no director with authority and know-how.

It is to the advantage of the actor to know his natural vocal range and cultivate it. He can then be heard best and most attractively under ordinary circumstances; he is always at home within that range and is never at a loss.

There are strange exceptions, however; I know one actress who can never use her beautiful and bewitching alto range because it cannot be heard — she has to shout herself up to a soprano range. To shift from range to range is to sing falsely, and tones strange to the harmony are disturbing because they introduce moods that do not belong.

Speaking so that it "sounds like theater" is something special that ought to be watched. The intonations do not belong to the role; they go alongside like loose horses that do not pull at all; "one sees the blue script in the air"; that is, the role has been merely memorized. It sounds memorized, and this means that the artist has not penetrated the role, that it is still not mastered.

Shouting often takes the place of poor enunciation, but the strange thing is that you can't hear shouts. At a general rehearsal I observed a great actor who felt he should portray the furious character he was supposed to play by shouting. But the more he shouted, the less he was heard. He drowned out his own voice.

The beginner often conceals his shyness by shouting, and one wonders why he is angry, because that's how it sounds, and that's how it looks, since shouting summons up all the symptoms of anger.

But in the third balcony of the old Opera House[22] I have heard an actress who whispered down on the big stage so that one caught every word. She had taught herself to speak by strict attention and by listening to herself and to good speakers.

Using the role as an exercise in speech, beating it to pieces, is not a good method. And reading the role to others can have the unfortunate result that the instructor's modulation, individual play of features, perhaps even his manner are acquired, too, and thus one stifles or suppresses one's own individuality. Better to go at it by oneself and try to cultivate one's own voice even if it is slight.

Verse is most suitable for exercises in speech; poetic form permits less carelessness since a skipped syllable immediately makes the verse limp. The verse even makes the speech take form so that one wins the legato, which also gives prose its attractiveness. This legato which I have so often asked the personnel of the Intimate Theater to observe means that all the words in the phrase steal after each other in rhythmic movement in keeping with one's breathing; it becomes a regular structure with attractive sounds and brings out the essence of the meaning without throwing away the nonessential; that is the most beautiful resource of the human voice and of the language, where the words form a necklace of pearls instead of lying in a heap and rattling like dry peas.

The direct opposite, or the beginner's staccato, resembles spelling and not combining; counting up the words instead of reading them; the shortness of breath, the stammering, which finally becomes jabbering or chattering.

(Staccato has its justified effect, as we know, when one is excited or angry and is gasping for breath.)

Mastering the role! There are several ways, but the surest is no doubt this: first, reading the script carefully, which used to be done at the initial group reading of the play, I consider necessary. I have seen with horror how great artists pick out their roles like grains from the sand and leave the rest [of the play] to its fate as if it did not interest them. I have also seen the results of such a procedure: they have misunderstood their roles or portrayed their characters falsely. Since they do not know what people say about them when they are not on stage, they do not know who they are. It often happens in a play that the others give the characterization of the one who is offstage and who can be a self-deceiver who does not know his value.

I have seen a great artist who lost his biggest scene because he did not understand what it was about. The audience, who had heard the preceding scene and understood the situation, caught the allusions but could not understand what the artist meant by his acting. He had not really read the play.

If the major character in a drama is characterized through what the others say, he must of necessity be bound by their characterization and correspond to it; consequently, he must know it; otherwise it clashes, becomes incomprehensible, and can become ridiculous. The following scene, I've been told, was acted at a rehearsal:

STAR: Why doesn't he come? Shall I wait for him any longer?

A VOICE: He can't come—he died in the preceding act.

STAR: Did he die? That's something else!

*   *   *

Analyzing and studying a role can be carried too far so that you see the designs and devices, which a frivolous artist can transform into tricks. A play can also be rehearsed so long that it loses its freshness. Theater art should be artistic, serious play, but not exercise and not philosophy. A little carelessness doesn't matter, for that provides room for improvisation, and I have seen roles so overloaded with technique that the tatters have flapped about the role.

The terms *character*, *depicting character*, and *characterization* have been misused so often that I must take a moment for clarifying them.

The actor—most often the favorite of the audience—who

plays up his own personality, which must be sympathetically appealing since he is the favorite, usually sacrifices the role and appears as himself without bothering to resemble the character except in make-up. That is one way, and it will go for a while. He does not present the character but something else that is interesting and attractive.

The character actor, however, forgets himself, steals into the role completely, and becomes the character he is playing. I have seen genuine magicians of that kind, and I have admired them. But the character actor can easily be tempted into creating types and transforming them into caricatures. The character is, of course, the essence of a human being's *inner* life: his inclinations, his passions, his weaknesses. If the character actor emphasizes the nonessential externals or tries to express the uniquely individual inner qualities of the role by means of strong external means the interpretation easily becomes a caricature, and instead of creating a character he creates a travesty.

People often equate character with the type or the original model and demand consistency in the characterization. But there are inconsistent characters, disjointed, broken, erratic characters.

To illustrate this I refer you to my latest *Blue Book*,[23] where I have pointed out how Shakespeare proceeds when he depicts people in all their facets in contrast to Molière, who presents types without life and limbs (the Miser, the Hypocrite, the Misanthrope, etc.).

*　　*　　*

Listening on the stage and silent acting. The one who is not speaking but who is listening to what someone else is saying must really listen. He must not look bored even if he has heard what is being said by the other actor a hundred times before;

he must not look as if he were merely waiting to speak or as if he were impatiently waiting for his fellow actor to get through talking finally so he could talk himself.

There are listeners who lower their eyes and look as if they were memorizing their next speech, which they are already going over to have it ready.

There are others who use the opportunity to count the people in the audience; still others flirt with the audience and with their eyes, shoulders, or feet say: "Listen, how stupidly he's talking; just wait till I come. Go on, reel it out; I'll be talking soon, and then you'll get it."

Others try to look interested, raise a glowing face but look merely hypocritical, moving their hands and lips as if they were listening to every word being said.

The one who listens is to remain what his role calls for, but his face must reflect what the other actor is saying, and the audience must be able to see what impression that is making. All this sounds simple and is elementary, of course, but it is very difficult, just as difficult as to pretend to be interested when one has to listen to a well-known story or anecdote. I have seen masterpieces in the art of listening and silent acting. I have seen Jean listen to Lady Julie's long autobiography as if he were hearing it for the first time although he had heard it 150 times. In the same play [Lady Julie] I have seen the cook listen to Lady Julie's death fantasies about an imagined happy future in such a way that I have had to applaud the cook.

Finally, I want to say this: it is as a listener that the selfish, malicious actor takes the opportunity to ruin or play down his rival. Through a carefully calculated absentmindedness, by making himself unreceptive, turning his back to his rival, looking skeptically impatient, he can transfer the interest from the speaker, detract from the latter's words and personality, and direct the attention to himself. But the speaker must not lose his self-control, not become angry, but take up the same tactics, adapt his acting to the silent rival's tricks, and take precedence if necessary and with a carefully suitable silent contempt unmask him. Then the audience will get the illusion that that is part of the play, and the situation is saved.

* * *

Positions. It is generally stated in the play how entrances and moves are to be made, but the author has often neglected this part of setting up the play. Then it is the director's duty to arrange this matter. But to set up an absolute plan ahead of time is considered impossible by the experts. The arrangement pretty much comes of itself during rehearsals. But when the best arrangement has been hit upon, it should be kept so that the actors will enter and exit through designated doors in order to avoid bumping into each other and ridiculous meetings. The big scenes are generally played near the footlights so that the actors will be plainly heard and seen, but sometimes the direct opposite has a greater effect. Explanations and settling of accounts are made face to face; longer explanations and speeches I most frequently have given at a table with two chairs. The table divides and unites the antagonists; the table also provides for natural, easy gestures, is restful, supports arms and hands. The chairs must not be too low, because the body then is cramped and the actor has a hard time talking. Sitting down on a chair gracefully and getting up from it requires forethought and care. The men have to be careful that their trousers fall attractively and cover their shoes and that they do not creep up revealing the garter or the sock; moreover, the knee should not have the profile of a pointed angle; the calf of the leg should not form a triangle with the foot.

The actors should be equipped with appropriate footwear since the audience on the main floor is on the level of the actor's foot.

In some theaters precedence acccording to rank is observed in positions on the stage so that the leading actors always take precedence over the younger actors, without consideration for the importance or value of the role. We disregard that sort of thing and let the role and the situation determine the matter.

Lining up the whole cast by the footlights when the curtain is to go down after the last act comes from [the tradition of] the old German comedy and begs for applause. Like anything frivolous, everything like that is banned in our theater although I saw it done as recently as in the revival of [Ibsen's] *The League of Youth* (*De Unges Forbund*, 1869).

*   *   *

Mannerisms. When an actor has hit upon a decidedly effective way of expressing the most common emotions and that way has been successful, he is tempted to use it both when it is suitable and when it is unsuitable, partly because it is comfortable and partly because it goes. But this becomes just a mannerism. The audience puts up with it in a favorite for a long time, but the critics weary first and label it by the fatal word [mannerism]. Some examples: there is an artist who keeps his mouth open [after his line has been uttered]; that expression came originally from a comedy where it was fitting, but when it is used in serious dramas it is out of place. The open mouth with a hanging jaw is the comedian's means of looking stupid in order to flatter the audience, but there is irony in it, too, that says: I'm not so stupid as I look; probably you're the one who is stupid. Afterward the gaping mouth became an appeal for applause. This sort of thing is not only a mannerism but also a lack of feeling for style; the play of facial expressions suitable in a farce has no place in a serious drama or a tragedy.

Another artist is constantly picking invisible lint from his sleeve; he does this with his eyes downcast as if he were up to something treacherous, insidious; that sort of trick can be used once a year but not every day.

Another shrugs his shoulders, supposedly at his fellow actors in order to court the favor of the audience and stand out as number one himself. Another looks at his legs; another stands with his mouth open and his face expressionless waiting for his fellow actor to get through talking; it's as if the actor's face were distorted because of his impatience to get a chance to speak. Instead his face should reflect by shifting expressions the other actor's speech.

Some years ago when a great actress hit upon bending her head way back and her jaw far up, it was effective because it was relatively new. But when the pose spread through all the theaters, the audience became tired of it especially when there was no justification for it. When I was young, people talked about Fru Heiberg's [24] handkerchief, [a device] which most likely had come from Paris. It signified double-dealing or treachery; her hands tore the handkerchief to pieces while her face smiled. We call this a mannerism nowadays. Or when the despairing father in [Friedrich von Schiller's] *Intrigue and Love* (*Kabale und Liebe*) with a smiling face tightens the violin strings until they break. Actresses fluttered their eyelashes for a time, but that trick was taken from a sculptor's plaque of a famous demimonde.

Vocal resources are often distorted into mannerisms. Someone has discovered his voice is beautiful; soon he is giving concert numbers with it. Another person has found that he can move [the audience] best by a solemn voice, and he stops with that; others laugh without motivation or produce sphinxlike smiles.

All unmotivated uses of effects are mannerisms: artificial pauses without point, false exits, hurried movements, motions with the arms, wriggling, making eyes at the audience, weeping without a valid reason.

*   *   *

Exploiting one's personality. An attractive, rich personality always adds something to the role so that the actor's individuality makes itself felt and people are eager to see his performance even if he does not play the character [but remains himself]. If such an actor can pick his roles, everything can go well to the end of his life although he is always the same and plays himself. But in that qualification lies the prerequisite for his success for, if he goes beyond the area of his ability, his weaknesses show up plainly.

The really great actor creates the role completely, but ennobled and magnified by his personality. And the genuine actor can recreate all roles and does so with more or less pleasure.

The actor who opens the play and utters the first speech ought to meditate for a moment in order to think himself into the situation and the mood so that he is immediately in the role. The one who answers him will have got the tone and must keep it up. If the first speaker has not caught it, the second one must try to catch it.

A drama should always be opened with slow and clearly uttered speeches, because the audience is not yet ready to hear and grasp [the plot], and, without having been introduced to the characters and having the exposition clearly in mind, the members of the audience cannot learn what the contents of the play and the course of its action are.

A very common mistake is made when the first speaker comes on stage, talks at random or toward no definite goal, a procedure that is reminiscent of the beginner's manner that "sounds like theater": a hesitant search for the tone which confuses the actor who is to make the second entrance or is to answer the first speaker.

If one word, particularly one name, is lost in the exposition, the audience cannot keep the characters apart, mixes them up, and cannot find them on the program since the auditorium is dark.

The one who is about to come on stage ought to be in the wings listening to the tone set by those on stage and not rush in bringing along an absolutely different mood. That often happens.

When the exposition, which is always a little didactic, has passed in exaggeratedly slow tempo, the actors must find the true tempo of the situation so that they do not get into the heavy, too slow tempo which makes the audience sleepy. Nor should the actors race along so that the audience cannot keep up with what is happening.

The one who is about to make his exit should prepare for it by prolonging the utterance of his speeches (*ritardando*), and not leap or rush out so that he cuts the action instead of ending [one scene] and preparing for a new one. (When stage directions indicate otherwise, this rule obviously does not apply.)

The end of an act requires a more careful exit, and toward the end of the play dialogue, the positions [of the actors], gestures, play of features, and bearing beautifully and slowly modulate to signal the final curtain. In a word, the audience is to sense in advance that the play is coming to an end and not get the final curtain as a surprise so that the members of the audience sit waiting for more.

The actor must control the role and not let the role control him: i.e., not let himself be so intoxicated or enchanted by the words that he loses his head. He must have full control over himself, not begin to rush, and he can do this first when the role is no longer merely memorized but a part of his imagination and consciousness. Then the role is definitely his, and his consciousness keeps watch over it. A role that has been merely memorized sounds hollow or empty, and comes out as false. But the danger here is being too conscious [of the role] so that one succumbs to cold calculation, speculation of effects, emphasis, signaling, display, etc.

The actor should be so strong that he remains unmoved by his fellow actors and does not let them tempt him into their strains. A weakness, temporary or not, can fool the actor into adapting himself to the one with whom he is talking so that he lets go of his role and begins to talk in several strains, according to the lead given by his fellow actor. Then everything becomes unsettled; "melodies strange to the harmony" creep in; the role is broken up and loses its authority.

* * *

The actor who has the leading role should not go out to be distracted either by reading or conversation, because both on stage and in the auditorium people are concerned with him in his absence. It is as if he were still on stage, and he has the invisible threads of the mood in his hand.

Therefore he ought to be particularly careful about his exits so that he does not take something along when he exits and leaves nothing behind, thereby tearing to pieces what has just been woven.

Every actor should watch for his own entrance; thereby he

gets a little restraint on himself so that he can catch the tone and the tempo while he is still in the wings.

When we at the Intimate Theater try to avoid what is stilted and affected, we must on the other hand watch out that we do not become banal. Our acting must be simple, but not common; easy, but not slovenly.

Even in our little theater the actor must always remember that he is not acting for himself alone up on the crowded stage but recall that about 150 people are sitting out in the auditorium and that these people have the right to *see* and *hear*. So it won't do to mouth the role; it must be spoken out in a magnified way as the public speaker must raise his voice and phrase what he has to say so that he will be heard and understood.

Even the most intimate scene must be performed with the audience in mind, without the actor playing *for* or *with* the audience. He must not give his eyes or his speeches to the audience but to his *moitié* or fellow actor on the stage, but not as if they were alone in the room. Every attempt to direct a phrase to the auditorium or to make a confidant out of a member of the audience, to play up to or to try to gain the favor of the audience should be prohibited.

The one who emphasizes or directs attention to a speech can easily hurt the member of the audience who wants to understand what is being said and not be the recipient of enlightenment or instruction.

The role itself shall determine when the actor is to speak with his eyes. Misusing one's eyes is called *"mit den Augen arbeiten"* in German. A declaration of love must always be directed at the person who is loved, face to face, and not toward the auditorium.

Turning one's back to the audience can be permissible if the role motivates doing so, but should not be misused when major conflicts are settled or disclosures are made. At such points the audience wants to see the play of the actors' features.

One wants to see a certain self-assurance in the actor, and self-confidence does impress one, but egotistic admiration of one-self and being cocksure on the part of the actor are annoying except in the audience's favorite who may do anything he wishes — for a while — without being criticized.

The actor is an illusionist, of course, and must give the illusion of being someone other than himself. If he has a strong, rich personality, that will be evident and be a plus which makes him great. It is this plus that can be defined only with difficulty and cannot be learned: a general heightening of imagination, obser-vation, feeling, taste, self-control. He is like the others, has no new miraculous qualities, but has everything in a richer measure.

At home he reads and meditates, but I have been told that the working out begins in ensemble at rehearsal, and that is no doubt true. If the play is serious, the rehearsal must be kept serious; if the play is a comedy, it becomes comic, but work in any case. There are large theaters where tragedies are rehearsed as if they were variety shows and where they even parody the play without its deserving such a fate. This poor tone remains in performance, and spitefulness and carelessness can ruin [the production of] a play in that way.

*   *   *

The director like the orchestra conductor is not a particularly popular person, because he is present only to criticize. He has to instruct even the mature artists and often gets tit for tat. Ex-perience has taught me that the artist can be right without the director's being wrong. In a questionable case a matter *can* be

[seen] in various ways. But then it's better for the sake of harmony to accept the director's interpretation since some solution has to be reached. And the director is usually the only one who knows the whole play thoroughly — the development of the plot, all intrigues, all roles; in this case he knows most, and for that reason he ought to have the final say. Even if he is not an actor himself and can not perform the part, he can know how it should be done.

The artist may certainly present his idea to the director and motivate it, but he must not ill-naturedly challenge the validity [of the director's point of view] or try to browbeat him, because that causes a tense situation and can cause enmities from which come uneasiness and restraint to make the whole project suffer.

As the author attending dress rehearsals I have many times seen an actor interpret a role quite differently from what I had intended. If his interpretation has proved a thorough characterization that does not destroy the play, I have not protested but have let him have his way. Far better that he should realize his characterization as he has conceived it than that I should tear to pieces his creation which is something whole and unified. The author, of course, ought to know his play best and know what he has intended. But he can have been away from it for such a long time that he has forgotten the details and for that reason may be wrong as opposed to the actor, who has the whole play fresh in mind. Then the author must admit that he is wrong. And as an author I have seen actors who have made a neglected character greater and better than I had dreamed of. Even after a dress rehearsal I've had to admit: this is certainly not my work, but it is just as good, in some places better, in others worse.

So I have decided: give the actor as much freedom in his work as possible; otherwise, he will remain a pupil all his life.

I have seen, you see, introspective directors who have drilled and threshed the play to pieces, and I have seen those who have wanted to force upon all artists, young and old, men and women, their own gestures, their own intonations, their own fragile voice, their mannerisms, yes, even taught them tricks. We never engage in that sort of thing.

So far as costuming goes, the actor usually understands that matter best, and he ought to have a measure of freedom in this, but if an obvious mistake has been made the director must have the right to insist on a change, or require it when there is no question about the matter.

In easily injured plays, particularly in costume plays, the director alone must select the colors to get them to harmonize and to be effective in the ensemble, but he should be willing to consult the major actors and will undoubtedly accept their points of view when they are sound.

*   *   *

The favorite of the audience is a strange but very common phenomenon. He is not necessarily the great talent, the ornament of the stage, the acknowledged first-ranking actor, unquestionably the greatest, but can be someone very insignificant. Something charming, attractive, in an insignificant human being who has an ingratiating nature, makes a clique launch him early; friends among the critics praise him to the skies; sympathetic roles that are not too complex are chosen for him and often forced upon a good-natured audience that considers itself flattered to be noticed or kowtowed to by a star of the stage.

Such an actor plays on a fortunate disposition, a pair of beautiful eyes, a couple of melodious tones, an engaging gesture, a daring expression, but does not play on his personality, because he hasn't any. He gives a sort of antispiritualistic séance, in which all the tricks are visible because they cannot be concealed, and can assume dimensions, be called "great" on big festive occasions, and as an illusionist he gives the illusion of talent. For such an actor or actress the art of the stage is a higher form of coquetry, and the auditorium is a real salon, in which the triumphs of salon life are celebrated theatrically.

I followed a comet career like that for eight years. I was urged to speak out the first year and admit he had native talent; won by his natural verve in movement, I could not, however, bend low before a talent that was not there, although I hoped that he would develop into something significant; I encouraged him. What I saw afterward was nothing. I heard nothing though I thought I did, and what I saw was unreal, vague, an image in smoke. But I was amazed when both the theater public and the critics praised him to the skies, and I refrained from expressing my judgment out of fear I was mistaken.

His next assignment was a big and serious one, but I did not detect any seriousness of purpose, did not see one expression or gesture observed, but [I did notice] in everything he did an ingratiating spirit which courted the audience, tried to get its support, and succeeded. When I said it was utterly false, I was outvoted. I stayed away for seven years. In the meantime his reputation had grown all out of proportion. The favorite had risen to stardom, and a bloody path on which small and great rivals lay trampled underfoot had been cut for his procession of victory.

Parallel with this, however, was an undercurrent of criticism and opposition so that the applause and approval were never absolute. The opposition would occasionally burst forth: "This is lack of talent; it amounts to absolutely nothing!" This made his supporters increase their claims still more, and soon the climax was reached.

One day I had to go along to see the wonder. I came and saw! Favorably disposed, ready to admire, prepared if necessary to be lenient in judgment, which I thought would be unnecessary. And I saw after eight years: a *raisonneur* without a voice, like a worn-out tenor, without being carried by any inner feeling, without excitement, without interest, lifeless, talentless.

There was simply nothing! It could not be set right, could not be improved because there was nothing to set right, nothing to work with. But it was a success anyway! The audience still saw its favorite as he had been but no longer was, heard a voice that did not exist.

This phenomenon can only be explained as a hypnotic séance, where weak heads are persuaded to see and hear anything at all, and where the audience gives the favorite the impression he is still a star, for one cannot call the whole thing a practical joke. So much the less as the favorite lives in eternal fear of awakening from his state of intoxication and losing his ability to create illusions, suffers by not being certain if he has talent or not. In moments of the deepest depression the doubt becomes certainty and grows into contempt for the art and for the audience, "which lets itself be fooled."

The mutual awakening is terrible. But the artist who first misused the stage for the public display of his vanity and sacrificed both his honor and his conscience for the favor of the moment can expect no other reward even if [others'] sympathy is genuine. What is hardest to understand about this phenomenon is that those who have been duped consider the favorite's flaws merits and see his weaknesses as perfections; and finally when the only things that are undebatable, his charming disposition, his youthful good looks, his smart figure are gone, they continue in blindness seeing—what is not

there. It is like distorting people's vision, practicing magic —
and the women favorites age into witches.

*   *   *

The director. His most important qualities are taste in selecting plays and judgment in casting. Reading a play is almost
like reading a musical score: it is difficult, and I do not know
many who can do it although a lot of people say they can. The
very arrangement of the text, where the eyes have to wander
from the name of the speaker to his speech, demands close
attention; the seemingly uninteresting exposition has to be got
through and carefully recorded in one's memory, since it contains the warp by means of which the whole weaving is set up.
The action noted within the parentheses delays and distracts
one, too. Even to this day when I read Shakespeare I have to
pencil in notes to keep the characters and particularly the numerous minor speaking characters straight, and I have to go
back constantly to the list of characters and to go back to the
first act to take a look at what the characters said then. A person has to read a play at least twice to have it clearly in mind,
and in order to be able to assign the roles one has to read it
carefully several times. Usually the author (*or* the translator)
and the director are the only ones who know the play thoroughly; for that reason they are the most competent in assigning the roles. But the director has been made director precisely
in order to experience the feeling of power in distributing the
roles; for that reason he accepts advice unwillingly, and that
is why the roles are often badly assigned — but also because
personal consideration, favoritism, ability, antipathy, and envy
are allowed to prevail. The person who knows the personnel,
every artist's disposition, ability, and limitations, sees immedi-

ately when he reads the play who should play each role. But there are directors who have not *seen* [my italics, W.J.] all the plays he has put on and therefore do not know what talents he has [at his disposal]; the assignment of parts then is hit or miss, the play suffers, and the artists suffer from uncongenial tasks.*

But even the conscientious director has a hard time dividing up the work, for he has to think of both the theater and the actor at the same time: so that the theater does not lose one of its talented workers and so that the actor is not without a role and is forgotten. Sometimes the director for financial reasons has to push ahead with the audience's favorite, "who is a drawing card," instead of exploiting a new and promising actor.

If the director is also the stage manager the theater can really be well looked after, but if the director is also going to act in plays it *can* go in a smaller theater but it is disastrous in a larger one.

The director does not have the freedom in selecting plays that actors and authors imagine. Depending on the prevalent taste, the financial or economic situation, or the mood, he is often forced to select a play that people want to see, even if it is not very good. How far he can go in giving in to poor taste depends on his artistic interests, the financial condition of his theater, and the traditions of his theater. If people are used to seeing good serious dramas at his theater, they do not want to see comedies or farces there, although they tolerate them in another theater.

Authors are often amazed when a really good play is returned to them. But the reason can be that [another play with] the same motif has just been playing at this or other theaters so

---

* The original, "*Men det finns direktörer, som icke sett alla sina givna stycken och därför icke känner, vilka förmågor han äger,*" is obscure. [W.J.]

that the motif is worn out and people do not want to have more of that sort. The play may be boring in spite of superb technique, or painful, or impossible to cast, or expensive to produce. An example from classic dramas is *King Lear*. All theaters would be glad to play that at any time, for it is interesting, lively, and well constructed, but how often does a theater have an old actor who still has the great powers required for this role?

Still: following the public's taste can be risky, because taste is forever changing and often changes very suddenly. One day people go in for uniforms on the stage; that sort of thing goes brilliantly for a couple of seasons. Then the director buys sight unseen an expensive military play with a very expensive production cost. It fails: the public taste has changed.

It is not easy to be adviser to a director. The only lead one can have in trying to find out "what the public wants" would be in contemporary problems, in contemporary literature, in everything that stirs up people's minds. But then, one fine day, people tire of the discussion and want to talk about something different, want to forget the wearisome quarrels; people long for peace. That is why an idyllic play such as [Ludovic Halévy's] *Abbé Constantin* (1882) could come very suitably right in the midst of the Nora controversy; [Fritz Reuter's] *Life in the Country* (*Ut mine Stromtid*, 1872) is used to this day as a lightning rod any time at all; [W. Meyer-Förster's] *Old Heidelberg* (*Alt-Heidelberg*, 1901) became an oasis in the march through the desert; and *Don Cesar* is always handy to put on when people want to break off an unpleasant controversy. But one has to have straws in the wind to know when the controversy is ripe for its end so that one does not come with a flop.

The director must also be able to sense when the public wants something classical. A theater with a government subsidy is duty bound to present a classic drama now and then. Enjoying such a play requires good will, a little education, and the ability to put one's ideas into historic perspective. Enjoying a classic play sincerely and thoroughly requires knowledge, of course, so that one has the prerequisites for grasping what is hinted at when references are made to matters generally regarded as well known. A person ought to know Antigone's story, know who she is, before he goes to see that last act in a tragedy.

The classics aren't fun, people say. But one ought to go through them, and for those who are growing up they make a rewarding and beneficial study. There are things which one does not need to see but must *have seen*: foreign cities, museums, cathedrals.

There are classic dramas that interest people in all periods, and the characters in them would arouse sympathy without make-up and costume. Hamlet is always understandable and his fate moving; *Faust*, I and II, ought to be produced occasionally, but not Part I alone because it has been worn to shreds as an opera text; [Schiller's] *Don Carlos* (1787), *Maria Stuart* (1800), and *The Maid of Orleans* (*Die Jungfrau von Orleans*, 1801) are not dated, and Schiller's strict, careful form, occasionally pedantic characterization, give firm authority to his dramas; Molière has his admirers although I have never liked him; Oehlenschläger's *Axel and Valborg* (1818)[25] was not loved by our unfeeling time, but it will return; [his] *Hakon Jarl* (1805) and *Aladdin* (1805) are waiting for the moment of revival; to Holberg's *Jeppe* and *Erasmus Montanus* could be added several of his plays, probably *The Lying-in Room* (*Barseltuen*, 1724), *The Fussy Man* (*Den Stundeslöse*, 1728), and others;[26] from Calderón one needs to know only *Life Is a*

Dream (*La vida es sueño*), but there are probably others worth putting on. I don't know if it would pay us to try Corneille and Racine, but their wines do not seem to bear either exporting or translation. The Germans have dug up Kleist and Hebbel, but for me they will remain fossils like Lessing.

But we must clear up the concept *classic*. A drama does not become superb because the author has a great name or is long since dead. Goethe was a theater director and an actor, but his sense of form failed him when he was going to construct a drama. *Egmont* is not classic in the sense of excellence. Its form wobbles, and it is carelessly constructed. People demand it occasionally so they can hear Beethoven's overture, just as people ask for *Antigone* because of Mendelssohn's choruses. *Clavigo* is miserable, in romance style; *Stella* like *Geschwister* goes because of inserted [material]. But *Goetz* in all its seeming formlessness is strictly conceived. Its fifty-six tableaux are a firm unit that lives and interests — Germans mainly.

Tasso is attractive, wise, fascinating, but does not bear translation. It probably will never reach the great public that finds poets and artists on the stage strange.

Blindly admiring everything signed by big names has the attendant danger that one appreciates what is bad and develops poor taste. Goethe himself admired his comedies, *Der Bürger-General* and *Gross-Kophta*, but posterity has called both rubbish. Several of Shakespeare's comedies *are* rubbish, and some years ago a Shakespeare comedy that had previously been admired became a fiasco. It was then completely exposed.

Of the old Greek tragedies there are probably others besides *Antigone*, and the turbulent Euripides deserves to be tried out to see if he could not move our time better than the calm Sophocles.

To the beginner. Many people select careers in the theater because they are amused by it, others because they are interested in it.

The former live in the delusion that a gay life free of artistic worries is led behind the wings. But that is not so. Life in the theater is a strict, heavy life of labor, all forenoon at rehearsal, all evening with make-up, costuming, and acting, ending toward midnight. In leisure hours — which never exist at some theaters — lines must be learned, the tailor and the seamstress visited. The actor who has parts in the repertory is almost never free during the season. For him there is no outside pleasure, no outside amusement, not even home life — if he has a home. He cannot accept an evening invitation, that is, at night, for then his work will suffer next day. He does not dare to accept a dinner invitation, "for he has to act that evening," that is: a few glasses of wine can extinguish his memory or exalt his spirits, and the whole thing can end with a lowering of the curtain, perhaps for his whole life.

But there is something else, too! He is always going about with roles on his mind, which is never free; and even if a play gets many performances and his work goes of itself, he can get ill, the program can be changed at six P.M., and a new play must be put on as if by magic. All this can never give the actor any tranquility, not to mention the natural uneasiness of mind which always has to precede an appearance before an audience, an audience that is new every evening, fickle, undependable, whimsical, sometimes getting out of hand so that it rejects the best and becomes contrary.

Finally, as an author I have come to thinking about how an actor is torn apart inwardly when he plays a painful tragedy, most likely many times in a row. People can say that this is imaginary torment, but imaginary suffering is just as painful as real, and the tears that are shed on stage are just as bitter and sincere as offstage.

In the happy days of the actor's success, he is the object of envy; but success soon fades away and can be followed by failure, which in one evening can wipe out the memory of everything great and beautiful he has done before. That is forgotten, is no longer talked about, is canceled. That is how fragile honor and fame can be.

Then come the fatal moments when the young man and the young woman have to leave their youth behind them. If youthful charm was all they had, their careers are over. If they had more than charm, they are promoted to a higher class, but an age class: the time for their playing character roles has come.

But youth does not have to pass *that* quickly; it can be preserved, but at what a cost! Fasting and mortification of the flesh, going to bed hungry, standing like a saint on a pillar in the middle of the floor after meals, never delighting the eye or strengthening the heart with a glass of wine. One's figure keeps its youthfulness for a while, but then the nerves begin to rebel, and one's voice fails for lack of nourishment. Then the doctor comes and prescribes—everything that can increase one's weight and so prevent keeping one's youthfulness. That is the dilemma that can never be solved!

But, even if everything about all this goes well, one's career has many other tribulations. The public can weary of one's best; new actors come along with new methods, sometimes merely with new tricks; the artist can lose public favor and become the object of the inexplicable hate of both the audience and the critics. If the actor happens to disagree with his director, he is frequently lost, because then he gets poor roles and he is on his way out. If he becomes sick or his memory is weakened, he is lost. And so on!

I have said all this to frighten the persons who select careers in the theater because they are amused by it and by the gay life. Those who want to become actors because they have a great desire to suffer and enjoy through reincarnating themselves and living the lives of many human beings on the stage will not let themselves be frightened. They go where their genius calls them, through fire and water, and they do not seek false honor but are sustained by the work itself, rewarded or unrewarded, with joy or without. The stage is their world and their home. The art they create cannot be displayed in store windows or in museums but is limited to the theater and to the moment, is transient, disappears in the sun like an unfixed ray of light, leaves behind it only a memory which can be wiped out by time or by still greater memories of others.

Those who are called to be actors know all this, but they do their jobs and die!

*　　　*　　　*

The beginner has to begin at the beginning so he gets the minor roles, most likely the parts which announce the coming of others.

I want to say at once that the author creates such roles intentionally. An important person is to be brought on stage, his entrance has to be prepared for to be effective, and the author wants to fix the audience's attention on this character. So it is very important for the play that the announcement be made clearly and distinctly in order that his name and his title will be heard. If it cannot be heard, the whole scene has lost its effect since the member of the audience will be annoyed by uncertainty about whom he has the honor of getting to know. So the beginner must not despise the announcement role, and

August Falck

Anna Flygare as Eleonora
in *Easter*

Anna Flygare (Nurse) and August Falck (Adolf) in *The Father*

he must also know whom he is announcing, the latter's significance in the play, and know if the coming situation will be calm or violent, decisive or not; all this should be heard in the announcer's tone of voice and tempo.

But there is also another reason why the pupil should not reject the little role. The director or the stage manager may be standing in the wings looking on. If he notices a true gesture or a genuine tone of voice on the pupil's part or discovers an attractive voice, a pleasant personality, seriousness and effort, absence of false pride, the young actor's fortune may be made. I have seen it happen that a talented actor has been discovered in the role of a servant, a voice among the people, a herald, a soldier.

On the other hand, the pupil should not do too much, not elbow his way ahead, not fix unnecessary attention on himself, not put himself above his role and look at it contemptuously.

I have been a pupil: it is not fun to hang about in the wings waiting for three hours to make one entrance in the fifth act. But the time can be spent usefully and relatively pleasantly if one follows what is happening on stage, listens and sees, sees and hears, how different the actors are every night, observes how different the audience is, how differently it reacts to the actors. *There* is a school and a place for studying especially if the pupil gets the opportunity of seeing how roles are alternated between two actors, so that he can compare different artists' different interpretations of the same role.

I advise against reading too many books about the art of acting. Your studies should be pursued in daily life by observing living human beings, in rehearsals, at performances. The person who is born with the gift of good delivery thinks the art of acting is easy; the one who has aptitude but is not trained finds it difficult; the introvert, bewitched within himself, soon finds it impossible, for there are inhibited people who are impossible on the stage.

*   *   *

To the personnel of the Intimate Theater:

Now that we are rehearsing a new play, *The Father*, I am going to take the opportunity to express my wishes about the pronunciation of the Swedish language on stage.

We are not putting on comedies or farces, and therefore the language must be held so high that it does not lose its resources as a means of expression because of careless enunciation.

All letters [i.e., letters representing sounds] must be pronounced distinctly from the beginning; afterward you will glide over them without omitting them.

So we are going to say *skall* (not *ska*), *är* (not *e*), *var* (not *va*), etc.—with discrimination, of course.

The consonants must be particularly protected. Examples: *fort* (not *fott*), *stort* (not *stot*), *s* must be pronounced *s* [voiceless *s*] and not *z* (lisping), *teatern* (not *teaten*), etc.

In general actors speak too rapidly in our theater; it is little and intimate, of course, but there are 150 people in the audience who have paid for the right to hear [what is said]. The actor is heard only if he pronounces every sound slowly and distinctly; if he uses *phrasing* and musical pausing, i.e., stresses more important words, does not emphasize less important ones, and divides the phrase properly; gives the nuances of rising and sinking [intonation], speeding up and holding back, pausing, legato, and staccato.

In order to be able to speak slowly and well, you should in general tie up all the joints and words of the line (legato) in such a way, however, that the inner punctuation can be heard lightly; staccato is to be used only when the role calls for it.

At the first rehearsals, which are used as exercises in speech, you should speak slowly to the point of exaggeration.

Afterward, when the tempo is increased, the pronunciation will still be distinct because all the sounds will be heard — they will have been learned.

In general you ought to speak from your chest and not only with your mouth, because with only the mouth one whispers.

To speak well — the chief thing on the stage — you need no lessons but merely observation of yourself and the actor playing opposite to you, listening to yourself, thinking about what you are saying.

When people have seen so much acting talent, almost heaped up, at the Intimate Theater, they have complained that the art of speech is neglected in several ways.

That is why I have wanted in good time to point out this flaw in order that we may try for perfection even if we do not attain it.

July 26, 1908   THE DIRECTOR.

SECOND LETTER

Introduction

WHILE the first letter to the personnel of the Intimate Theater was designed primarily to clarify Strindberg's concept of an intimate theater not only for the actors but also for Strindberg himself, the second aimed at broadening several matters that had been touched on but not fully developed in the first. Taking an approach that is at once subjective and cooperative in spirit, Strindberg presented what he considered matters basic for the development of skills and engagement on the part of everyone concerned with the production of plays at the theater. Addressed to coworkers whom he considered intelligent human beings seriously interested in drama and theater, Strindberg explained how he analyzed a play, indicated the importance of such a study, applied what he had to say to the recent production of his own *Queen Christina*, commented on Shakespeare's method of characterization and concept of the world, indulged in a number of digressions on topics that he could never wholly escape, and, finally, returned to his point of departure, *Hamlet*.

The letter is not a set of pedantic instructions on how to analyze a play, how to think things through, or how to act. It is instead a very personal document that suggests and illustrates how Strindberg analyzed a play, how he came to conclusions, and what he believed are some of the secrets of good theater. Since it is a letter, it, more-over, reveals as effective letters do a great deal about the personal preferences and thought patterns of the letter writer himself.

What Strindberg has to say about *Hamlet*, "the most interesting and the greatest of Shakespeare's work," merits serious considera-tion by any student of either dramatist. While, for example, Strind-berg may have misunderstood why Hamlet dragged Polonius' body off stage, Strindberg did not err in his attempts at penetrating the mystery of Shakespeare's "artlessness in art," nor did he err in as-signing scholarly commentaries to their proper secondary role and insisting that, if one is to get to know Hamlet, one must study the play itself.

Strindberg's discussion of Shakespeare's methods of characteriza-tion is doubly interesting because of what Strindberg had said about his own methods (primarily in the important preface to *Lady Julie*, 1888) and had applied in his historical plays and in his plays of the 1880's and the early 1890's. His insistence in the letter that at best the dramatist can merely suggest the rich nuances of a dynamic and complex character is essentially the same as what he says in the preface about the presentation of "characterless characters." Strind-berg's choice of Ophelia as an illustration of the result of "an un-conscious attempt at giving in summary form a character with all its nuances" is particularly happy, it seems to me. His defense of Po-lonius is surely worth consideration; his analysis of Hamlet is bril-liant. Can any one quarrel with Strindberg's conclusion? "Briefly and summarily: Shakespeare depicts people, in all their phases, just as inconsequent, self-contradictory, tattered, self-torn, illogical, and incapable of being understood as people are. But he does not do this always, and not completely, for one cannot!"

Strindberg's conclusions about Shakespeare's concept of the world are probably more open to qualification. There is no question that Strindberg believed that Shakespeare revealed himself in his works, was a devout believing Catholic, was a pessimist at times, and on occasion doubted the reality of life. One example will illustrate the point: the fascinating little section of the letter called "King Lear's Wife." As every student of Strindberg knows, Strindberg was personally engaged with the whole problem of woman and her relationship with man to the point that he could rarely if ever escape from the question. There is at least a hint that Strindberg hesitated a little to read his own thinking about the matter into Shakespeare and state flatly that such and such were the details of Shakespeare's concept of woman.

Strindberg admits that *Hamlet* had had a very great meaning for him when he was young. The passage in *The Son of a Servant* to which he refers in the letter reads in part:

> The melancholy Hamlet had a profounder effect. Who is this Hamlet, who still lives, after having seen the footlights [first] during the age of John III [of Sweden] and has always remained just as young? People have interpreted him in many ways and have used him for all possible purposes. Johan [Strindberg] immediately took him over for his own.
>
> The curtain goes up; the king and the court in brilliant costumes; music and pleasure. Then comes the pale young man dressed in mourning and opposes his stepfather. Ah! He has a stepfather! That's at least as damnable as having a stepmother, John thinks. Hamlet's my man! And he's to be crushed, and they want to torture him into having sympathy for tyrants. The youngster's ego rises. Rebellion! But his will is crippled; he shakes his fist, but can't strike. He punishes the mother! Shame it wasn't the father! And has a bad conscience afterward! Good, good! He is sick with thought, becomes introspective, considers his actions until they dissolve into nothing. . . . John begins to doubt he's an exception! . . .
>
> But it was wonderful to get to weep over one's destiny and see one's destiny wept over. Hamlet didn't, however, become more than the stepson for the time being; later on he became the man who broods, and still later the son [who is] the victim of family tyranny [*Strindbergs Samlade Skrifter*, XVIII, 182–83].

Young Strindberg identified himself with Hamlet, and throughout his lifetime Strindberg had the conviction that *Hamlet* was one of the masterpieces of world literature.

In this letter he shows the members of the company why that is so: a superb structure, unsurpassed characterization, and universality of ideational content — all of them so important that he felt that *Hamlet* might well be put on without any cutting, without scenery or with a minimum of scenery, but with an abstract frame and perhaps draperies used as Falck had used them in producing *Queen Christina* at the Intimate Theater. What Strindberg implies is that every word in *Hamlet* deserves to be heard. If anything is to be sacrificed in a production of Hamlet, it must not be the lines themselves. [W.J.]

Hamlet
A Memorial on November 26
Our Anniversary, Dedicated to
the Intimate Theater

It is not tempting to write about Shakespeare when every date and fact that concerns his life and work is questioned. For that reason the Danish critic began his great book about Shakespeare[1] by confessing that practically nothing is known about Shakespeare. No one knows when he was born or how he spelled his name, and at the end of the nineteenth century some people even doubted that he had ever existed; [some] people thought Lord Bacon had written the plays until Bleibtreu[2] in our time has "proved" that it was not Bacon but another lord (whose name I don't have at the moment) who wrote them. All this seems strange to me, for Shakespeare was never known by any other name in his own day, still less unknown, and contemporary writers (Ben Jonson) mention him with admiration and appreciation. They knew his name at the club (The Mermaid) at which he flourished; and his friends (later enemies) Burbage and Greene were famous. In David Brewster's *Edinburgh Encyclopedia* I read recently a long "guaranteed" biography with family trees and data galore, so I have no doubts of the poet's existence; and even if certain youthful escapades such as poaching should be false, it would not matter in the least to me — either way.

I have admitted elsewhere (in *The Son of a Servant*) that about 1866 *Hamlet* was a revelation and a milestone in my unhappy life mainly for personal reasons, but I have also acknowledged that Shakespeare did not then become my favorite. There was something foreign to my nature in Shakespeare, something I cannot explain which made me keep him at a distance although I later had to pound some of his tragedies — in the original English — into me and have them destroyed because of [the instructor's use of] experiments in comparative linguistics (Diez's method).[3] That was in the 1870's. About 1880 I saw *Macbeth* performed, but I was not delighted with it; the text had been cut, and I was disturbed by the trick mirrors and the trampolinelike structures, and the old actors who were trying to achieve the "grand style" did not have the proper reverence for the play. Since then I have seen only *Othello* and *A Midsummer-Night's Dream*. But at the end of the century[4] I was at the university and repeated my study of a number of subjects, including Shakespeare. My enjoyment was not unmixed, but I was determined to study his method of constructing a drama. It was at that time that I noticed that his structure was both formless and at the same time strictly pedantically formal. All his plays have the same cut: five acts, with four or five scenes, but one cannot really see how this is done. He begins at a certain point; then the play develops in a straight line to the end. The technique does not show, no effect is calculated, the great strokes are there after a beautiful development, and then comes the peaceful settlement with drums and trumpets. Someone has said that it all seems like nature itself, and I agree.

What we call a scene (*en scen*), according to the French (Sardou) concept, is the result of calculated strategy and refined tactics. We younger dramatists have to work with foreshadowing and preparation, minutely detailed exposition, reversals, peripateia, stratagems and counterstratagems, parallel action (that is my strength!). Shakespeare is blunt, telling everything he knows in Act I. There is Hamlet about whom we know nothing. In the first scene of Act I comes a ghost, who tells everything, even what Hamlet does not know.

Look at *Richard III*: in Act I the murdered Henry VI's corpse is brought in; his widow walks beside the body. Stop: Richard (Gloucester) woos her, and after eight printed pages she has almost said "yes" to the murderer. All this is done in such a masterful way that it becomes believable, and there is nothing to criticize about that; I have simply studied the scene for a similar objective. But a contemporary Frenchman would have used all five acts to have brought forth this "yes" from the victim's widow to the murderer; and that effort alone would have interested the Frenchman. But it is merely a detail for Shakespeare, and he goes beyond it to no one's harm. Those are simply two different approaches, the one as good as the other!

In the comedies, too, intrigues are planned and fashioned; in them the characters reveal at the beginning that they intend to play a trick, a comedy within the comedy, and they reveal the whole plot in advance.

Shakespeare does not bother about what we call the architecture or structure of a play, but he tells a story directly, and that is that.

It was this artlessness in art that annoyed Voltaire; but during periods when the drama has become artificial it is a good thing to renew oneself in nature, and Shakespeare is nature itself. Naked as a child, he shows unveiled what would be offensive if veiled. No matter how carelessly he composes what he writes he is always sustained by an innate sense for form and a never failing buoyancy. Shakespeare never goes to work without motivation; he does not write for the sake of writing; he is not one of those writers who always have to be scribbling away, understanding the art of writing about nothing or writing to please somebody, or just to show others there is nothing special to it. Shakespeare is always deeply engaged; he loves or hates, rages against destiny, submits, rages again, but whatever he does his major interest is this: to depict human beings, and he does this from above so that for him all people are alike without his being a friend of the mob just because of that. He cannot be, of course, but, just as he heaps scorn on the arrogant (not the justified) claims of the mob in *Coriolanus* and *Julius Caesar*, he ridicules the godlike pretensions of kings and queens in most of his historical dramas.

Although he is everywhere present, he embodies himself in the person who is talking at the moment and takes his point of view even against himself. In *King Lear* he defends adultery in the bastard Edmund's monologue: "Thou, nature, art my goddess" (I, 2), but afterward Edmund is shown to be a monster when he among other things has Cordelia hanged, and he dies at his brother's hand, but the older son Edgar is presented as a finer nature. Their father Gloucester, who has boasted about his beloved bastard (Edmund), has his eyes opened when they tear his eyes out: "Oh my follies! then Edgar was abused" (III, 7). The bastard has betrayed him.

There Shakespeare plays nemesis without squeamishness, and when one cites Edmund's monologue as a defense of adultery, omitting what follows, one is falsifying the source.

Now I come to *Hamlet!*

I suppose I have read twenty commentators, but I have discovered that a careful examination of the text is the only way to form a judgment of *Hamlet,* the most interesting and the greatest of Shakespeare's works.

The composition is like that of a *novella* with its subplots and digressions as Goethe said in *Wilhelm Meister,*[5] and I have speculated on whether the subplots should be eliminated or not. The actor who plays the title role would, of course, like to cut whatever obscures his own role. But we may not take that point of view, and Shakespeare had his own difficulties with actors, who pursue "the art of borrowed feathers."

In order to get a clear answer to this difficult question, I will examine the content (the plot) of the play. But I must first make two important comments. In the first printed editions of *Hamlet* in folio and quarto the texts do not agree, and insertions seem to have been made: author's additions to give especially effective "numbers" to the actor, capricious changes by directors, actors, and even scribes. So one must not be too respectful of the text, for one can easily blunder if out of respect for the author one keeps a false passage and cuts the original. Wilhelm Meister was not faultfinding when he wanted to exclude the following: the rebellion in Norway, the war against young Fortinbras, the mission to the old uncle, the settled controversy (?), young Fortinbras' expedition to Poland, and his return at the end; Horatio's return from Wittenberg, Hamlet's wish to go there; Laertes' trip to France, his return;

Hamlet's mission to England, his capture by sea pirates, the death of Guildenstern and Rosencrantz because of the Uriah letter. "All these," says Goethe, "are circumstances and events that make a novel broad and inclusive but hurt the unity of the play to the highest degree and are flaws, especially since the hero does not have any definite plan."

These cuts most likely had been made in the play I saw at the Royal Theater about 1867, and I did not miss anything to mar my enjoyment of the play which I knew in its complete form.

But just about then Dietrichson[6] in *Det skönas värld* (*The World of Beauty*) began to call for Fortinbras, and that call has been made ever since but has not been heard except in Munich,[7] where *Hamlet*, every last word of it, is given in its entirety. Initiated people considered this experiment in Munich successful, but I do not think it served as an example, though that may depend on the public's opposition to new ways in spite of its desire for novelties.

Now if I examine the action in *Hamlet* I can arrive at my own point of view on whether the play should be performed in its entirety or cut.

ACT I

Scene 1. The guard at Elsinore is changed. Horatio asks if the ghost has appeared again; when they talk about it, it appears, and then disappears. We learn that Denmark is preparing for war against Norway where Fortinbras has rebelled; that is also the reason for the strict watch. In his day Hamlet's now-deceased father Hamlet I had defeated Fortinbras the elder. If this is to signify anything by way of nemesis (the sins of the father visited on the children), I do not want to state yet. The ghost comes a second time and disappears. Horatio says he wants to go to tell Hamlet about the apparition. (All exit.)

Scene 2. A room in the palace. The king is speaking, among other things, about young Fortinbras' rebellion; Cornelius and Voltimand are sent on a mission to Norway. Laertes asks leave to return to France. The king asks Hamlet if he has any wish. Hamlet, who got this stepfather a month ago, asks only for permission to return to Wittenberg. The king advises him against this. The queen supports the king's opinion, and Hamlet says he will obey his mother. The king becomes more cheerful.

Hamlet's first monologue:

> How weary, stale, flat and unprofitable,
> Seem to me all the uses of this world!

and

> Frailty, thy name is woman!

etc. — Horatio enters and tells about the ghost. Hamlet decides to go to the ramparts to meet his father's ghost.

Scene 3. At Polonius' home. Laertes warns his sister Ophelia about Hamlet. Polonius enters, says farewell to his son Laertes, who is going to Paris. Then Polonius warns Ophelia about Hamlet's courtship.

Scene 4. Hamlet's meeting with the ghost, who merely signals to Hamlet for him to go aside.

Scene 5. On a remote part of the terrace, the ghost tells what Hamlet does not know: that Hamlet's father was murdered by his brother, who had first tempted Hamlet's mother successfully. The ghost asks Hamlet to seek revenge. Horatio, Marcellus, and Bernardo swear to Hamlet (1) never to reveal what they have seen and (2) never to expose Hamlet when he plays insane to find out if the king is guilty.

Act I is a thorough first act: all the major characters are introduced; all threads are tied up; everything one needs to know one has learned. But there is a plus: Hamlet's character has developed; from having been a melancholy cynic he has become obsessed and has a goal for which to live — revenge. A decision has been made, and the act ends with a promise that makes the audience want to hear what is to follow. Thus this first act is perfect as exposition and composition even if one feels that the preparation for Hamlet's meeting with the ghost is too detailed.

ACT II

Scene 1. Polonius asks Reynaldo to keep an eye on Laertes in Paris. I do not understand why this scene was written unless it was to characterize Polonius as somewhat cunning. Ophelia tells her father that Hamlet has become insane. Polonius believes the insanity is a result of Hamlet's love for Ophelia, and goes to tell the king.

Scene 2. The king asks Guildenstern and Rosencrantz to distract Hamlet from his melancholy. Polonius reports that the ambassadors have returned from Norway and that he has discovered the reason for Hamlet's insanity. Voltimand and Cornelius enter and report that Fortinbras has been arrested by his uncle but has escaped and intends to go on a campaign to Poland. Now Polonius tells about Hamlet's insanity and shows a letter he has written to Ophelia. Hamlet has been repulsed by Ophelia and he

> Fell into a sadness; then into a fast,
> Thence to a watch, thence into a weakness,
> Thence to a lightness, and, by this declension,
> Into the madness wherein now he raves,
> And all we mourn for.

This is a very important point, because even if Hamlet has decided to *act*, this new motif — Ophelia's rejection — could

have made him mad. Therefore Hamlet can both be acting insane and be insane — the commentators have argued about both
notions. Hamlet's love letter to Ophelia begins with pretended
foolishness — "To the celestial, and my soul's idol, the most
beautified Ophelia" — but his reason is in good condition in
these lines:

> Doubt thou the stars are fire;
> Doubt that the sun doth move;
> Doubt truth to be a liar;
> But never doubt I love.

Now the king and Polonius decide to listen to Hamlet behind a tapestry to find out if he really loves Ophelia. When
Hamlet enters, Polonius is alone and the conversation begins.
Hamlet is supposed to act insane here, but Shakespeare lets
go his intention and has Hamlet talk like a court fool: ironi-
cally, satirically, wittily, but not insanely, and Polonius does
not believe he is mad either. Hamlet talks as Yorick, the court
fool, would have done, the clown who had been Hamlet's
companion in his youth and whose skull he later finds in the
churchyard. Edgar's pretended insanity in *King Lear* is genuine, for he talks pure nonsense. For example:

> The foul fiend haunts poor Tom in the voice of a nightingale.
> Hopdance cries in Tom's belly for two white herring. Croak not,
> black angel; I have no food for thee.

Rosencrantz and Guildenstern enter; and now begins an exchange but no madness; Polonius and the players enter, and
Hamlet says the wisest words that have ever been said about
theatrical art. Then he continues with a soliloquy: "O, what
a rogue and peasant slave am I!" Doubt has seized this Witten-
berg-trained casuist, who has to seek the ultimate basis of everything, and he now begins to wonder if the ghost was only a
devil that wanted to entice him into sin:

> . . . The spirit that I have seen
> May be the devil: and the devil hath power
> To assume a pleasing shape; yea, and perhaps
> Out of my weakness and my melancholy,
> As he is very potent with such spirits. . . .

This soliloquy resembles Richard II's (Act V):

> I have been studying how I may compare
> This prison where I live unto the world. . . .

This second act ebbs out in Hamlet's decision to use the play to trap the king's conscience. With that one has gone ahead quite a bit to reach the climax in Act III.

ACT III

Scene 1. The king asks Rosencrantz and Guildenstern about Hamlet's condition and orders that he be amused by means of a play. The queen expresses her hope that Ophelia may "be the happy cause of Hamlet's wildness." The king and Polonius, who both are justifiably spies, decide to spy on Hamlet anew. But the king's conscience has awakened: "O heavy burden!" Hamlet enters; the soliloquy "to be or not to be," expressing an infinite contempt for this world and ending [with consideration of] suicide, is interrupted by Ophelia. The duet follows, whereupon Ophelia expresses her conviction that Hamlet is mad. The king, not believing that Hamlet is insane, orders that he be sent to England to collect tribute. Polonius proposes locking him up.

Scene 2. Hamlet strikes out at actors and their art; against loud mouthing and artificial gestures, but warns them against tameness and asks them not to "overstep the modesty of nature."

Horatio enters; Hamlet characterizes him, saying among other things that he has "good spirits," which is never illustrated by Horatio on stage. He performs like a flabby soul and a shadow, not to say a yesman of the same cut as Rosencrantz and Guildenstern, whose "Yes, my lord" is repeated to the point of weariness by Horatio. And Shakespeare has been careless about Horatio, for he shows him as a yesman and not as Hamlet characterized him. Horatio is urged to keep an eye on the king in order to study his behavior while the play is presented.

The king, the queen, Ophelia, and the court gather while Hamlet is ironic and plays the fool.

Now comes the play, which is a little masterpiece that is usually carelessly and ineffectively presented. It is in rhymed verse, and it is full of fine little observations, thoughts, and discoveries. The play has the desired effect: the king gets up and leaves. The mine has exploded as it should in Act III, and now the stone rolls downhill. Guildenstern and Rosencrantz ask Hamlet to visit the queen in her rooms; the king is ill ("with drink?" asks Hamlet). Polonius, too, comes on the same errand, and Hamlet promises to go to his mother. But now he is stirred up: "I could drink hot blood," but immediately afterward he comforts us by saying, "I will speak daggers to her, but use none."

Scene 3. The king sends Rosencrantz and Guildenstern to England (with the secret Uriah [8] letter); Polonius hides behind the arras. The king confesses in the soliloquy, "my offence is rank," in which he shows he is very human: "Bow, stubborn knees!" and arouses our sympathy and pity. Hamlet enters, wants to kill the king, but falls into his casuistic university method of philosophizing about the matter, and therefore postpones it.

Scene 4. The queen's room where the reckoning with the mother takes place. Hamlet is coarse and cruel when he exposes his mother's shame, and he has forgotten the ghost's warning (Act I) to spare his mother; for that reason his father's ghost crosses the stage to interrupt the unpleasant performance, when Hamlet has murdered Polonius, and to spur him on to seek vengeance soon against the king. Why Gertrude cannot see the ghost is a question that I cannot answer.

In Act I, crude soldiers could see the ghost, [a power] generally considered to be restricted to refined natures. The mother's inability to see [the ghost] is not, I suppose, a flaw in her, stemming from a sensual nature. Shakespeare may have meant that the dead husband wants to spare her from horror and simply wants to give Hamlet a reminder. Or has he used this device to motivate the following discourse, where the mother says that Hamlet's having seen the ghost is proof of his madness, whereupon Hamlet demonstrates the contrary, reveals that he has been pretending, and asks his mother not to tell the king?

Hamlet weakens a little and almost begs for forgiveness: "I must be cruel only to be kind."

Hamlet goes, dragging Polonius' body behind him. This crude detail is not an addition, because it is mentioned twice in the next act, and Hamlet is said to have hidden the body in a stairway in the gallery. This repulsive act is so unlike Hamlet that scholars have guessed that it represents an outbreak of genuine insanity. But even this lack of logic in his behavior pattern—he hesitates about murdering the guilty king, but without hesitation or pang of conscience kills the innocent old man and dishonors his body—is a symptom of insanity. Besides, Polonius is the father of Ophelia, the woman he loves, and great love usually radiates over those closest to its object. Therefore this wild outburst of hate against an innocent, good-natured man seems to be insanity. If Hamlet had believed it was the king, his anger should have subsided after his discovery of the mistake and a feeling of gentle regret should have appeared. The scene is hard to interpret, and the dragging out of the body should be cut without comment.

ACT IV

Act III was effectively composed, as we say; in Act IV the matter is complicated, old motifs are shifted contrapuntally, a reversal takes place, the theme is varied in new ways, and new motifs are introduced.

Scene 1. The king and the queen talk about Hamlet, and the queen tells about the murder of Polonius, "the good old man." The king does not become angry, but just feels sad about "This mad young man: but so much was our love, we would not understand what was most fit." That Shakespeare means that the king is hypocritical when he says this I do not believe, for his conscience has awakened, and the king laments in his confession soliloquy that he cannot attain to genuine repentance. The king decides to counsel with "our wisest friends" to decide Hamlet's fate and set the matter right.

Scene 2. Rosencrantz and Guildenstern meet Hamlet and are taunted, whereupon they ask where the body is and ask Hamlet to go to the king.

Scene 3. The king talks to his retinue. He has had people try to find Polonius' body; he thinks it dangerous that Hamlet is at large. But now we learn:

> He's lov'd of the distracted multitude,
> Who like not in their judgement, but their eyes;
> And where 'tis so, the offender's scourge is weigh'd,
> But never the offence. . . .

Hamlet enters and answers the king's questions unkindly, but has nothing against a trip to England. He leaves.

Now the king reveals his intention to have Hamlet killed

in England, but he reveals this in a soliloquy, not to Rosencrantz and Guildenstern.

Scene 4. Then young Fortinbras finally appears in a seemingly insignificant scene. But this young Fortinbras, young healthy Norway, is to end the play when rotten Denmark has been buried. I assume Shakespeare has wanted to present him before that, and in earlier parts of the play there has been talk about Fortinbras. Fortinbras tells his captain only that the Danish king has granted him permission to march through Denmark on his way to Poland. Then Fortinbras exits. But this little scene seems also to have the object of influencing Hamlet or of giving him a reason for comparing his fate with that of Fortinbras. Hamlet asks the captain what the purpose of the expedition to Poland is. The captain answers that it concerns only a little patch of land not worth five ducats. Fully sane, Hamlet says it is insane to sacrifice two thousand men for a straw. And in the soliloquy:

> How all occasions do inform against me,
> And spur my dull revenge! . . .

he broods about his brooding:

> A thought which, quarter'd, hath but one part wisdom
> And ever three parts coward. . . .

Then he admires Fortinbras, who for the sake of honor dares risk his life for an eggshell, and rebukes himself for hesitating about meting out justice for the murder of his father and the defilement of his mother:

> . . . O, from this time forth,
> My thoughts be bloody, or be nothing worth!

Scene 5. The queen comes with Horatio, who at long last can speak out, even though what he says is very little. He tells that Ophelia has become insane. Notice that Ophelia is really insane, but that Hamlet has only pretended to be. May one believe that something psychological is concealed here? Has Hamlet made her insane? Has he infected her? Or was her losing both father and the man she loved enough? Then the king speaks to the queen in private and relates a new motif: the people have rioted because Polonius has been buried quietly, and the king is suspected of having murdered him. Laertes has secretly returned from France and has been persuaded that the king has killed his father: this is a trace of nemesis — the king has had an unjustified charge of guilt thrust upon him while he has escaped from being charged with his own crime.

There is noise; a lord rushes in to report that Laertes has overcome the guards and is heading a host of rioters who call him prince and who are calling for the election of a new king, "Choose we, Laertes shall be king!"

Here we face a violent antithesis (in Victor Hugo's manner): Laertes has received Hamlet's personal affliction: having to avenge his father. There is a fugue in the action, when Laertes picks up and carries Hamlet's voice, but now in bass (Hamlet was a tenor).

The doors are broken open. Laertes and armed men enter. "Where is *this* king?" — "O thou vile king, give me my father!" — The king now behaves in a really royal fashion and is not cowardly, knowing that

> There's such divinity doth hedge a king,
> That treason can but peep to what it would,
> Acts little of his will. Tell me, Laertes,
> Why thou art thus incensed. . . .

Laertes rages on; the king says he is innocent. The scene is then interrupted by Ophelia's entrance. Thereby the audience is spared a painful explanation, for Laertes would never have accepted the king's word; the scene would have become one tremendous quarrel which would have ended with swords drawn. So this scene is strategically a masterly move, a diversion, which conducts the struggle into new areas instead of draining strength in pointless struggle about an impregnable position.

The interruption has succeeded. Laertes listens when the king again swears he is innocent.

Scene 6. A sailor gives Horatio a letter from Hamlet telling about his trip: they had been attacked by pirates and Hamlet alone taken prisoner. He asks Horatio to come to him.

Scene 7. The king tells Laertes that Hamlet killed Polonius and has tried to murder him [the king]. Laertes believes him, but asks why the king has not proceeded against Hamlet. The king answers:

> . . . The queen his mother
> Lives almost by his looks; and for myself —
> My virtue or my plague, be it either which —
> She's so conjunctive to my life and soul,
> That, as the star moves not but in his sphere,
> I could not but by her. . . .

and:

> . . . The other motive,
> Why to a public count I might not go,
> Is the great love the general gender bear him. . . .

Laertes accepts this explanation but calls for revenge. The king is just about to tell Laertes what measures he has taken against Hamlet (the Uriah letter), when he is interrupted by a messenger. Two letters are delivered, one to the king, the other to the queen. In the king's letter, Hamlet tells he has been set ashore naked on the Danish coast and that he will explain the reason for his return next day. Frightened by Hamlet's return, the king and Laertes jointly plan the murder of Hamlet. The king suggests fencing, Laertes tops this by proposing a poisoned

sword, and the king adds a poisoned drink. Laertes has undergone a violent change in character, thoroughly motivated, however, by his father's death and Ophelia's insanity; and the king
has spurred him in a diatribe against Hamlet's indecisiveness:

> . . . that we would do,
> We should do when we would; for this "would" changes
> And hath abatements and delays. . . .

Laertes agrees: "To cut his throat i' the church."

The queen enters and says that Ophelia has drowned herself.
With that Laertes' decision is final, and he leaves.

The act ends when the king lies to the queen: "How much I
had to do to calm his rage!" (Laertes' rage, which he had stirred
up: "Revenge should have no bounds.")

One might ask what became of the rebellion motif and why
Laertes' election as king did not take place. Well, one could
say it all drowned in the whirlwind stirred up by Hamlet's unexpected return.

And some curious soul probably ought to ask, too: What was
in Hamlet's letter to the queen? I can answer that: That does
not concern us! Or: You can guess! Briefly, it is an indifferent
matter like a polite remark, whose explanation should not
delay us.

ACT V

Scene 1. The gravedigger's scene is a restful interlude that
one would not want to do without, for it is pleasant to talk about
something else when one has been exposed to painful matters
for quite some time. Besides, this retrospect on all of life as the
great nonsense, *die grosse Verachtung* — from the point of view
of the grave — is salutary, in *Hamlet's* own style.

The courtiers come to bury Ophelia, who as a suicide cannot
receive the full funeral ceremony.

Hamlet and Laertes clash. The king ends the scene with the advice to Laertes to be patient in view of the previous day's conversation.

Scene 2. Hamlet tells Horatio about his trip: how he changed the Uriah letter so that Guildenstern and Rosencrantz lost their heads. Hamlet states his feelings about Laertes:

> But I am very sorry, good Horatio,
> That to Laertes I forgot myself;
> For by the image of my cause, I see
> The portraiture of his. . . .

(Parallels!)

Osric invites Hamlet to fence with Laertes. Hamlet accepts the challenge, in spite of unhappy premonitions:

> HAMLET: . . . But thou wouldst not think how ill all's here about my heart: but it is no matter.
> HORATIO: Nay, good my lord, —
> HAMLET: It is but foolery; but it is such a kind of gain-giving, as would perhaps trouble a woman.
> HORATIO: If your mind dislike anything, obey it: I will forestall their repair hither, and say you are not fit.
> HAMLET: Not a whit, we defy augury: there's a special providence in the fall of a sparrow. . . .

The king, Laertes, and the court enter. The king puts Laertes' hand in Hamlet's and asks them to be reconciled. Why? He is either false or he does not want Hamlet to die without reconciliation. Hamlet begs Laertes for forgiveness and blames his insanity:

> . . . What I have done,
> That might your nature, honour and exception
> Roughly awake, I here proclaim was madness.

Can one believe him this time? Or is he improvising again? I don't know.

Then the bloodbath, which many have found fault with,

begins. But it proceeds logically so that everyone gets his deserts; and all of rotten old Denmark is laid on the bier; in a word, the house is swept clean, and finally young Fortinbras comes, the one to whom the dying Hamlet has given his support in the election of a king. And now we learn something important:

> I have some rights of memory in this kingdom,
> Which now to claim my vantage doth invite me.

says Fortinbras. This is intimately connected with a bit of information in Act I — that Fortinbras' father had been defeated by Hamlet's father; in a word, justice has been done, the misdeeds of the fathers for which the children have suffered are now atoned for, decency has been revived, and the heritage has been restored. This means Fortinbras, and now I, too, want to call him in! All the way through the drama rotten Denmark has awaited him as a liberator. May he come then!

When I now consider the composition of the play, I find it simple but not artless. It forms a symphony, polyphonically developed with independent motifs, which are beautifully woven together; it is fugued as I have already said. The andante of Act I tells us everything we need to know; the second movement (act) develops the theme, which is varied in the third; Act IV's largo maestoso (Ophelia's madness) finds its transition in the gravediggers' scherzo only to pour forth in the presto of the finale.

After having spent three days preparing the simple review above, I have concluded that *Hamlet* can be presented uncut. But if you are going to enjoy all of this powerful tragedy you have to prepare for it as if you were preparing to see an opera: you should study the play first, try to interest yourself in the action and in its background. And so as not to be distracted by small talk during intermissions, the play should be produced with only a couple of intermissions in order that there will be time for all twenty scenes, which should follow closely upon each other; the Shakespeare staging used in Munich in the 1890's should be followed consistently. This is an absolute must: no scenery! An abstract architectonic frame that can serve as rooms, a street, or a square, when the curtain is pulled to; when it is pulled to the sides, one is out in the open country.

The staging of Shakespeare in Munich had an extensive reputation.

If furnishings — tables and chairs — are needed, these can be brought in; if properties are used, they can be procured. Otherwise not. The spoken word is the major thing; and when Shakespeare's highly sophisticated contemporaries could do without scenery I suspect we would be able to imagine walls and trees. Why, we can *read* the play silently and enjoy it, imagining we hear voices, seeing the changing scenes; and when the actors pretend to be kings and queens, we can certainly pretend it is a room in a castle or a forest we have in front of us. Why, everything is pretense in the theater.

The experiment Director Falck undertook without my help in staging *Queen Christina* at the Intimate Theater[9] was absolutely successful, I think. As the author of the play, I am the expert, because I certainly know best how I want it; besides I am a veteran in my profession since I have written plays over a forty-year period and have had them produced. So my word weighs heavily in settling this question! Act I of *Queen Christina* is set in Riddarholm Church according to the printed text; but when we had cut all references to the church, the setting needed to be only a room in which people gather; and I did not miss what had been cut. The Treasury in Act II was allegorized by two shelves with account books on them. It was enough for me; and the sets were among the most beautiful I have seen in a theater. The last two acts were just as superb, and the whole production was a delightful surprise, a successful experiment and innovation which will be recorded in Swedish theater history. Since I did not have a thing to do with the production, I have not been praising myself, but giving simple justice to the one who deserves it.

As no scene was set out of doors, no background curtain to conceal the landscape was needed.

Falck's drapery staging had several advantages. Since it was not necessary to bring in and carry out scenery, the mood of calm and reverence on stage that is extremely important to the actor for whom the stage is his study where he realizes his art was sustained. The open wings (three on each side) provided nuances of light and shadow, and made unnecessary all opening and closing of doors; entrances and exits were made without disturbance of any kind. With a soft carpet added, the artists at the Intimate Theater lived in a carefree, pleasant milieu, in which they felt at home and could create their roles undisturbed by the noise and commotion of the theater and the stagehands' bustle which otherwise is part of it. I know that the personnel of the Intimate Theater consider the days *Queen Christina* was produced among their best hours, which could not be embittered by shouts of ill will—an organized outrage that shames the community we live in, and that for a moment is experienced as a collective crime against all justice and decency. *My* acknowledgment of the director's scenery, his beautiful costumes, of all the artists' excellent performances could hardly erase the depressing effect of this attack against a beautiful and successful attempt at renewing the stage and making it possible to present plays that otherwise are usually hard to produce.

If someone should ask me how *Hamlet* ought to be produced, I can only answer: That depends on personal preference and taste. The connoisseur and the actor could, of course, on occasion get an uncut *Hamlet* on the drapery stage for the sake of study; and an impatient contemporary public can very well enjoy an arrangement of the Wilhelm Meister variety. There are two sides to the matter, and there is no point in arguing about it, so much the less so when one cannot be certain about the integrity of the text since a *Hamlet* by an unknown writer is probably the basis of Shakespeare's, and some scholars think that the earlier play had been written as early as 1589 and that it became an integral part of the *Hamlet* we have. Yes, some of them say Shakespeare simply reworked the older play, which they say was composed by a man "who had previously devoted himself to law."

It is the idea that Shakespeare *took* even the dramas of his contemporaries and rewrote them in his own fashion that has given rise to these strange stories about Shakespeare's being only a pseudonym. I am beginning to believe that there is a secret behind Shakespeare's writing when I see that scholars insist there are no longer extant originals behind most of his plays. Although textual criticism does not amuse me, I do want to cite Israel Gollancz' investigation of 1906,[10] although I cannot judge its reliability.

The authorized text of *Hamlet* rests on the quarto edition of 1604 and the first folio of 1623.

A comparison of the two editions shows that they stem from two independent sources, but neither one is a copy of the author's manuscript.

The first quarto edition contains only 2,143 lines compared to 3,719 in the later quarto; in the first quarto some scenes are not in the same order; the queen swears she did not know about the murder in a scene with Horatio, a scene that does not appear in later editions; Polonius has the name Corambis, and Reynaldo is called Montano. This edition was a pirated edition based on a transcriber's manuscript.

Some believe that this edition is an incomplete copy of a *Hamlet* Shakespeare may have written in his youth; others believe that the first quarto is a mutilated version of an old *Hamlet* Shakespeare had reworked. Gollancz agrees with the latter opinion. On the other hand, he thinks the lost *Hamlet* should be ascribed to Thomas Kyd (*The Spanish Tragedy*).

*

As a curiosity, I shall finally state my speculations about *Hamlet*, which occurred to me first when Bleibtreu concocted a new Shakespeare myth in the Bacon fashion, but I do so only as a curiosity. My point of departure was the name Polonius, the name of the councilor from Lübeck, who participated in the election of Gustav Vasa as king of Strängnäs. This Lübecker had the name of Polonius (Germanized to Plönnies in Swedish history).

But in 1585 Lord Leicester's actors visited Denmark; and three of them—Kempe, Bryan, and Pope—later became members of Chamberlain's Company and appeared in Shakespeare plays. Some scholars have wanted to trace Shakespeare's knowledge of Denmark in Fredrik II's time to his acquaintance with these actors.

*

Dear Mr. S.[11] My research about *Hamlet* is continuing. The Guildenstern who was sent to England with Rosencrantz *could* be my Gyllenstierna in *Erik XIV* because he (like Hamlet, Guildenstern, and Rosencrantz) studied in Wittenberg and *was sent to England* to court Queen Elizabeth for Erik XIV in 1564 (the year Shakespeare was born). It is strange that a certain

Holger Rosenkrantz (born 1586) was a member of a mission *to England* to attend the coronation of James I. He was married to Lena Gyldenstjerne (born 1588). Shakespeare took rumors and contemporary tavern talk and gossip as motifs! Ask Bleibtreu if he knows this, and ask him to send me his resumé of the Rutherford (or Rumford or ???) theory, and I'll give him a new theory.

*

Dear Mr. S. What made me suppose Nils Gyllenstjerna's possible identity with Guildenstern in *Hamlet* was not only that he was sent to England (by Erik XIV to propose to Queen Elizabeth) but also his absolute lack of faith and character, which coincides with Guildenstern's (and Rosencrantz'): in my *Erik XIV*[12] I have characterized him as Lord Back and Forth; that's how Swedish history has recorded him. But yet a parallel: Erik XIV proposed that Gyllenstjerna go to England to murder Leicester. Guildenstern (and Rosencrantz) are sent to England to murder Hamlet! It is strange that Erik XIV is a Hamlet with a stepmother and (pretended) insanity, frivolous courtships, etc.! Nils Gyllenstjerna had Danish ancestors, and is sometimes called Guldenstern (studied in Wittenberg as Guildenstern did). Lingard's *History of England* tells about Erik XIV's courtship in England.

Erik XIV is a Hamlet. Stepmother (= stepfather); murders Sture (= murders Polonius); Ophelia = Karin Månsdotter; Erik XIV dies poisoned as Hamlet does; insane or simulating insanity like Hamlet, vacillating, judges and rejects his judgment; his friend Horatio = Erik's friend Göran Persson — faithful unto death; Fortinbras = Dukes John and Charles; Hamlet was loved by the uncivilized masses. Erik, too, a hater of the lords and the people's king. Who is Polonius? Dionysius

Beurreus, who was assassinated on Erik's order, an intriguing courtier?

*

Dear Mr. S. When I read Hamlet again, I found that Polonius (scene 3, Act I) where he blesses Laertes (in an Old Testament manner) cites *Hávamál*,[13] which Shakespeare had probably learned to know through Saxo, from whom he took Hamlet secondhand. Has Bleibtreu noticed this? Further: Our Plönnies (from Gustav Vasa's time) had the name Polonius. Is there any connection? Hamlet's father was Örvendel, and the paternal uncle Fengo, but Shakespeare calls Fengo Claudius, and Horatio says he's a Roman. Shakespeare probably got his plot from an Italian tale (by way of Saxo Grammaticus). In *Hamlet*, Shakespeare is a thorough Christian; the ghost says he comes from "sulphurous and tormenting flames" (although he was a good man). Shakespeare seems to have been a Norman or Roman, for he expresses hatred of the Danes in several places.

*

Before I proceed to Hamlet's character and Shakespeare's way of depicting human beings, I want to insert a few passages previously printed in *A New Blue Book*.[14]

Characterization
(*From* A Blue Book, *Part II*)

Notice how many shots must be taken in sequence by the cinema photographer to reproduce a single movement, and even so the image is blurred. There is a missing transition in every vibration. When a thousand shots would be needed for one movement of an arm, how many myriads would not be needed to depict a movement of the soul? The writer's depiction of human beings is for that reason only summaries, contour sketches, all of them imperfect and all half-false.

A genuine depiction of a character is therefore difficult, almost impossible, and, if a person tried to make it absolutely true, no one would believe in it. One can merely suggest.

Ophelia in *Hamlet*, for example, seems to me an unconscious attempt at giving in summary form a character with all the nuances that the crowd calls inconsequences, and which make all actresses in all countries fear the role as difficult.

Ophelia is sweet — that can't be helped, but she can't be sweet all day long.

When she makes her first entrance with her brother Laertes, she defends without submissiveness her natural free behavior (with Hamlet), but she is just as sweet, though she does use the word *libertine*.

In her second scene, with Polonius, she accepts her father's warnings submissively. That is not an inconsequence; it is a new phase; she has been frightened, and she has to observe a behavior toward her father different from that toward her brother. Hamlet's somewhat cynical declaration of love she receives with an innocent lack of understanding, just as Juliet is untouched by the Nurse's vulgar speeches.

OPHELIA: . . . O, woe is me,
To have seen what I have seen, see what I see!
. . . .
HAMLET: Do you think I meant country matters?
[Hagberg's translation is the equivalent of "Did you think I meant something indecent?"]
OPHELIA: I think nothing, my lord.

August Falck as Edgar in *The Dance of Death*

The treasury scene in *Queen Christina*,
showing the use of drapery setting

The interior of the Intimate Theater

That is the right answer! She does not reflect about a feeling, which cannot be analyzed, and she rejects Hamlet's cynical manner of destroying his love by being skeptical about it:

OPHELIA: You are naught, you are naught: I'll mark the play.

She thereby averts further attacks. But, when the prologue is over, she says merely: "'Tis brief, my lord." "As woman's love," answers Hamlet. But then Ophelia is without an answer, for she knows she will die of her love.

But when Hamlet comments on the play being presented, Ophelia becomes ironic: "You are as good as a chorus, my lord."

The sweet girl becomes sarcastic! Why not, for a moment?

HAMLET: It would cost you a groaning to take off my edge.
OPHELIA: Still better, and worse.

Ophelia seems cynical when she deigns to answer Hamlet's crude remark. Still I believe she answers without meaning anything but to cut off such talk, for I do not find any meaning in her answer, and do not want to read any into it.

Then comes Ophelia's so-called madness, when she sings songs of a kind and with words that are out of keeping with the sweet girl. What does that signify? They undoubtedly lay concealed, suppressed, and, when her heart broke, they rushed out with her blood. Why not? That is a new phase.

Through his vulgarity Hamlet has killed her love, and his evil spirit, which he has tossed into her, now speaks through her sweet mouth.

That is a terrible accusation against Hamlet the man, but it is difficult to retract. Let us listen to how beautifully innocent brotherly love speaks and how beautifully Laertes has seen his fair sister:

. . . O rose of May!
Dear maid, kind sister, sweet Ophelia!

. . . .

> Nature is fine in love; and where 'tis fine,
> It sends some precious instance of itself
> After the thing it loves.

I would interpret these lines in this way: when Ophelia has let the very best in her fly out to seek her beloved, her spirit has left her body and cannot find its way back. For that reason it is only the frail, relatively impure vessel that gives forth sounds without thought.

Anyone who has ever been in ecstasy knows how it feels: as if one's heart wanted to fly out of one's body, the spirit is released; that must be like a beautiful death!

Then comes Hamlet's way of characterizing Ophelia, whom he has murdered with his skepticism. In the first acts he is only mocking toward her. He does not, of course, read his own ugly thoughts into her, but he takes up out of her essential fineness the flame which there is in her, and the way in which he sees her is not that of madness, for he is only pretending to be insane, but his vision is perverted; he probably commits soul-murder by pretending to be insane.

But then she dies, and by the grave Hamlet declares his love:

> I loved Ophelia: forty thousand brothers
> Could not, with all their quantity of love,
> Make up my sum. . . .

Should we believe Hamlet loved her, when he had treated her like a prostitute, and had said to her and about her the most shameful things?

To that I answer without qualification: Yes, he loved her in spite of everything!

There is not any inconsequence; it is just a matter of different ways of seeing: changes of perspective for one's point of view, the ones the surveyor seeks in order to get a genuinely complete picture of his terrain.

Simple souls always talk about contradictions and inconsequences, and every living thing and being is put together with elements that are not homogeneous, but must be contradictory in order to hold together, just like the forces that attract unlikes to each other.

In that fashion Hamlet himself is simply made up of apparent contradictions, good and evil, hating and loving, cynical and enthusiastic, mean and indulgent, strong and weak — in a word: a human being, different every moment just as every human being is.

That is how it is with Polonius, whose fate is certainly too hard: to be murdered without being avenged. Why, he is a good father, irreproachable toward his children, faithful to his king; careful about his daughter, whom he naturally would be glad to see married to Prince Hamlet, as long as the latter is sane. That the father becomes frightened by a crazy person is certainly obvious, and the worst thing he stoops to is listening for his master behind a drapery in order to catch dangerous secrets when Hamlet on good grounds is suspected of stirring up the people to rebellion. What else is there [to justify] that Polonius should always be played by a comedian? His little foolishness as a courtier? But this quality can easily be converted into a social virtue called affability which is highly valued in social circles. And the little professional weakness sits just as loosely on the courtier as the gilt on his coat. Polonius' agreeableness on such trivial matters as what the clouds look like is not characteristic; it is merely a kind of behavior. Compare his beautiful farewell to his son Laertes in Act I. That deserves to be noticed, for it seems to be taken out of the *Hávamál* but mixed with Old Testament formulas for blessing people:

> The wind sits in the shoulder of your sail,
> And you are stay'd for. There: my blessing with you!
> And these few precepts in thy memory
> Look thou character. Give thy thoughts no tongue,
> Nor any unproportion'd thought his act.
> Be thou familiar, but by no means vulgar.
> The friends thou hast, and their adoption tried,
> Grapple them to thy soul with hoops of steel;
> But do not dull thy palm with entertainment
> Of each new-hatch'd, unfledged comrade. . . .
> . . . .
>
> Give every man thine ear, but few thy voice:
> Take each man's censure, but reserve thy judgement.
> . . . .
>
> This above all: to thine own self be true;
> And it must follow, as the night the day,
> Thou canst not then be false to any man.
> Farewell: my blessing season this in thee.

When I read this manly, attractive speech, I wonder if Polonius is not joking with Hamlet when he says yes to everything, and if the old man pretends to be foolish, for he is very shrewd and worldly wise when he gives Reynaldo a great many rather harmless directions for keeping an eye on Laertes in Paris.

Polonius is "familiar but in no wise vulgar," and does not himself "give his thoughts tongue." And a man who dares to say to his son, "To thyself be true," is no fool, though he can be foolish or pretend to be!

And what about the king? Is he completely black? He cannot be, for he has won a woman's love. He is a murderer, but according to the thinking of ancient days—he is like most people. Hamlet himself commits murder (Polonius) without being challenged, and is vulgar enough to drag out the corpse himself.

Briefly, and summarily: Shakespeare depicts people, in all

their phases, just as inconsequent, self-contradictory, tattered, self-torn, illogical, and incapable of being understood as people are. But he does not do this always, and not completely, for one cannot!

Shakespeare's Concept of the World
(*From* A Blue Book, *Part II*)

Was Shakespeare a pessimist?

Yes, at times, not always, like the rest of us. In *Lear* he says when the king dies:

> Vex not his ghost; O, let him pass!
>   He hates him
> That would upon the rack of this rough world
> Stretch him out longer.

Rack!

In *Hamlet* he says, of course:

> . . . To die . . .
> .   .   .   .
> . . . 'tis a consummation
> Devoutly to be wish'd. . . .
> .   .   .   .
> . . . who would fardels bear,
> To grunt and sweat under a weary life,
> But that the dread of something after death,
> .   .   .   .
> . . . makes us rather bear those ills we have
> Than fly to others that we know not of?

Or when he bids Horatio live "And in this harsh world draw thy breath."

In *The Tempest* he goes still further and like the Buddhists doubts the reality of life:

> . . . We are such stuff
> As dreams are made on, and our little life
> Is rounded with a sleep.

So, too, in *Macbeth*, but still worse:

> Life's but a walking shadow . . .
> . . . it is a tale
> Told by an idiot, full of sound and fury,
> Signifying nothing.

In *Timon* he expresses a hate, or contempt for human beings, that reminds one of Schopenhauer's or Hartmann's:[15]

> Commend me to them,
> And tell them that, to ease them of their griefs,
>
> . . . .
>
> In life's uncertain voyage . . .
>
> . . . .
>
> I have a tree, which grows here in my close,
>
> . . . .
>
> . . . tell my friends,
> Tell Athens, in the sequence of degree,
> From high to low throughout, that whoso please
> To stop affliction, let him take his haste,
> Come hither, ere my tree hath felt the axe,
> And hang himself.

Timon's personally composed epitaph includes:* ". . . a plague consume you wicked caitiffs left!"

Was Shakespeare a freethinker or atheist?

No, he was a devout believing Christian, with periods of deepest doubt and despair, when God had concealed Himself from him. In *Richard III*, which Shakespeare wrote when he

---

* Strindberg says, "ends like this." [W.J.]

was thirty, thus a work of his youth, since he began at twenty-eight (with *Henry V*), he lets Richmond, the attractive hero of the play, say:

> God and our good cause fight upon our side;
> The prayers of holy saints and wronged souls,
> Like high-rear'd bulwarks, stand before our faces.

And about Richard:

> One that hath ever been God's enemy.
> Then, if you fight against God's enemy,
> God will, in justice, ward you as his soldiers. . . .
> God and Saint George! Richmond and victory!

And when the evil Richard has fallen, Richmond closes the drama with thanksgiving and prayer to God because the thirty years' war of the Roses is over:

> O, now, let Richmond and Elizabeth,
>
> . . . .
>
> By God's fair ordinance conjoin together!
> And let their heirs, God, if they will be so,
> Enrich the time to come with smooth'd-fac'd Peace,
>
> . . . .
>
> Abate the edge of traitors, gracious Lord,
>
> . . . .
>
> That she may long live here, God say amen!

At the age of thirty-eight we rediscover the poet in Hamlet. In Act I he believes in the ghost, for he troubles Marcellus by refuting Horatio's doubt:

> MARCELLUS: Horatio says 'tis but our fantasy,
> And will not let belief take hold of him
> Touching this dreaded sight. . . .

Horatio sees the ghost and is convinced:

> Before my God, I might not this believe
> Without the sensible and true avouch
> Of mine own eyes.

Then Hamlet himself sees the shadowy form of his dead father:

> Angels and ministers of grace defend us!

This is Shakespeare himself, for he certainly knew from Saxo that the characters of the drama were ancient pagans. Then the father comes, directly from Purgatory:

> My hour is almost come,
> When I to sulphurous and tormenting flames
> Must render up myself.

This shows that Shakespeare was a Catholic, since he believed in Purgatory, which the Protestants reject.

This emotional need of purification in fire before one enters the company of saints is attractive, of course, and a Catholic is not amazed to find the splendid hero and superb man in such a situation. And the father comforts his son with the assertion that it is a necessary transitional stage even for the righteous, since he was torn away through a sudden death before he had had time to do penance for his sins of weakness:

> Doom'd for a certain term to walk the night,
> And for the day confined to fast in fires,
> Till the foul crimes done in my days of nature
> Are burnt and purged away. . . .

It will not do to say that this depends on the time of the action of the play, for that was pre-Christian; nor on Shakespeare's age, for that was godless; people have wanted to make Shakespeare a so-called man of the Renaissance (a pagan) and a freethinking disciple of Giordano Bruno,[16] with no other basis than a few botanical reflections (at the moment I cannot recall where).

Furthermore: Hamlet swears by St. Patrick, the patron saint of Ireland, but even by "so help you mercy" [the Hagberg translation makes it the equivalent of "as true as God would help you"].

The thirty-eight-year-old poet has certainly doubted, and for a moment he believes the ghost is a delusion of the devil who because of his heaviness of spirits has affected his senses.

This doubt of everything, of God and His goodness, is expressed in the soliloquy; and anyone who has experienced anything like it wants to attribute Hamlet's vacillation to the fact that he has let go the anchor, which is God. A godless human being torn between thoughts of vengeance and comfortable forgiveness behaves in just such a characterless fashion.

At the height of his despair he begs Ophelia to include him in her prayers!

Hamlet swears moreover (III:2) by the Holy Virgin ["but by'r lady"], who was not popular in Queen Elizabeth's reign.

And he is at least not a materialist in the soliloquy in Act IV:

> What is a man,
> If his chief good and market of his time
> Be but to sleep and feed? A beast, no more.

In Act V Hamlet's godless doubt has been disspelled, and in scene 2 he preaches:

> . . . and that should teach us
> There's a divinity that shapes our ends.

But the poet (Hamlet) has even discovered the finger of Providence in the trivialities of everyday living (V:2):

HORATIO: How was this seal'd?
HAMLET: Why, even in that was Heaven ordinant. I had my father's signet in my purse, which was the model of that Danish seal.

So it was not a matter of chance, just as the ghost was not a figment of the imagination!

In the same act, the same scene, Hamlet bursts out again after he has made his discovery: "There's a special providence in the fall of a sparrow."

There is Christianity, pagans!

Although a Roman, Horatio is just as devout as Hamlet became: "And flights of angels sing thee to thy rest!" he says to his friend at the moment of death.

A fairly unnoticed figure is Shakespeare's Maid of Orleans in his first work, *Henry VI*, Part I.

The concept is absolutely orthodox Catholic.

She begins with a miracle which the others have doubted. She has to live a pure life in order to keep in touch with the spirits and to be able to see into the future. Whether she becomes emotionally involved with the Dauphin I cannot decide, because they lie about her so often in the play. But in Act V, Scene 3, she is harassed by evil spirits when she feels her power diminish, and here her fall from grace probably takes place, for she promises her body and soul if they will help her. But:

> My ancient incantations are too weak,
> And hell too strong for me to buckle with. . . .

In this speech is revealed the English concept of the witch who, on that basis, too, was sentenced to the stake.

She is allowed to free herself in a speech of self-defense (V:4) in which she says that she is of royal blood, and that through the inspiration of heaven she has become a virtuous and holy chosen one to perform many a glorious miracle on earth.

> But you, that are polluted with your lusts
> . . . .
> You judge it straight a thing impossible
> To compass wonders but by help of devils.

As far as one can tell from inaccurate world history, Jeanne d'Arc was a divinely inspired seeress who completed her mission "to crown the king at Rheims." But, when she let herself be persuaded to go beyond that, she had troubles and misfortunes until she fell. That is a tragedy, and Schiller has understood it. Shakespeare was young when he took hold of the difficult figure, and he carelessly lost it at the end, when she says she is pregnant and claims to have several lovers in order to escape the stake. But he is not a Protestant, for the Protestant concept is absolutely crude — that she was an impostor.

What really supports the idea that Shakespeare was a Catholic is his interpretation of Cardinal Wolsey in *Henry VIII*. Henry was the Reformation king, of course; but the drama deals only with his first divorce, his second marriage, and the birth of Elizabeth. Cardinal Wolsey is a rascal, not because he is a Catholic, but because he was a "rascal." The other cardinal, Campeius, is sympathetic and worthy and is on Henry's side, although he is accused of wanting only to promote Wolsey's plans with the pope.

Henry strikes out against Rome one single time, rather mildly, and we know Henry remained just as Catholic after his separation from the pope, for it was Rome he wanted to become independent of, and not the Catholic Church. Mary the Bloody reintroduced Catholicism immediately afterward. And Elizabeth, during whose reign Shakespeare flourished, preserved the Roman liturgy and the Catholic dogmas (through the Thirtynine Articles) to the great annoyance of the Protestants. Shakespeare frequently ridicules the Protestants (the Puritans), too.

It should not matter to us what faith Shakespeare belonged to, but one matter is important: that he be acquitted of atheism, since he was not godless. This [I address] to the neo-pagans, who have stolen Shakespeare, just as they have stolen Goethe.

They could not steal Schiller, so they have been content to ignore or belittle him!

Aging: The Beautiful and the Ugly
(*From* A Blue Book, *Part II*)

Since life has so little happiness to give human beings and the earliest portion is that of being in love for the first time, they ought to be taught to care for it as if it were the most delicate of flowers. The quiet, festive melancholy that accompanies the awakening of love is an angel who keeps watch at the gate of eternity, which stands slightly ajar, because it is an axiom that we feel happiness will last forever. But a skeptical word, an untimely jest, a passing thought, a careless word can destroy it all in a flash; the angel flees; and the gate is slammed shut forever.

Shakespeare, who otherwise does not deal very tenderly with love (the Nurse in *Romeo and Juliet*), in his last play *The Tempest*, the best fruit of his late years, has presented a little bit of wisdom, surely based on a dearly bought experience. The poet was probably too old to use the hard-won experience late in life, but he donated the hint, surely with sincere good will, to young people who could use it (but probably do not). The aging Prospero tells Ferdinand when the latter gets Miranda as his bride (= betrothed):

> PROSPERO: Then, as my gift, and thine own acquisition
> Worthily purchas'd, take my daughter: But
> If thou dost break her virgin knot before
> All sanctimonius ceremonies may

With full and holy rite be minister'd,
No sweet aspersion shall the heavens let fall
To make this contract grow: but barren hate,
Sour-eyed disdain, and discord, shall bestrew
The union of your bed with weeds so loathly
That you shall hate it both: therefore, take heed,
As Hymen's lamps shall light you.
FERDINAND: As I hope
For quiet days, fair issue, and long life,
With such love as 'tis now; the murkiest den
The most opportune place, the strong'st suggestion
Our worser Genius can, shall never melt
Mine honour into lust; to take away
The edge of that day's celebration,
When I shall think, or Phoebus' steeds are founder'd
Or night kept chain'd below.

Why, that was nice of the old man who, grieving because he was helpless about doing anything for himself, wanted to teach his children how to win the sort of happiness he had thrown away. If one can see anything ugly, selfish, mean, or ridiculous in his doing so, one is abnormal.

However: Ferdinand keeps his vow, and the aging Shakespeare shows this in an attractive little scene, in which the two young people sit in Prospero's cell—playing chess.

Shakespeare, emancipated man of the Renaissance that he was, arrived at that conclusion when age gave him wisdom he did not have time to use himself. When he saw his own young people approach the altar, everything that was beautiful in the dreams of his youth came back to him. Everything reappeared in a new sacred light, even "the solemn ceremonies."

Isn't it more appealing to see an old age with rewon common sense and innocent childlike faith than to hear a cynical old man in a gutter on the verge of the grave still singing about his father's bed and his mother's folly?[17] Tell me. But be honest.

King Lear's Wife
(*From* A Blue Book, *Part II*)

A number of daughters and sons-in-law and a father-in-law who is quite demanding appear in Act I, but there is no mother, and no one mentions her by name. So she is dead! But people generally in family get-togethers recall a dead mother in an unguarded moment. But here there is complete silence! Aside from Cordelia, the daughters are not pleasant, and the Fool characterizes Regan and Goneril in his blunt fashion when he sees Goneril coming: ". . . here comes one o' the parings."

I have never been attracted to King Lear. He demands love, though love is something one gives, without payment, without thanks. Giving in order to get is buying! Giving in order to give is love.

Of course, he does give away his kingdom with one hand, but he reserves a juicy bit of it with the other when he makes the provision that the newlyweds are to support him and a garrison of one hundred men. That is lack of common sense on the part of such an old man, and Goneril is right when she complains about the riotous life led in her new home by one hundred knights:

> Men so disorder'd, so debosh'd and bold,
> That this our court, infected with their manners,
> Shows like a riotous inn: epicurism and lust
> Make it more like a tavern or a brothel
> Than a grac'd palace.

Lear answers, "Darkness and devils!" and then he says it is a lie. His retinue consists of "men of choice and rarest parts"!

Has Goneril lied or exaggerated? Or is the old man exaggerating? I do not know: but Goneril demands that he cut his retinue by fifty men. Then her father curses her! Does that make sense?

Later Regan wants to cut the retinue to twenty-five or less. But the old man becomes crazy and goes out on the heath. And there he delivers his great soliloquy, but this time not against the ingratitude of children (his daughters) but against woman, against women in general.

There's his wife, I thought, because he has no reason for concerning himself with his daughters' erotic life:

> Down from the waist they are centaurs,
> Though women all above:
> But to the girdle do the gods inherit,
> Beneath is all the fiends'; there's hell, there's darkness.

There can be no doubt that an unhappy memory has come into the old man's brain and that in his daughters' cynical attacks on Edmund he has recognized their mother, whom they probably take after.

There is a speech in Act II that is not clear, but may give a hint of the sort of secret a man is not ordinarily anxious to reveal. Regan comes in and greets Lear:

> I am glad to see your highness.
> LEAR: Regan, I think you are; I know what reason
> I have to think so: if thou shouldst not be glad,
> I would divorce me from thy mother's tomb,
> Sepulchring an adultress.

Regan is false when she says she is happy to see her father. For she has just recently explained to others that she intends to go away when her father is coming as a guest. Lear does not believe her and becomes ironic; but the inversion of the phrase is so daring I think it reversed or doubled or misfired!

Let that go!

Shakespeare's supposed hatred of women is beautifully disproved in Act V when Cordelia has come back to him:

> We two alone will sing like birds i' the cage:
> When thou dost ask me blessing I'll kneel down
> And ask of thee forgiveness: so we'll live,
> And pray and sing, and tell old tales, and laugh
> At gilded butterflies. . . .

In good and evil, with her roots in the dirt and her flower in the light, the most beautiful grafted to the most ugly, the masterpiece of creation but utterly spoiled, hating when she loves, and loving when she hates, that is how Shakespeare depicts woman, the sphinx whose riddle cannot be solved, because it is unsolvable or does not exist!

But I have a real need of thinking or imagining that Cordelia is her mother's beautiful image which survived her, a palette of pure gold on the black slate, and which the eighty-year-old had seen in his youth with the sharp eyes of love, ripped out, framed, and hidden in his heart!

How else could he have loved Goneril's and Regan's mother?

*

Who is Hamlet? He is Shakespeare; he is man when he leaves childhood, enters life, and finds that everything is quite different from what he had imagined it. Hamlet is the awakened youngster, who discovers that the world is out of joint and feels called upon to set it right, and becomes desperate when he puts his shoulder to the stone and finds it immovable.

Hamlet's character is depicted in the text in many places by fellow players, and that is the reason why an introspective actor, who studies only his own role, never grasps Hamlet's whole character. Ophelia says:

> O, what a noble mind is here o'erthrown!
> The courtier's, soldier's, scholar's eye, tongue, sword:

The expectancy and rose of the fair state,
The glass of fashion and the mould of form,
The observ'd of all observers, — quite, quite down!

. . . .

That unmatch'd form and feature of blown youth
Blasted with ecstasy. . . .

The king calls him "gentle . . . free from all contriving."
Horatio calls him "a noble heart."

FORTINBRAS: For he was likely, had he been put on [the throne],
To have proved most royal. . . .

How Shakespeare portrays Hamlet and how he reveals his nature through his actions is clear in the text, but I want to point out to the actor some essentials, let us say *leitmotivs,* which are conclusive in the creation of the part if this is to be something more than a superficial "playing insane" and getting to blurt out a lot of malicious remarks.

At the beginning of the play Hamlet is mourning his father; he is therefore sad and dressed in black, of course; but he has a stepfather, and what an offspring never notices in the marital relations of his parents even a little child notices when a "bastard marriage" has taken place. Hamlet feels that his mother's debasement is incest or adultery. But the young man's whole being is revolted by *his* having a new father and his mother a married lover; his filial ties with his forefathers have been broken, not by gentle bearable death but by something contrary to nature, something unnatural, unclean, which tarnishes his memory of his father and his mother's dignity. He has lost his respect for his mother, his origin — the womb from which he came; so Hamlet at the very beginning is broken. When he cannot believe and respect, he doubts and defames. Later, when he learns that a crime has been committed — one or two — because it is never revealed if his mother has been her

brother-in-law's mistress and if she had known about the murder — he becomes wild, and this wildness, called insanity and
causing him to be beside himself, must be considered a kind
of mental disturbance. So there are two factors in Hamlet's
insanity: what he actually is and what he pretends to be.

But in the very nature of this young man, who probably
from the start was not quite at home in "this prison" and "vale
of tears," there is a really divine quality — for him, all people
are the same. He is democratic in spite of being successor to
the throne. He has associated with Yorick, the court fool, and
with actors and students, and, when he talks to the humble
gravediggers, he is polite and not proud. He is adored by the
little people or all the people so that the king is afraid of *that*
popularity, but Hamlet is not democratic in the sense that he
kowtows to the "vulgar masses" to achieve power. His point
of view is so universally human that he is above everything —
throne and court, community and the law. If he had had a
coarser nature, he would not have murdered his stepfather
but would have started a rebellion, overthrown the king, and
had the murderer legally decapitated. But he is a noble, good,
fine nature, so he does not know *die Kunst Weh zu thun.* He
suffers when he has struck, and he asks both his mother and
Laertes for forgiveness. His doing so is no weakness; it is moral
superiority; therefore he drowns in the general meanness. Hamlet has pretended, merely to find out if his uncle is guilty, but
an absolutely unexpected gain appears to his credit. Experience teaches us that as soon as a person is considered not quite
"all there," he gets to know everybody's secrets. Because people believe he does not understand anything, they come in
droves and reveal themselves, strip themselves, show, without
wanting to, all their defects and vices. All mankind marches

by Hamlet, putting on his altar all their meanness, which he has undoubtedly sensed but does not know: "the calamity of so long life" becomes clear to him; he is made to feel "the spurns that patient merit of the unworthy takes." Even Ophelia exposes a flaw in her fine soul, but to save humanity Hamlet (Shakespeare) creates a Horatio. As fiction, a categorical postulate, the sheet anchor, Horatio therefore becomes a vague figure, while all the other characters, the ghost included, come alive.

Hamlet is the tragedy of man, written when Shakespeare was about forty, the psychically critical age in a man's life. Luther says a man is a child until he is forty. He means that a man lives like an unreflecting sleepwalker, dependent, working by means of other people's thoughts and ideas which he learned as a child and imagines are his own. Then he awakens, his eyes open, he sees through the deception and the illusions, rages about having been fooled, and has to revise his whole philosophy. It is a sort of measles at forty—a closing of accounts that prepares for the coming of age and wisdom.

To Shakespeare's third period, his period of doubt and suffering, belong *Julius Caesar, Hamlet, Othello, King Lear, Macbeth, Antony and Cleopatra, Timon,* and *Coriolanus,* in other words, his most powerful works. His fourth period, when he shows how a person broken by misfortunes or crimes attains harmony through suffering, includes *Cymbeline, A Winter's Tale,* and *The Tempest.* (*Henry VIII,* which I heard interpreted at the University of Uppsala, probably was written by Fletcher for the most part, a thought I find reasonable since Shakespeare would hardly have stooped to flattering the ghastly Elizabeth.)

But Hamlet is also a prototype of Faust; a thinker who tries to get at the very basis of the simplest of matters, a philosopher, who gets his Gretchen (Ophelia), and Valentin (Laertes, her brother). After having accepted the ghost's orders uncritically in Act I, Hamlet begins philosophizing — in the very midst of his effort to avenge his father — about the problem of the ghost, whether the latter comes from the devil and fooled him. In the churchyard he speculates about the problem of material existence; in Ophelia's presence he analyzes love, which in its very nature is unreflected synthesis that cannot be analyzed. He wants to know what one is not permitted to know; and because of arrogantly wanting to know God's secrets which have a right to remain secrets, Hamlet is punished by the kind of madness called skepticism, which leads to absolute uncertainty, and out of which the individual can be saved only by faith: childish faith which through the sacrifice called obedience one gets as a sort of Christmas-gift wisdom, the absolute certainty that surpasses understanding.

Faust attained that in 1830 (Part II), but Hamlet did not in 1600!

*

Every serious young actor's dream is to get to play Hamlet, but nowadays the role is assigned as a reward to aging stars so that the ideal of a young Hamlet has been corrupted. "How then should Hamlet be played?" a young fellow asks himself. Well, that matter is clear: read Shakespeare's advice to the actors! That tells us!

Hamlet says:

> Speak the speech, I pray you, as I pronounced it to you, trippingly on the tongue: but if you mouth it, as many of your players do, I had as lief the town-crier spoke my lines. Nor do not saw the air too much with your hand, thus; but use all gently: for in the very torrent, tempest, and as I may say, the whirlwind of passion,

you must acquire and beget a temperance that may give it smoothness.

and not

split the ears of the groundlings,

but

> Be not too tame neither, but let your own discretion be your tutor: suit the action to the word, the word to the action; with this special observance, that you o'erstep not the modesty of nature: for anything so overdone is from the purpose of playing, whose end, both at the first and now, was and is, to hold, as 'twere, the mirror up to nature; to show virtue her own feature, scorn her own image, and the very age and body of the time his form and pressure. Now, this overdone or come tardy off, though it makes the unskilful laugh, cannot but make the judicious grieve; the censure of the which one must, in your allowance, o'erweigh a whole theatre of others.

I thanked a young actress who recently was highly praised for her performance in one of my plays. She answered modestly and frankly, "Well, I was praised though I didn't do much about it—I merely followed the text."

Merely followed the text!

If one thinks about the acrobats who dart about with a mutilated Hamlet, who jump up on chairs, raise their heads or lower them forward, act the serpent-man out of *Fliegende Blätter*,[18] open their shirts as if they were about to be executed, as if a bullet could not go through both a coat and a vest, twist themselves as if they were corkscrews, in other words, play Hamlet in a way directly opposite to Shakespeare's directions, one will have to admit that the attractive image of Hamlet needs to be restored. But this can happen only through the restoration of the original form of the drama by means of the drapery stage and by not assigning the role to a tightrope walker who makes the play secondary, the acting primary, and converts all his fellow players into extras by cutting their parts.

Follow the text! Yes, this is the art of acting: play the part, and no more!

It is strange that an author gets nowhere with *great* actors, and that all plays in which stars are to be featured are second-rate. If a masterpiece is to be a vehicle for a star, the play is mutilated. The attempt by the art of acting to isolate itself, to free itself from natural dependence [on the text] is the beginning of deterioration. For the star becomes visible only if the major planet is darkened. The star robs the play of interest, plays down the author, and transforms his fellow actors into extras. The foolish head of pride shines through borrowed feathers, but the mob, which is duped by frivolity, is immediately ready with applause and flowers.

I have seen the greatest now living star;[19] I came with youthful respect to learn and honor. The play was a drama of character, which I had seen before. There was an armed guardsman at the door, a tribute most likely arranged by some undisciplined alcove-favorite. I saw no characterization in the drama of character: but I saw costumes, lace handkerchiefs, powder, and make-up. She was a peacock, not with her own feathers, but adequately so for concealing both drama and fellow actors. I must admit the audience that day was select, for not one hand moved in the places designed for applause; the star was obviously annoyed by this, took her handkerchief, and blew her nose to show us her profound contempt for our poor taste. And in the next big "number," she put her hands on her hips like an angry cook and literally "bawled out" the actor playing opposite her. We sat silent, and left the theater in silence. We had seen "the beast," on whose face there was not a trace of the human, only paint and false pride, and the only thing I remember vividly is a train that ran out through the doorway like a serpent's tail under a rock.

*

I have always had the bad taste of liking good actors but not being able to stand great ones. The good actor always plays his role, is adequate without going to excess, fulfills his duty of acting according to the text. But human frivolity is so great that the good actor never is given a big name, never gets flowers, but is treated as if he were just average, is called useful in a derogatory sense.

A serpent-actor has been traveling about creating a furor, but they say he has improved lately because his taste has become better. As soon as people in Germany see that the technique is beginning to show and the actor is "destroying" the role, they say, "*Der schauspielt! Der Hund is ja ein Schau-Spieler zur Schau.*"

The extra something that an actor has the right to give is his significant or winning personality if he has any; but it shows through unintentionally and is not put on. As soon as one *sees* the technique or notices that the actor is puffing himself up, shouting, or making an unnecessary movement, the whole thing is sick. His intention is clearly something other than creating the role, and the audience that came to see the new play gets instead an actor who is strutting and courting its favor.

To return to Hamlet: a few reminders to the actor.

Hamlet is young; he is called young Hamlet; Ophelia says: "The expectancy and rose of the fair state." And one can figure out that his mother, who can still attract the king, is not said to be old. If one estimates the limits of her charms to be thirty-five, Hamlet can be twenty, the right age for a Wittenberg student. Ophelia thinks he is handsome, and we can believe her.

Is he blond or dark? Either. The play does not say.

Is he fat or thin? Answer: he is thin because he is mourning and because he is in love. The line in Act V where his mother calls Hamlet *fat*, Gollancz in his latest English edition of 1906 says was inserted to make it possible for the fat and obese star Burbage to play the part. So we can eliminate this line until we need it for another fat and obese forty-year-old.

Large or small? Not too large, because he himself says he is not a Hercules.

The king's sensitivity of conscience and his genuine love for the queen show that he is no theater villain. He says:

> . . . The queen his mother
> Lives almost by his looks; and for myself —
> My virtue or my plague, be it either which —
> She's so conjunctive to my life and soul,
> That, as the star moves not but in his sphere,
> I could not but by her. . . .

The queen is a weak woman, who loves her husband and her child and who in the play did not know about the murder.

Finally a word about the ghost. It says "the Ghost" in the list of characters, so he is a role and must be seen. In Act I he is tangible because he is seen at the same time by four people. Wilhelm Meister tells how his company arranged it so that in Act IV Hamlet's mother did not see the ghost.

The actor who has played the ghost has made himself noticed occasionally. D'Israeli[20] says (in *Litt. Cur.*) that Booth played the ghost opposite Betterton, who as Hamlet acted so superbly that Booth forgot his lines out of consternation.

Right now three companies are said to be touring Sweden giving *Hamlet* in the provinces. People say all three Hamlets are good. Why not? The role carries itself, is easily played, because it was so well written by Shakespeare; to ruin it one has to be an unusually artless person with disadvantageous looks and a crude manner!

I heard a sensible old theater director say: "How do you get actors? Give them roles! Then they'll be actors (if they have what it takes, of course!)."

That is how it is! And I've always thought people are petty about actors. A thing can be done in any of several ways occasionally. He had come to this conclusion because of the difficulty of always having on hand a variety of talents to select from. When I as the author am satisfied, in whose name is the critic justified in being dissatisfied? You may well ask!

I shall end this little memorandum with a couple of words about the acting at the Intimate Theater.

When I have been satisfied in general at dress rehearsals, that should be adequate testimony. People have then asked me to be critical, and I have answered: When my play has been played so well that I haven't noticed the actors as such, the performance has been good. I saw the painful tragedy *The Bond*; when the performance was over, I had had an experience. I could not make suggestions. Falck, Flygare, Wahlgren[21] had given the illusion [of being the characters]. A judge among my friends and a friend of theater declared afterward: "All criticism is silenced; this is not acting; it is something else! It is absolute reality." I agreed! And if you ask me why, I think the answer would be: Their acting is honest, unaffected art, created by young, natural people, who have gone through a difficult school, who are not spoiled, who have not learned tricks, who are not arrogant, who do not try to play down the drama or each other. They have just the right amount of unselfishness to interest themselves more in the play than in their own success. Miss Björling and Miss Flygare are willing to go from major roles to playing extras cheerfully and voluntarily in a play where a pupil has the title role; where the actresses have not been able to afford dressers or hairdressers, they have helped each other. This is what we call a good spirit, and it is that that has helped us through this terrible year, when more stones have been placed in our way than roses along the roadside.

Thank you at the Intimate Theater for the first difficult year, and a good new one!

STRINDBERG

THIRD LETTER

Introduction

IF Strindberg had a deliberate plan for encouraging and informing his fellow workers at the Intimate Theater, he could hardly have devised a more effective approach than the one he uses in the third letter. Convinced as he was that the actors should know the plays in which they appeared but not analyze them to death, he provided an analysis of a second Shakespeare play that is personal and informative without being pedantically didactic. Then in the two other sections he discussed matters of very great concern to every member of the company — acting, dramatic criticism, and the state of the contemporary theater world in Stockholm. With its digressions, personal touches, and informality, the letter combines some of the best features of the friendly letter and the informal essay.

While everything he says in the first section about *Julius Caesar* merits consideration, the really important matter is his direct and indirect acknowledgment of his debt to Shakespeare. No writer could ever more frankly summarize the nature of the reasons for his gratitude toward a predecessor than Strindberg has in these lines:

I shall end with a confession and an admission which I have long since made. Shakespeare's manner of depicting historic persons — even heroes — intimately in *Julius Caesar* became the decisive pattern for my first big historical drama, *Master Olof,* and, with certain reservations, even for those written after 1899. This freedom from "theater" or calculated effect . . . I took as my guiding principle.

If one recalls what Strindberg had had to say about *Hamlet* in the second letter, considers what he has to say about *Julius Caesar* in this one, and then examines the fourth letter which is devoted to several Shakespeare plays, one can, it seems to me, come to only one conclusion: what Strindberg says he owes to Shakespeare is primarily the courage to do as Shakespeare had done — present the historic dead intimately and realistically. If one examines the rest of the section (or for that matter the other material on Shakespeare in this volume), one can clarify what Strindberg meant by his statements: Shakespeare had thought of the historic dead as flesh-and-blood human beings; on the bases of records and his own imagination he had recreated them for the stage as people who felt, thought, and acted as people of his own time did; and he had presented them within the limitations of the stage. Strindberg does not admit borrowing lines and scenes and the like (although there are echoes of Shakespeare on rare occasions in both historical and nonhistorical plays). The nature of Strindberg's debt to Shakespeare is a far more important and subtle influence than slavish borrowing and imitation.

*

"Treat them like artists, not like laborers or schoolboys" must have been a delightful point of view for the actors at the Intimate Theater at a time when many people still considered most if not all actors members of an inferior social class. Well aware of the fact that human beings need to be reminded time and again of what is highly important, Strindberg considers some of the matters he had already pointed out in the first letter: his emphasis here is placed on the differences between good and bad acting; the need for clear, distinct enunciation; and various other problems actors face.

What is most important in the section, however, is what Strindberg says about the perennial problem that faces living dramatists and all theater people, and, among them perhaps above all, actors: dramatic criticism in the form of reviews of actual productions and performances. No other playwright could have better qualifications for speaking frankly about the subject than Strindberg. Since he himself had served as the dramatic critic for a Stockholm newspaper for a time in his younger years, he knew the difficulties involved in having to have a review ready for publication a few hours after an opening; he knew that such judgments must be hurried and improvised. He knew, moreover, that there is something decidedly unnatural in the situation in which the critic is involved: the critic is there not to enjoy but to evaluate many things, among them the performances of all the actors, the staging, the play itself, and the production as a whole. Besides, as a playwright who had not curried the favor of either reviewers or critics and had irritated many of them and other influential Swedes by blurting out what he thought and felt on innumerable occasions, Strindberg was in a good position to speak not only about the inadequacy of most reviews but about downright flaws in the whole system of dramatic criticism.

His blunt assertions that the dramatic critics of his day were not trained for their work and that some of them had selected reviewing as a career out of sheer pedantry and/or love of power are obviously accurate, as anyone familiar with the criticism printed in Strindberg's own time knows. His awareness that the people who review any one production after its opening frequently disagree in their judgments reflects a situation as true now as it was back in 1908. His advice, based on the conviction that actors should not have to be exposed to biased and unjustified criticism, that actors should disregard the reviews was perhaps comforting — but only to a slight degree, for actors, like other performers in various fields of human activity, do want to know what is said about their achievements.

Theater people today should be interested in Strindberg's direct as well as implied suggestions for a solution to the problems of dramatic criticism. His ideas that the reviewers should be professionally trained for their calling and that what is particularly needed is a professional journal are certainly sound. Such a journal, edited by and contributed to by experts should, he felt, be devoted to all the dramatic and theater arts and would do much to inform the people of the theater about all aspects of theater art and help materially to protect them from the more or less disastrous results of amateur, incompetent, and biased reviewing. That his suggestions would not be a complete answer to the problem of protecting those engaged in an art the very nature of which implies the ephemeral Strindberg knew only too well; he knew, moreover, that man is finite.

The third section of the letter is less interesting, perhaps, for Strindberg's personal discussion of the crisis that faced the Stockholm theaters in his time than it is for its revelation of Strindberg's concept of theater and of his sane and sensible answers to practical questions that always have and perhaps always will be problems for most theaters. To be sure, what he has to say about Stockholm theaters in the closing years of his life is historically important, but the problems have since been appreciably solved, frequently very happily as the present highly healthy state of most Swedish theaters testifies.

Even though he was the great experimenter within the modern theater and is generally recognized as one of the most stimulating forces in twentieth-century drama, Strindberg was remarkably realistic and practical in his answers to some very matter-of-fact questions: fitting the repertory to the times, setting the times for performances to suit the convenience of the public, and modernizing the seating arrangement. These were all matters Strindberg felt had been nicely taken care of in the Intimate Theater.

Strindberg believed that the theater should be a theater for the people, an institution that would provide both entertainment and education not only for the fortunate few but for the masses. If the institution were to survive in a constantly changing world and face the competition of such forces as the movies, it would, he insists, have to renew itself to fit the needs and wishes of its potential public. Not that the theater should be at the complete mercy of a weary, relaxation-hungry public; as a vital force in the community, it could educate its public to appreciate good fare even while it was entertaining its audiences. That, in brief, is precisely what the Intimate Theater tried to do. [W.J.]

Julius Caesar
Shakespeare's Historical Drama
Together with Some Remarks
about Criticism and the
Art of Acting and an Addendum
about the Theater Crisis
and the Theater Muddle
Dedicated to the Intimate Theater

When one is going to write a historical drama, it is a little like writing an assigned composition in school about a definite topic, to write a variation of a theme on an already composed piece. Shakespeare's *Julius Caesar* was one of his most popular plays even in its own day and has continued to be played in all civilized countries. This, although the play is not amusing. One knows everything ahead of time, even what will happen to the heroes; even love, which adds spice to the simplest and driest concoctions, is lacking; there is no clown who amuses, no intrigue that holds one's attention, no troll, only a ghost, which amounts to less than Hamlet's. But the play is interesting all the same, as is everything Shakespeare wrote, because it is sustained by an inner buoyancy that nevertheless slackens here and there.

When I used *Julius Caesar* as a textbook in English in 1869 (although I could hardly pronounce the sounds of that difficult language), the play had been selected because the English in it was easy and the play did not contain anything coarse. We youngsters, who were highly critical, commented at once that the play should have been called *Brutus*, since Caesar fades away in Act III; and we found that the world's greatest hero, whom we knew from world history and his own *De bello gallico*, had been badly depicted: a wretch who believed in signs and apparently was henpecked so that he wanted to stay home from the senate because his wife had had bad dreams and had asked him—a general—to be careful. These major criticisms from twenty-year-olds have certainly been made before and since by famous commentators, but now, when at the age of sixty I reread my *Julius Caesar*, which because of the commentaries I know best of Shakespeare's plays, these same weaknesses came to mind.

When I again examined Caesar's role in detail as I had done before, I again found a certain weakness in his characterization, which must not be called a merit just because one likes Shakespeare.

Let's take a close look at the weaving, separating the warp from the woof to examine the shafts.

In Act I, Caesar appears in a public place with his wife Calpurnia. One knows that one does not talk about Caesar's wife, and a Roman did not show off his wife on the street. When

Caesar, conqueror of the world, opens his mouth, he does so to ask his wife to stand in Antony's way in the races so Antony may touch her:

> . . . for our elders say,
> The barren, touched in this holy chase,
> Shake off their sterile curse.

Scholars have explained this by stating that Caesar at fifty-five is so tired or exhausted he is getting quite simply superstitious. Couldn't one instead believe it means this: Caesar is at the height of his power—*imperator, pontifex maximus*, condemned (literally) to be worshiped as a god, but he has no children by his wife (although he has Caesarion by Cleopatra), and now when he senses he has not long to live, he wants to live on in descendants or to found a dynasty?

Then comes the soothsayer and warns about the ides of March, but Caesar does not want to listen and calls him a dreamer. So he was not superstitious in *that* sense. All this happens on one page and was presented too early, as we more modern people would think.

After a while (also in scene 2) Caesar comes back and gives some sharp characterizations of the conspirators, a fact that indicates he suspects them. The commentator says that his knowledge of human nature is thereby revealed. Then Caesar leaves again and does not appear any more in Act I.

The conspiracy is developed, and in scene 2 of Act II Caesar appears in his nightgown (and slippers), frightened by the thunderstorm and by Calpurnia's screams in her sleep. He sends a servant to the priests to ask for a sacrifice and prophecy (out of the entrails of the sacrificed animals). This is not superstition but a Roman religious practice, like the oracles in Greece. Calpurnia comes out of the bedroom. She has never believed in signs before, but now they frighten her, and she asks her husband to be careful. "When beggars die there are no comets seen." She's right about that.

The servant returns and says that the priests when sacrificing the animals found one that did not have a heart.

Caesar answers in a boastful way that is not in keeping with the sensible, highly cultured man and therefore strikes us as false. He says:

> . . . danger knows full well
> That Caesar is more dangerous than he.

The Julius Caesar who wrote the dispassionate history of the war in Gaul did not say anything like that.

Calpurnia, a tender and not at all unwomanly wife, begs him not to go to the senate: "Call it my fear that keeps you in the house." Caesar does as his lovable wife wishes so as not to upset her, and there is not a trace of his being henpecked here. Then their close friend Decius Brutus comes and succeeds in rousing Caesar's masculine pride so that he changes his mind and puts on his toga to go to the senate. The conspirators enter, and Caesar greets them without visible suspicion. To Brutus he tosses a barbed question that could be without significance: "What, Brutus, are you stirred so early, too?" They all go to the Capitol.

Act III. The Capitol. The soothsayer warns [Caesar] again. Artemidorus hands him his supplication. In vain: Caesar enters the senate. Metellus Cimber begs for mercy for his exiled brother. Caesar becomes brutal. Brutus and Cassius press forward and join in the plea for mercy. Caesar answers like a braggart or *Vielgeschrei*: he is as immovable as the North Star:

> But I am constant as the northern star,
> Of whose true-fix'd and resting quality
> There is no fellow in the firmament.

. . . .

> So in the world, — 'tis furnish'd well with men,
> And men are flesh and blood, and apprehensive;
> Yet in the number I do know but one
> That unassailable holds on his rank,
> Unshak'd of motion; and that I am he.

And then he is cut down! With the words "Et tu Brute," which Hagberg translates into Swedish. So: in scene 1 of Act III the hero of the drama has gone, a fact that has always been objected to as a flaw in the composition. But now twentieth-century critics come along to say that that is not a flaw, although not all of them agree. In his edition printed this year (1908), Gollancz presents the information that "Mr. Fleay (whom I do not know!) thinks that the present form of the drama comes from 1607, and that it is an abbreviated version of a more complete play and that Ben Jonson did the cutting."

This is the mysterious quality about Shakespeare, that as soon as one starts writing about him one runs into controversies, with authorities both for and against. I cannot decide if *Julius Caesar* is Shakespeare's own as it stands, and limit myself to considering the play as we have read it from childhood on.

The major criticism, that the hero disappears at the beginning of Act III, can be met by simply saying, "Call it *Brutus* or what you will," and that's taken care of! One commentator has strained himself by explaining that Caesar is not gone in Act III, because he appears again in both Acts IV and V as a ghost, and that his powerful personality lives on in people's memory and engages and occupies the minds of the other characters to the very end. Why, Brutus' last words are:

> Farewell, good Strato. Caesar, now be still:
> I kill'd not thee with half so good a will.

Well, he could put it that way!

But what about depicting the world's greatest hero as a coward? How does that fit in with Shakespeare's aristocratic way of thinking? One can answer: The human qualities, including the frailties, are what interest us. How would *you* depict the conqueror, the statesman, the historian on the stage? Is he to appear with his legions on the battlefield? Is he to sit at a table drawing up laws, or perhaps be writing *De bello gallico*? That is not dramatic, so his private life remains. But involving him in a love affair — for example, with Cleopatra, would not be pleasant, and not significant for Caesar, for he got over Cleopatra while Antony was caught in the net. So all that is left is "Caesar *intime*," at home, as Shakespeare has done, even if he is in the bedroom with his nightgown on. We see Caesar as a good husband, yielding in little things; as a friend; as a statesman and conqueror, in the senate. You cannot drag his leading of an army on stage; it takes battlefields and armies for that. Cassius' depiction of Caesar's character is only a faithful expression of the demagogue's constant delusion that all people are alike. Caesar's calling for help when he was about to drown is in the democrat's eyes proof of lack of heroic courage; Caesar's catching the ague in Spain and calling for a drink while feverish makes him a feeble being, Cassius thinks. The whole petty depiction becomes merely a depiction of Cassius' pettiness and envy, for Shakespeare seems to have had a naïve admiration for Caesar, and he could just as well have told the anecdote about "Caesar and his luck" in the boat.

The difficulty in writing a historic drama is to find just the right mixture of the historic and the intimate. History in the large is Providence's own composition, and Shakespeare is a providentialist just as the ancient writers of tragedies were, so he does not neglect the historical but lets divine justice be meted out to the point of pettiness. For example: Caesar has overthrown Pompey his cotriumvir; Caesar is struck down at the foot of Pompey's statue. Cassius has jabbed Caesar with his sword, and the same sword cuts Cassius down:

> . . . Caesar, thou are reveng'd,
> Even with the sword that kill'd thee.

But Shakespeare has also slavishly followed history as Plutarch wrote it, and he has even copied whole passages (listed by Gollancz, 1908). So far as the central character of Brutus goes, he is an ideal figure related to Hamlet, who was created in about the same way. Brutus philosophizes about everything he undertakes and speculates about his destiny and the problems of existence. Brutus has no flaws, but commits a big mistake when he interferes with the plans of Providence and murders Caesar; it is this act that causes his fall after it has dawned on him what a rabble he had been working with and what the men who succeeded the tyrant were like. Antony tampers with Caesar's will; Cassius is avaricious and accepts bribes; Lepidus is an ass. The people who in scene 1 of Act I have been cheering for Caesar had shortly before "climb'd up to walls and battlements" to shout for Pompey; after Caesar's death they cheer for Brutus, shortly afterward for Antony, and then for Caesar again when his will is opened. Brutus has sacrificed his friend's life for the fickle mob; on the altar of abstract freedom of the people he has liquidated the abstract concept tyrant, which is simply a bad translation of ruler.

As you know, Caesar kept all the republican forms, but made himself absolute ruler. That he arrogated to himself worship as a god (apotheosis) a writer of Greek tragedy would have used as an adequate motif for his overthrow (*hubris*).

Shakespeare's manner of characterizing his hero is not successful, for instead of letting the character be revealed through action, he has Brutus tell who he is; and in his famous little quality, his thoughtfulness about the sleepy servants, he poses as noble, a little too sentimental for a Roman, I think. Brutus declaims, we would say nowadays, and he is too hasty in his praise of the dead Caesar, whom he has just exposed as an avaricious petty soul:

> The last of all the Romans, fare thee well!
> It is impossible that ever Rome
> Should breed thy fellow.

That is the partisan's way of praising himself in his fellow criminal.

The depiction of the new men's cruelty when they have come into power and pass sentences of death in Antony's house is harsh. Octavius demands that Lepidus condemn his own brother; Lepidus agrees without protesting. Lepidus demands that Antony's sister's son Publius is to die. "He shall not live," says Antony; "look, with a spot I damn him." Compare this with Caesar's refusal to reprieve Metellus Cimber, the refusal that became the excuse for Caesar's death! Now the new men commit the same crime, without embarrassment. Things did not change! Commentators have always seen as a weakness in the depiction of Brutus the fact that Brutus merely accepts Cassius' call and becomes his tool, remaining under the lesser man's influence.

Caesar's friendship for Brutus is not emphasized in any scene, but Brutus' boundless love for Caesar is strongly emphasized. We do not know what sort of love it was; an uncertain tradition has made him Caesar's natural son, something that used to be implied through the free translation "även du min Brutus" [even you my Brutus] (Et tu Brute! is translated by Hagberg: Du också, Brutus).* Who is Brutus then? Shakespeare,

---

* Gollancz says that according to Plutarch Caesar cried out to Casca: "O vile traitor, Casca, what doest thou?" but Suetonius has Caesar apostrophize Brutus (in

who did not suffer from excessive learning and who takes things rather lightly (he calls Decimus Brutus "Decius"!), makes Brutus a descendant of Lucius Junius Brutus, who expelled Tarquinius Superbus and was himself the nephew of Rome's last king (after Lucretia's adventure). I thought so, too, in my youth, but now I learn that Caesar's Brutus, Marcus Junius, was the son of a tribune of the same name and of Servilia, the half-sister of Cato the Younger. In passing I point out that the elder Brutus acted as if he were mad in order to get away from the persecution of Tarquinius, and that Shakespeare possibly got his Hamlet motif when he was busy with Brutus (*Julius Caesar* preceded *Hamlet*).

Shakespeare's Brutus is in any event a splendid man, just, humane, unselfish, and not even his enemies suspect him of bad motives. He says of the murder: "As Caesar loved me, I weep for him; as he was fortunate, I rejoice at it; as he was valiant, I honour him: but, as he was ambitious, I slew him." That is approximately the same as Hamlet's assertion that he must be cruel out of pure love.

But there is an important person in *Julius Caesar* who should have been presented properly, since he plays the same conciliatory role as Fortinbras in *Hamlet*. That is the one whom Shakespeare calls Octavius Caesar but who later becomes the Emperor Augustus. Of course, his name first was Caius Octavius; he was Caesar's adopted son, but also the son of Caesar's sister's daughter, and later called himself Caius Julius Caesar Octavianus; and in the drama at Philippi he should have been called Octavianus. (In the year 27 [B.C.] the senate and the

Greek): Even you, my son? *Teknon* does not mean that Brutus was Caesar's son, for son is *huios*, but *teknon* is a term of endearment like our *kära barn*. Paul uses *teknon* in writing to Timothy, who was not his son (II Tim. 2:1). In David's son, son is *huios* and child *pais*. The error *Decius* for *Decimus Brutus* may stem from a misprint in Amyot's French translation of Plutarch, which was the basis of North's English translation which Shakespeare used. [A.S.]

people gave him the honorary title Augustus). Well, I know how dangerous it is to correct Shakespeare because one generally gets a counterblow in the text itself, but I am going to try. When Caesar in scene 2 of Act I is presented, he complains that he has no heir since his marriage with Calpurnia is childless. He is surrounded by a crowd of people (Cicero is an extra!), but his adopted son is not there. Caesar does express his hope of getting a son with Calpurnia and asks her to stand in Antony's way at the races. Since he is murdered immediately after that, the adoption must already have taken place. There was a good opportunity to prepare the presentation of Octavianus here so that he would not simply tumble down on us in Act IV. I wondered for a moment if Shakespeare knew who his Octavius Caesar was, but the question and the comment can be dropped as impertinent since it is quite possible that the missing scene was eliminated when the play was cut. I would have eliminated Cicero since he is a neglected figure in spite of his talking Greek; and I do not want to listen to Cicero talk for six hours in a pulpit — his terrible oratory tortured me throughout my youth.

But the man who is to become Emperor Augustus is neglected all the same although he is not even present at the murder.

He appears first in scene 1 of Act IV and demands that Lepidus' brother be killed. He puts in a good word for Lepidus, whom Antony compares first to an ass and then to his horse.

Then he does not appear again until Act V at Philippi; there he is already arguing with Antony about the arrangements for battle. "Why do you cross me in this exigent?" The conqueror-to-be who will defeat Antony at Actium answers: "I do not cross you; but *I will* do so." And shortly afterward, sensing his destiny, he answers: "I was not born to die on Brutus' sword."

After Brutus' death Octavius Caesar takes all of Brutus' men into his service and, a generous victor, he delivers his tribute to his fallen enemy:

> According to his virtue, let us use him
> With all respect and rites of burial.
> Within my tent his bones tonight shall lie.

That is fine! But the audience ought to know that this is Augustus and that he is to defeat and succeed Brutus, because thereby the drama would give one endless perspective, without beginning, without end, something of world history's eternity, in which the actors succeed each other but the theater remains; the audience is always new, but the old play keeps the stage: "where Caesar died and became dust. . . ." Pompey, Caesar, Brutus, Antony, Augustus. That is a series in which each term is as if it were the root out of the one preceding it.

*

The composition in *Julius Caesar* is noteworthy because it is simple, almost classical; it pleases tired people to be able to survey the whole work of art easily. There is no lack of form — the murder is prepared for in two acts, takes place in the third, and the tragic consequences unfold toward the catastrophe, which is followed by renewal and the perspective of the future. Caesar lives on in his ghost (revenge or justice), memory, and his adopted son.

Calpurnia and Portia are, in keeping with the common sense of Shakespeare and all other healthy people, genuine women, feminine, mindful of honor, devoted to their husbands, submissive. One forgets Calpurnia, but Portia is more of a Roman woman than the weaker variety. But both are treated well by their husbands, as true friends, whom one listens to but does not always obey. There is a so-called good relationship, which in Caesar's marriage is not even disturbed by Calpurnia's barrenness.

Cassius, the third character, is power hungry and cannot bear to have anyone above him, but he does not seem to be so very much dedicated to the people. This "dry Cassius" is also an avaricious person and something of a joker.

Casca is a duplicate of Cassius and is unnecessary; he probably got in through a scribal error, for when we read Hagberg's translation, in which the names are abbreviated Cass. and Casc., we used to confuse them. Shakespeare must have noticed the weakness, because he goes to the trouble of presenting several characterizing details about Casca without succeeding in interesting us in him. He is said to be dull; he gossips; others say he is a contrary person and a hypocrite. Then he is out of the story.

Decius (Decimus) Brutus I cannot understand, and the minor characters are too many to be kept apart; probably the author did not expect that, either; like our contemporary directors he wanted to have the list of players exhaustive. And one does Shakespeare a disfavor by praising his little shortcomings.

In *The Two Gentlemen of Verona*, Shakespeare has, as Hagberg has pointed out, included two Eglamours. "Possibly Shakespeare had forgotten that in the beginning of the play he had given this name to one of Julia's suitors." Things like that happen!

Gollancz thinks that in *Julius Caesar* Shakespeare had the same sort of lapse when Lucius seems to be confused at one point with Lucilius. From that I take the liberty of believing that the *two* Cinnas in *Julius Caesar* have come into being in the same way. They are minor flaws the director can correct without pedantic critics attacking him for sacrilege.

There is one little scene I think particulary well put together — scene 3, Act IV,* in which Brutus arrives at an understanding with Cassius. That scene is instructive as the type
or model for a quarrel.

Cassius has extorted money and sold positions. Brutus tells
him so bluntly. Cassius denies the fact at first (typical!). "I an
itching palm!" When he cannot avoid the issue any longer, he
appeals in this way: "I am a soldier, I, / Older in practice, abler
than yourself / To make conditions." Brutus cannot admit that.

CASSIUS: I am.
BRUTUS: I say you are not.

Then they go to name calling. Brutus: "Away, slight man!"
Then they begin to boast, and after that they bicker:

CASSIUS: I said, an elder soldier, not a better.

[He is lying, because he had said "older in practice."]

CASSIUS: Did I say "better"?

[Both of them have forgotten what they have said, for Cassius
said "abler than yourself to make conditions" and not a better
soldier!] Brutus answers as the custom is when the quarrel has
culminated: "If you did, I care not." (About time!) Then they
begin to be ashamed, feel sorry, and proceed to reconciliation.
What did Shakespeare mean by this little scene? That Cassius
was not unselfish in his pursuit of liberty but that Brutus was.
Or that all people, even the greatest, are afflicted with weaknesses, and that a human being without weaknesses would not
be human. Shakespeare could not bring himself to make Caesar
a god, but he has not lowered him because of that. Shakespeare
assumes we know about Caesar's heroic deeds; in the drama
we get to see the human being, who does interest us.

* Strindberg says Act III. [W.J.]

In his *History of England* (London, 1818 reprint, VI, 191–92), David Hume says:

> If Shakespeare be considered as a *Man*, born in a rude age, and edu-
> cated in the lowest manner, without any instruction, either from the
> world or from books, he may be regarded as a prodigy. If represented
> as a *Poet*, capable of furnishing a proper entertainment to a refined or
> intelligent audience, we must abate much of this eulogy. In his com-
> positions, we regret, that many irregularities, and even absurdities,
> should so frequently disfigure the animated and passionate scenes inter-
> mixed with them; and at the same time, we perhaps admire the more
> those beauties, on account of their being surrounded with such deformi-
> ties. A striking peculiarity of sentiment, adapted to a single character,
> he frequently hits, as it were, by inspiration; but a reasonable propriety
> of thought he cannot for any time uphold.

*

I have to admit I have never understood Shakespeare's sonnets, which supposedly deal with homosexuality. C. R. Nyblom,[1]
who translated them into Swedish, says in his introduction that
he understood them. Oscar Wilde says these sonnets had the
same influence on him that Plato's works had had on the young
men in a certain university city. In Shakespeare's plays, as far
as I can recall, it is only in *Hamlet* that the touchy subject is
mentioned. The matter is touchy because, if one tolerantly says
he understands it, then one becomes suspect; and, if one speaks
disapprovingly about it, one is accused — of something else. In
scene 2 of Act II, Hamlet says to Guildenstern and Rosencrantz:

> HAMLET: . . . man delights not me; no, nor woman neither, though
> by your smiling you seem to say so.
> ROSENCRANTZ: My lord, there was no such stuff in my thoughts.
> HAMLET: Why did you laugh, then, when I said, "man delights not
> me"?

Does it mean what I have suggested? I do not know, and I have
seen no commentator's interpretation.

I shall end with a confession and an admission which I have long since made. Shakespeare's manner of depicting historic persons — even heroes — intimately in *Julius Caesar* became the decisive pattern for my first big historical drama, *Master Olof*, and, with certain reservations, even for those written after 1899. This freedom from "theater" or calculated effect which I took as my guiding principle, was long held against me until Josephson[2] at the Swedish Theater discovered *Master Olof* in 1880. But even as late as 1899 Molander[3] did not understand that my *Erik XIV* was playable. After reading the play, he exclaimed: "Am I to put on this play? Why, it has only two scenes!" Molander was so conditioned to French technique that scene meant effect to him. I do not remember if Molander saw the production of *The Three Musketeers* at the Swedish Theater. In that play all the old effects were assembled, and the director expected a smash hit. But the play was received coldly; the effects seemed to be only tricks, which were immediately exposed.

Grandinson[4] went beyond Molander's "externals" and admitted I was right when I was right, seeing that the effect or the impact of the play depended on something other than what was piquant in the situation and the scenic effects. Grandinson's refined but simplified taste for the "internal" made it possible for me, after Fredrikson's[5] retirement, however, to get such plays as *There Are Crimes and Crimes, To Damascus I, Easter, Charles XII* produced at the Royal Theater, all of them under Grandinson's direction. *To Damascus* was something new and a masterpiece by way of direction!

*

I have always had a hard time getting my own final judgment of a stage production. The art of acting is the child of a series of flashes, sciopticon images that disappear when the stage lights are extinguished, something half real that one cannot take hold of. I was the dramatic critic[6] for a daily during a few months, and I did not find it pleasant after the performance was over to sit down at my desk to put down on paper improvised judgments that on closer scrutiny I felt could be expressed just as well in another way. When I wanted to postpone my judgment in order to sleep on it, the editor explained that the printers were waiting and that I had to write my review right away. When I still was hesitant, he advised me rather to give the performance the benefit of the doubt than to damn it. I envied the people who could go to a restaurant to talk about the evening's performance, and I wondered why my judgment had to be printed when I — at the age of twenty-odd — had seen so little of the art of acting. If I go to enjoy art, I am in an unreflective, receptive, sympathetic mood, ready to get something. If something displeases me, I pass it by and go on without determining the reason. If something pleases me, I enjoy it, but do not want to disturb my own enjoyment through analysis. But the critic proceeds in the very opposite way. He steels himself to judge, to determine why this pleases and that displeases, and that is why he so rarely enjoys anything. Since the theater is an institution for the creation of illusion, there is nothing easier than to make oneself unreceptive to the illusion. One is contrary, the illusion does not come, but with that the purpose of going to the theater is counteracted, and the critic might better have stayed at home when he did not want to receive the delightful illusion that here a bit of life was presented.

If I go to see a traveling magician, I pay to be pleasantly duped; but if some critically inclined person in the audience would get up to say that the goldfish did not come directly out of the hat but had been in the magician's coat pocket, I would not be grateful for the information. He would have spoiled my pleasure.

That is why people in the theater world ask what they have to do with criticism. The director, the stage manager, and their comrades undoubtedly understand the matter best, and their judgment is an education. The public understand pretty well, too, if the characters resemble human beings, and if the actor can move, shake, or simply entertain his public; the artist knows if he has done well or not, and, if it did not go well today, better luck next time.

If the critic has any claims to being a judge, he should know the rules and must be impartial. If the critic appears as an instructor, he must have studied his profession and take his task as a calling accompanied by responsibility. Nowadays a paper hires a man as dramatic critic because he can write or has an easy style. He is not asked if he has been backstage, attended rehearsals, or composed a drama. He does not even need to have been interested in theater but can come from a totally different calling. But the job is not always accompanied by the gift, so one often gets to read the most outrageous evaluations which theater people would laugh at if their bread and butter and reputations were not at stake.

A blind person is not eager to judge colors, but, if he should permit himself to do so at an art exhibit, he would have to put up with the reminder that he is blind even if it is cruel to remind anyone of a bodily defect. If an intoxicated or deaf person comes to the theater and sets out to write a review of the play after *one* performance, I as the accused have the right to challenge the witness or judge: "He's drunk! He's deaf! Out with him!"

An author was recently charged with the absurdity of having had an infant in arms go to the cupboard and eat mustard.

Either the critic had written this deliberately to injure the author or he had not heard right. The first is unforgivable, the second indefensible.

One critic (or several) felt that Riddarholm Church in *Queen Christina* was not like the real church. Either the critic did not attend the performance or he did not notice that Riddarholm Church had been eliminated. "Drunk or deaf! Out with him!"

There is a special breed of critics who select the career out of pedantry or love of power in the false notion that the public buys reviews. A professional journal should be edited by experts in the field and really give the reader a review of everything in the foreign and domestic theater, facts, notes, realities that could benefit theater people and not only contain praise for friends of the house or stones for personal enemies.

People who quite often have another completely different profession are frequently seized by the inclination to express themselves in print about the theater, and the job is often done like that of the executioner, with the great pleasure of decapitating [others] without risk of cross action.

The actor's work involves his personal attitude; he stands there with body and soul, defenseless, a target, every man's outlaw. He meets evil glances, little contemptuous laughs, remarks against his eyes, nose, and mouth. — Don't you pity him? He is put together as we are, he has feelings and passions, he does his best, for he does not dare do anything else. He is not good tonight; yes, but he may be ill and not dare to say so, he may have grief, which he wants to talk about still less!

People have organized societies for the protection of ferocious animals. Can't public opinion begin to protect the actor, not from the printed review but from undeserved insults from the audience? Recently a decrepit old man sat on the main floor loudly insulting an excellent actress through a whole act. Human cowardice was so great that evening that not a single voice was raised against the wretch, though the disapproval was general.

*

As I said, I was a dramatic critic for a few months. It was not fun; and I can comfort actors with this: when my opinion was in conflict with that of my colleagues, it was like living in a wasp's nest. I lost friends, people did not answer me when I said "Hello" to them, and, when the editor got worried about me and told me to praise what I did not approve, I had to give up the job.

The job is not enviable, and the position could be eliminated as superfluous when there are directors, managers, and actors who understand the matter better. The director particularly. He has seen probably thirty rehearsals, he knows the play thoroughly, the way in which to say what is to be said, he has been in on considering the production and discussions about it for thirty days, the movements on stage have been tested, and changes in nuances have been thought through. The public, which knows as much as the critic, wants to make its own judgment and keep it and the pleasure it got out of a performance, and, if a theatergoer looks at a review, he does so to have his judgment confirmed, not to have it set straight.

When an actor has complained to me about the injustice, errors, and deliberate distortions in the newspapers, I have told him merely: Quit reading the stuff!

Criticism can never be objective or universally pertinent as long as kinship and friendship, sympathy and antipathy, coteries and special interests exist. A couple of years ago a subscription get-together was held to demonstrate against my *Dream Play*;

a year ago warnings about my chamber plays were issued. A
half year later the public was urged to go to see a potpourri of
all these and a little more, a production which they then labeled
a masterpiece by the plagiarist. That sort of thing is not criticism; it is poor taste based on the principle of personality; it is
the blind confusion that comes from hatred or self-inflicted
stupidity!

*

When can an actor be said to be bad? Well, when he *is* not
the character he is playing; when he is distrait, inattentive, slack,
uninterested; or when he does too much, forces himself forward, sticks his own head through the role to look at himself
or the audience, isolating himself from the role.

Being the character portrayed intensively is to act well, but
not so intensively that he forgets the "punctuation"; then his
acting becomes flat as a musical composition without nuances,
without piano and forte, without crescendo and diminuendo,
accelerando, and ritardando. (The actor should know these
musical terms and have them constantly in mind, because they
say almost everything).

But there are fine, modest people whose acting can easily
seem colorless because they forget the enlargement the stage
requires. If they look at the scenery to see how large it is painted,
they can see how the acting, too, must be kept somewhat magnified and not in miniature manner. The work that is entirely
too fine does not stand out against the background; it is a painting on ivory, which one gladly picks up in one's hand but does
not hang on the wall.

One knows that a superb actor is excellent the minute he
makes his entrance. When he comes in, he immediately carries
and elevates; he radiates power that transfers to his fellow actors;
he attracts the interest of the audience without playing for its

special attention. The strong personality has an indescribable plus—of intelligence, knowledge of the ways of the world, culture, humor.

The *great* actor is frequently uneven. He acts on inner steam, but, if he does not get the steam up, he can be miserably poor, flat, nothing. That is called acting by inspiration, but I think the word ought to be disposition. And one can make the effort to seek disposition, or one gets it by attention to oneself and by not combating the coming of disposition. It will not do to go from a gay dinner to dress in a hurry and run on stage to play Hamlet. When a person is merely going to read a work, he goes aside to pull himself together and get into the mood. The so-called inspiration will certainly come after a little effort and exertion of one's will. A person who is lazy or careless by nature will never make a good actor. Too thoughtful a person sinks instead of stepping on stage in rapport with what is being played.

There is a kind of tendentious actor and actress who cannot create a role or enjoy creating it if he or she cannot in so doing teach some idea or other. There are the political actor and the suffragette actress. They are miserable when the role does not call for a sermon, either about socialism or about the woman question. Lugné-Poe was a bad actor who became interesting when he could teach, preferably about woman but even about platonic anarchism, but then he preached.

The person who considers himself an artist, that is, looks at his art as art and does not brood about universal suffrage or emancipation, who does not speculate about world problems and zoology, will become a good actor. If the actor can live unre-flectively, naïvely, a little carelessly, not read too much, rather be with people but not to study them but really live with them now and then, and have fun, his art will benefit most. With studies and reflection comes calculation, which in turn becomes speculation, and the studied can seem too studied. He does not need to use dramas for his reading; novels are just as good, sometimes better. I think Dickens would be a good teacher, because his depiction of human beings is more thorough than the dramatist has time for and because he motivates action endlessly. But he has something else the actor can use: he supplements every character's actions with a wealth of gestures and play of expressions that are incomparably fine. I have recently reread *David Copperfield*, and my admiration for the teacher of my youth goes beyond words. With only a few sparse printed words he calls forth the same illusion one gets at the theater with its large apparatus, or, more correctly stated, he gives me the illusion of actual experiences.

*

When I, as the author, see my play performed and I have been satisfied with the performance, I have never been able to understand how the critic could be dissatisfied. But when I see how one critic has been delighted by the same performance the other one has attacked, I have understood that the difference rests on purely subjective grounds. An actor's personality attracts me, but somebody else finds him unattractive. Furthermore: the member of the audience is indisposed, the content and the intention of the play go against his grain, and he transfers his animosity to the actor who is innocent; or the actor is badly "off," probably not through the whole performance, but only in certain scenes, and he transfers his dejection to the audience; or the actor has been assigned a role that is not suitable to his nature, and he therefore does not become believable.

But there can be one person in the audience who has come for a contrary purpose; he may be such a strong person that he can affect a certain actor so that the latter will feel the hatred, awaken from his trance, and become bad in his role. An older actor has told me that he can feel when an enemy is in the audience before he sees him; when he locates the source of the hatred, he dedicates the role to him and usually succeeds in "playing him" down but does not always succeed in pinning him down. If the members of a coterie show up (after a big dinner, including drinks) in an unusually hostile mood, they can destroy the whole evening for both the audience and the actors. It is, of course, a touchy and sensitive thing to create art, and all artists seek solitude and the closed door; the actor alone works with the curtain raised, publicly, and for that reason people ought to be merciful toward him. There once were so-called concert-painters, but although their performance was mechanically studied and fixed ahead of time, music had to be used to keep disturbing influences at a distance.

But there are also purely personal motivations for unjust treatment of actors. I know one actor who is always good; he always creates his role, destroys nothing, makes the special efforts needed to be the one he is playing, and succeeds. But when he is excellent, people say nothing; when he is competent, he is abused and jeered at. People pick on him, although he irritates no one by being arrogant. I do not fully understand the reason for all this. He is admittedly a lone wolf and does not belong to any coterie; he is also independent [financially] and does not need to kowtow to anyone. I believe he has to bear the burden of hatred of a notorious relative who is not liked but has the same name. Even his colleagues nag at him, but, when I meet them and we talk about him and I ask, "But isn't he a good actor?" they answer in chorus, "Yes, of course, he's good!" — Yet he never gets recognition or acceptance.

I know another actor who is always excellent, recognized by

everyone; but he never gets "the big name." We specialists are amazed by that, but we cannot explain it.

To receive recognition as a star requires, I suppose, a little extra personal goodwill from a group of friends who are interested in seeing to it that one of them is great and thereby casts reflected glory on those about him.

*

During many years of association with actors, directors, and producers, I have received varied explanations of the following simple little fact. I asked one theater employee who had had to see the same play sixty times running if the actors always acted in the same way evening after evening. He answered: "No, they're not the same any two evenings!" — Other specialists have asserted the contrary or that the actor's acting is fixed. I have not had the chance to judge very thoroughly, but when I recently again saw one of my plays at a dress rehearsal, I found the same flaws I had commented on six months before — uncorrected. When I asked the director why the willing and cooperative actor had not corrected the flaws, he answered: "He can't — though he wants to. They're part of him."

Then I came across a bad habit. The actor usually has a lot of ideas that cannot be got rid of. For example: as soon as an actor in a Protestant country puts on a monk's cape and the monk catches sight of a woman, the actor immediately thinks it is a question of Tartuffe or some other joker. If I tell him that in this case it has nothing to do with Tartuffe, that does not help. That is a bad habit and conceit.

When my *Saga of the Folkungs* was going to be produced, I found the actor playing King Magnus decked out as Christ. I explained to him that Magnus Eriksson, who admittedly was called Magnus the Good in Norway, was no Christ, and I asked the actor not to carry the cross on his back as the Saviour did on His way to Golgotha. But he knew better, for in his youth he had seen Udhe's[7] paintings (Christ the teacher, etc.). So that was that.

In the final scene of *Gustav Vasa* in which the Dalesman Engelbrekt comes in drunk, I asked the actor to refrain from staggering. He staggered anyway. I pointed to a passage where it says, "merrily drunk, but steady in his movements." — He staggered anyway! I explained that a merrily drunk person can in an important moment — as before a king — become sober, and that a drunk person above all tries to stand straight when he tries to look sober. It did not help, although the whole play was in danger because of this bit of behavior.

I have heard that Norway's greatest dramatist [Ibsen] used to hand slips with instructions to the actors after the dress rehearsal, but not one of them was followed.

Is acting so mechanized after the many rehearsals that it cannot be changed? That is possible, but I suspect that the actor acts so unconsciously, so much like a sleepwalker that he literally does not understand what the director says. When I have made a polite suggestion, I have often been answered by a perplexed smile as if the actor thought I had said something silly. But the actor also has the little professional weakness of getting the false notion that he has written the role himself. And the playwright seems to him an unauthorized intruder, who should merely be grateful and make no critical remarks.

When the author pops up at the dress rehearsal and offers suggestions, they answer: "It's too late!" When I have appeared at an earlier rehearsal, they have answered: "It isn't ready yet! It's too early to criticize!"

So I have concluded: let them do as they wish just so they do not do anything absolutely crazy that distorts the meaning of the play. — Freedom in the free arts!

And I think that method has been successful at the Intimate Theater, where no director has torn the play to bits. A few days ago I met a forty-year-old poet whose plays have been performed. He had seen my latest play, and when I asked him about the acting, he answered: "I didn't notice the acting; it was so honest and unaffected the acting wasn't noticeable." — He did not know the name of a single actor, either. — This made me ask in a meeting with the actors how they would feel if their names were not listed on the billboard. After some hesitancy they told me the public would soon find out the names anyway! If I had asked further if they preferred a quiet incognito before "the execution block," I do not believe they would have been ready to answer. Why, every première is a test, and it can be tiresome to continue as a schoolboy through life; but it does lend suspense and keeps up one's interest so one does not have time to get old. On the contrary, one gets younger with every new assignment! If theater people could select, I think they would choose the present, with its annoyances and disadvantages.

*

It is impossible to set up valid rules for theatrical art, but it ought to be contemporary in order that it may move contemporary people. I mean this: if the time is skeptical, insensitive, and democratic as ours is, there is no point in using grand airs or sentimentality. Then a light skepticism, a certain insensibility which can look like coarseness to many have to be prevalent in the theater. During such a period people are not likely to weep over *Axel and Valborg*,[8] *King Lear* will seem unmanageable, and Timon does not arouse pity when he is deserted by paid flatterers. Even tragedy itself will use light conversational dialogue, verse gives way to prose, the levels of style are blended, and kings do not dare walk on stilts any more than "the barbarian mob" does; all speak the same language. All words can be used anywhere. The acting in such a repertory will be obvious; if the text is followed, there will be a search for reality or nature, truth, words that have been misinterpreted but whose meanings need no explanation. I saw the very opposite of this art at the Theâtre Français toward the end of the 1870's. Everything in tragedy was stilted. The play was *Rome vaincue*, in verse; it contained general observations, *loci communes*, which had become mere phrases: effusions and eruptions of feelings. The acting was in keeping. Mounet-Sully did esthetic gymnastics, created plastic art; he could stand for five minutes as the Borghese Fencer with his head stretched far back, the veins in his throat swollen, and emitting a shriek "as if fire had broken out," his eyes rolling and frothing at the mouth.

This was, strangely enough, Goethe's first ideal as a theater director in Weimar: "Beauty first, then truth." But I did not find it beautiful, possibly because I was not a Frenchman, because no other art is so closely linked to what is national as the art of acting. But when Goethe had survived this first sort of thing, which was a reaction against a crude German naturalism, his beauty ended up in a killing formalism, which did away with the individuality of the actor and which was self-caricatured in Goethe's *Rules for the Art of the Stage*. It is from that that we have inherited the pathetically excessive, large manners, artificiality, and extravagance, all of which are now called "provincial."

The requirements of our time are not those of the time that

is coming. If there comes a period when people become more sensitive and another view of the world succeeds the biological we have passed through, there will be needed another repertory, which will have to be acted in another way. So it is not worth drawing up any rules which will quickly enough be discarded; the wise will listen to the voices of the time when they begin to be silenced by the voices of the age coming into being, and keeping up with his own contemporaries is the duty of the growing and ever self-regenerated artist. As far as beauty on the stage goes, I have to admit I do not like to see just anything at all on the stage. When a man of culture keeps close watch on himself in daily life and does not behave in an unbecoming fashion, I do want to see the actor, too, conduct himself with dignity and self-respect when he is playing a man of culture. A prince should not strike himself on his chest with all of his fingers spread like a goose's foot, nor should he sit on a chair with his legs forming a triangle. A lady should never "bite" or be sullen even if her role is oppositional; a lady should always be attractive, even when she is furious. This is an example of that beauty which is truth. Weimar-Goethe went too far in setting up rules when he forbade all playing in profile or with the back to the audience, ordered the stars to take the right side as more distinguished, to walk on stage only when talking — not directly across, though. Even careful arrangement of placement was criticized — the whole thing became something like a chess game. But what was justified in Goethe's attempts at reform lay in his opposition to a cheap or vulgar conversational tone, which quickly became mere chatter that could hardly be heard, and which had reduced the actor to being a reporter of the content of the play. Goethe demanded that the dialogue be heard and seen, and he cured the unsatisfactory state of affairs by means of excesses, some of which survive in our own day.

When I have reacted against too fast a pronunciation, one that has approached chatter, at the Intimate Theater, I have also warned against the very opposite — speaking so slowly as to cause sleep. In music there is indicated within a slow tempo an inner movement (*mouvement*) by an *agitato,* for example, which does not increase the speed, but strengthens the speech, lends excitement from within, causes the speech to vibrate and pulsate. This is what makes the slow tempo bearable.

I have even pointed out the lack of new nuances, which follows rapid speaking. If one hears a long role uttered in only one tone, in a single allegro, without pauses, without ritardando or accelerando, then one gets weary and bored. That is to report on the play, not to act it. If the actor would make his observations in daily life, observe how a conversation is carried on, a conversation in which the speakers take time to think before they speak, he would notice the difference between that and the memorized talk one very often hears on the stage.

The actor speaks too rapidly for several reasons. He thinks the audience will get impatient, but the opposite is the truth; for, if it goes too fast, it becomes tiring to grasp the meaning of the many words. A certain fear of losing the train of thought keeps him from pausing; the memorization at rehearsals lingers on, and this memorization of a lesson which was the major task then remains from habit during the performance. For that reason both the learning of the lines and the mastery of the role should come at the same time. When one only hears a lesson recited, it is an amateur show; the actor's art begins where the lesson ends; and that is why one expert has said that a production is never ready on opening night and isn't until about the fifth performance. Therefore I have asked even the actors to use every performance as a rehearsal, develop, modify, invent, fill in, and not make their acting mechanical. Experience has brought me to the point where I would rather hear flaws in memorization than an entirely too well memorized lesson; and I think that the prompter's presence adds the feeling of security needed to keep worry about forgetting one's lines from leading to speeding up one's speeches. One is generally too quick to criticize the actor, the public less so, but the dramatic critic is proud when he discovers small lapses in memorization. If one only does not skip an important passage, to which the dialogue later refers, it does not bother me if there is a little faltering. Once I heard a famous actor deliver a speech several printed pages long. He forgot his lines a few times. I went backstage and found the actor beside himself. I comforted him by pointing out that we, the audience, had not noticed that anything had been omitted and that his speech sounded more natural: "What human being can deliver such a long speech without stumbling?"

I have heard and seen excellent actors who never knew their lines completely but always had to be prompted. But they acted! And I want to risk saying this: "The lesson" can kill acting.

I know a superb actor who never reads his lines at home but uses the rehearsals to learn his part. He says reading his lines at home without getting others' lines in return can never amount to anything.

I have even said to my actors: Tamper with your speeches if you can get them to go better; stretch them a bit, if you want to, but see to it your speeches fit with the others'.

People are generally too demanding of the poor actors, petty even. Thereby one robs them of the necessary self-confidence, frightens them. And there probably is too much rehearsing; the play is threshed to pieces. "Treat them like artists, and not like laborers or schoolboys!" They learn more from one performance than from thirty rehearsals, and in an empty theater with a director and a prompter no play can take shape, least of all if the director sits there breaking the mood the artist has gone through inner agony to summon up.

One should not correct anything but what is absolutely wrong. And when something is expressed in several ways the artist should independently decide what is right for his purpose.

Freedom without license, play gladly, but "seriousness in the acting, king!"

*

When the Intimate Theater got along without a special director until this fall and everything went all right, even with such difficult plays as *The Ghost Sonata*, *The Bond*, and *Queen Christina*, I immediately found myself almost superfluous as the regular director. The actors tried their best at the rehearsals, smoothed out each other's acting under the director's guidance, and arrived at good results with *The Father* and *Swanwhite*. If I add that I could not bear hearing my own words out of the past drummed into my ears day after day and if I confess that my writing fascinated me, I have stated the principal reasons for my withdrawal as director although I remain that in title.[9]

About the Theater Crisis and the Theater Muddle

There are public secrets, and among them is the position of our theaters right now. The theater owner reveals nothing, issues denials, and lies until he has to feel sorry for himself. The personnel is loyal and does not spread the sad fact that the attendance is poor. Performances can even be canceled without the public's getting to know about it, but somehow or other the public does learn about it and it becomes known the theaters have not been doing well for some time.

Rumor has it that the Swedish Theater [10] has done well, and that has been attributed to the closing of the Royal Dramatic Theater. But, since the latter reopened, it has gone badly at both of them.

People blame the crisis on the poor economic conditions nowadays, but they have always been bad as far back as I can remember in this sense: the capitalists have complained about low profits in good times, and borrowers have complained about the shortage of money and high interest in bad. A philosopher (I think it was Buckle himself) has discovered that people seek amusement when they either are bored or have difficulties, for people can always raise money for entertainment. Attending the theater is not classified as an actual form of entertainment but has been considered as part of the intellectual diet in life. As a youngster, I thought of a theatrical performance as an experience which I made my own and collected along with other essentials in life. Briefly: there is something special about the theater. If one merely talks about it, others are interested, and, if one writes about it, one is read as never before. The theater is the chronicle of the contemporary world in living images, charades in action, silhouettes of living people, sometimes portraits, echoes of significant events, even the questions of the time. When the theater was still considered an educational, cultural institution, the state came to its aid and supported it as a commendable undertaking. That was true even in Sweden up until recently: the support ended when the misuse of public funds caused the government to end its support of theatrical activities. Yes, it used to be that the theater was considered so valuable that the state reserved the theater as a monopoly as they still do in Denmark.

We have not had a national theater since 1888;[11] free competition then became the rule with this qualification: the government rented its theater at Kungsträdgården to private citizens (Fredrikson and Personne) for a fixed rent, which is said to be merely two thousand crowns, a figure I find unreasonably [low]. And it probably was not the state — i.e., Parliament and the government that gave this present to private citizens, but apparently the minister of finance, who does not have the legal right to give away public money. If the official auditors should clear up this affair, both Fredrikson and Personne would have to pay up what the state has lost if the minister of finance himself would not have to. I cannot testify to the accuracy of all these details, which I have been given by a reliable authority, for it is possible secret funds do exist, even though I know nothing about them.

The Royal Dramatic Theater lost its "Royal" on the billboards in 1888 because of well-known unsatisfactory conditions and then ceased to be a national institution. When everything about it, including the building itself, had become run down, the authorities condemned it but allowed the theater to continue its activity in the biggest firetrap in town after the sheet-metal marquee had been propped up by a few iron bars and a few changes had been made inside. In recompense for making these changes, the rent was remitted — competitors estimated this to be some forty thousand crowns a year. Such an arrangement cannot be called free or honest competition, and the Swedish Theater had a hard time of it about 1900 as a result, but succeeded all the same in topping the record financially, while Personne's private theater lost money, which the generous minister of finance covered, partly by means of the emerging lottery.

From this same lottery Fredrikson probably had his equally large shortages covered while he had his private theater going the last time. That Fredrikson was not in the service of the state during the last period, he himself testified in the suit for his pension, which he declared in court he had coming because he conducted his theatrical activity only as a private citizen! I do not know if Director Ranft[12] has received any support from the minister of the lottery, but I doubt it, because the minister *almost* never attended the Swedish Theater but frequently attended Oscar's Theater.[13]

When the Dramatic Theater was condemned, the lottery[14] was set up to provide a new theater building. That was fine and commendable, but the whole project quickly became a mess, and in business there should be order.

In the first place, the lottery council acted like a private patron. The Dramatic Theater was to get a new house as a gift. But the Dramatic Theater had ceased to exist as such, and, if one asked if all this meant that the Fredrikson Company should get a new house, one got no answer.

The lottery council simply explained that there would be a twenty-million-crown lottery and that from this sum two and a half million would be used to build a new house and that this house would be given to the state for resurrecting King Gustav III's Swedish Theater.[15] (Sometimes they call it the National Theater.)

Well: this council, which still was private, began to act as a government institution, expropriated land as if it were for national and generally useful purposes, got a committee set up, and was working under the supervision of the minister of finance, who appointed inspectors of the construction, etc.

The building was finished! It is beautiful and, in terms of our circumstances, splendid. But the cost, it is said, ran to six

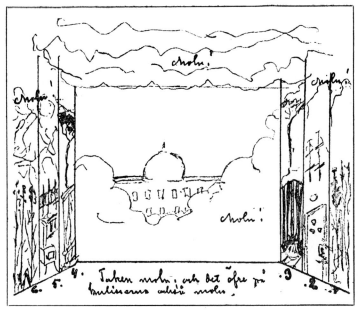

A Strindberg sketch for *A Dream Play*

Intima Teatern

Pelikanen.

Kammarspel i 3 akter af

AUGUST STRINDBERG.

Personer:

Modren Elise, enka... Fröken Svea Ahman.

Sonen Fredrik, juris
studerande .... Hr Aug. Falck.

Dottern Gerda......... Fru Manda Björling.

Magen Axel, gift med
Gerda .... Hr Johan Ljungqvist.

Margret, tjänarinna... Fröken Alexanderson.

Carl Kylley

Program for a production of *The Pelican*

million instead of two and a half, and the outstanding expert
has told me its value is two million. I cannot testify to the accuracy of any of these figures, for the report on the lottery has
not yet been made public. But I put this down anyway, with
these qualifications, with the hope it will help get the facts made
public. The public has a right to get such a report.

The building was to have been handed over to the state when
the committee had completed its work, but no one dared to offer
the dangerous gift, not even the minister, for people knew ahead
of time that Parliament feared the Trojan horse that always
had shortages in its stomach. The gift was not presented to the
Fredrikson Company either, for Fredrikson was left out and
his company broke up.

The theater did open under the name of the Royal Dramatic
Theater. The word *royal* has two meanings in our country:
either it refers to the state (the Royal Department of Foreign
Affairs, for example) or to the court (the Royal Stables), etc.
The Dramatic Theater is neither a national nor a court theater.
What right has it to be called "Royal"?

And who owns the Dramatic Theater? A council that has
constituted itself a corporation under the name of the Royal
Dramatic Theater. This is improper and irregular since it is
not clear. Does the corporation own the house, and does the
corporation count on interest on its shares? Has the corporation
been given a charter by the government? Under what department does the theater function? When I have asked, I have
always been told "the minister of finance." Then I have asked:
When it is neither a national nor a court theater, is it a ministry
theater or a corporate theater or a private one? That they do
not know, but some say it is *res publica* or the public's theater
since the public bought the twenty million lottery tickets. Others

believe that the theater is *res nullius*, that no one owns it and it should, like the property of a person who dies without heirs, go to the state (which does not want it!)*

The council did, however, make its first announcement: (1) the old Dramatic Theater would be sold and the proceeds go to the operation of the new Dramatic Theater (but surely Mr. Holm[16] and his friends cannot sell the state's building, can they?); (2) that a fund of 700,000 or 1,000,000 (the figures vary) out of the lottery money would be set up for the operation of the theater.

Then Mr. Michaelson[17] was appointed director, and the choice proved a good one. He has long been a friend of playwrights and the theater and, on occasion, a director. He had both knowledge and enthusiastic interest, he was used to big business and supervising people, and he had a liking and a knack for dealing with subordinates.

When he shouldered the burden, it became clear that some accounts were not accurate. The theater, which should have opened in September, 1907, did not open until February, 1908. When the actors went to work in September, 1907, and there was no money with which to pay their salaries, a corporation was set up to operate the theater. But its slight capital of 100,000 [crowns] seems to have been exhausted because of the expenses for five unproductive months when the salaries alone amounted to 20,000 crowns a month. (Note well: I put a question mark after each one of these figures!) The fund of 700,000 (or 1,000,000) [crowns] was to be used to balance the opera's losses. The new theater director protested, amazed (1) by the fact that the fund and the losses (at the opera) were identical and (2) that the Dramatic Theater was to pay the deficit at the opera.

---

* I have jokingly called it a raffle theater, and that is probably most accurate, but then the theater ought to be raffled off. [A.S.]

But his protest did not help, and Michaelson had to begin his career by spending what he did not have.

Since the fund was not available and the old building has not been sold, the new Dramatic Theater has had to operate in a difficult financial situation. The director soon calculated that, even if he had a full house every day, the theater would not be self-supporting.

The theater was opened, and the attendance was less than expected.

The reasons? There are many — People said the auditorium and the corridors were too elegant. A person in everyday clothes felt embarrassed in this luxurious setting; the acoustics were poor; people could not hear the consonants; it was hard to see close up in front and from the sides; the stage lacked depth; there was not room to store scenery comfortably, etc. People have complained about the repertory (I do not!). People have commented that in this festive hall with its unbelievable luxury only costume and period plays can be given; that colorless modern rooms and modern clothes are not adequately effective in such a frame of gold and brilliant colors. Fine! But neither *Master Olof* with its splendid staging, nor *Antigone* with Mendelssohn's choruses, nor *King Lear* has attracted people. So it was not that! Berger's *Syndafloden*[18] with its stage marvels that were talked about all over town still did not attract people. What is wrong then, especially since Michaelson has tried to meet the public by offering them both tears and laughter?

When one cannot find the cause of an unfortunate state of affairs, one usually tries to find deeper reasons. Since I wrote the Preface to *Lady Julie* in 1888, I have speculated about the theater now and then. I have wondered if the theater and the drama have not too long retained old forms without renewing them or adapting them to the needs of the time or the wishes of the public. Is it reasonable to expect people who have worked hard all day and who keep old-fashioned bedtime hours will leave their homes for intellectual labor that ends at midnight? A tired person demands entertainment or rest. He is happy to settle for a neutral place (the tavern or his home) among his own kind to reflect quietly about the labors of the day. But to dress up and appear at a public gathering, expose himself to hard intellectual activity and emotional experiences, that is something else again. About 1880 I saw *Faust* at the Swedish Theater; it began at seven and ended at twelve. That was ghastly! In Shakespeare's day and Goethe's the performance, I understand, started at five-thirty and ended at bedtime — nine o'clock. That was all right! Now, to keep up their strength, people have combined the tavern and the theater, but that has not improved the situation. The Intimate Theater tried to be up to date and shortened the labor — from eight to ten, and this seems to agree with the taste of people of our day. Another fact is that the theater is not a theater of the people. It is aristocratic in its old-fashioned seating of the members of audience according to their importance or according to what they pay for the tickets, so that the "better" people sit in the best seats and the less wealthy have to sit way up where they can neither see nor hear. I suppose that is how it is all the way through life, but in the theater it is *too* obvious. Such an arrangement does not become obvious in church, in the courtroom, or in Parliament, but you can see it in a theater even if you do not have opera glasses. People have told me that in the old Dramatic Theater people in the third balcony never saw a backdrop. Making people pay for what they cannot see is not nice.

The result has been that the balcony public first disappeared and turned to the movies. The modern institution called the movie house fitted in with the spirit of the age and made terrific headway. It is democratic: all seats equally good, priced the same, no charge for the cloakroom. For a very low price, one can select the time for a little distraction, even for a bit of news or pure entertainment. Since we can learn from everything, the Intimate Theater has borrowed two principles from the movie house: all places are equally good, and the time for our performances has been set at a suitable time which does not approach bedtime.

The movie house is the first nail in the theater's coffin, and the high prices are its second; the third is the late hour — even for those who do not go to bed early; and the fourth is the long play which Frenchmen call "machine."

Then there is a very natural cause of empty houses. There are too many theaters, and the theater [world] is too little to divide, Alexander [the Great] would have said.

With the appearance of the large Oscar's Theater, Stockholm obviously had too many theaters. The Opera had already expanded; the Östermalm Theater[19] had started; and the Vasa Theater,[20] which did not exist in Josephson's day, had taken over the whole new part of town, Vasastaden. When the Dramatic Theater also enlarged its house, what has happened had to. If one also takes into consideration the rapid development of the People's House,[21] its setting up of a theater, and the Intimate Theater, the causes of the crisis become more evident.

Premières of good and well-known plays before half-empty houses are unparalleled in our theater history, but they have become very common in our time.

How can the crisis be solved? Crises resulting from overproduction used to be solved by crashes and decreased production since demand cannot be increased by production. One or more theaters will have to go under. That is the cruel law, for an increase in population cannot be arranged right off.

When all our theaters are having a bad time, the crisis threatens to become chronic. When it does not pay to operate a theater, one closes it or is forced to close it, unless the owners of the theaters form a syndicate and control the production either by each one taking on one branch or by closing some theaters—which is not conceivable, human beings being what they are.

The Dramatic and the Swedish Theaters are the sharpest competitors and are most dangerous to each other, since the new Dramatic Theater has invaded the Swedish Theater's more ambitious program, and the latter has come out with Brussels carpets and costumes in imitation of the Dramatic. Specialization would not be impossible for those two if the Dramatic Theater would be subsidized by the lottery as it could put on what the Swedish Theater does not want to and hardly can put on.

The Dramatic ought to specialize in, say, Schiller, Goethe, Shakespeare, Oehlenschläger, Holberg, and Molière, and let the Swedish Theater have its Shaw all to itself.

If the Dramatic Theater does not get anything from the lottery and cannot manage, what will happen? A new manager cannot do anything about that, no matter who he is; I suspect that in thinking about the fate of the beautiful theater people will raise a cry for its getting a subsidy from the state.

State subsidies! Why Michaelson's company and not others?

And with state subsidies will come government bureaus, cliques of favorites, bureaucracy, little work, big pay, long vacations, and then deficits. No parliament will agree to that. We know that from a hundred years' experience. Then the fate of the Dramatic will be a question which because of tradition will be put alongside that of the Opera.

Now I must say something about the Opera, although it will

be mainly in the form of questions since nothing is less certain than the available information.

In the foyer of the new opera house [22] is (or was?) a marble plaque with an inscription in gold. It lists the members of the council and says that these men handed over the building to the state. But it does not say that the state refused to accept the dangerous gift. The land, which was the property of the state, was given (?) to the Opera, with the expectation that the building would belong to the state.

Now it is asked: Who owns the building that the public paid for? And who owns the land, which the state turned over with the expectation of getting it back with a building on it?

A corporation called the Royal Theater appears as the owner of the building and rents the Opera to Director Ranft. As director of the corporation, the Marshal of the Royal Court, Printzsköld [23] stepped forward during the court orchestra's strike to declare that the opera was not a government bureau but a business that wanted to make ends meet. There we found out! But even so the name of the minister of finance appears now and then as having cast an inexplicable veto as if the Opera were under his department.

About 1900, personnel of the Opera said that there is a fund of one million (the figure varies) and that the interest on this goes to help run the Opera. This has since been denied, and the fund declared a deliberate lie. There was no fund when Ranft became director, but shortly afterward there was a deficit of 700,000 crowns, which was to be covered by the lottery of the Dramatic Theater, and against the irregularity of which Director Michaelson protested.

It is none of my business who owns the opera house, and when the highest authority on government buildings in the country has told me, "No one knows who owns the Opera," I have quit asking. But the state pays the fire insurance, it is said!

But the Opera has never made ends meet, is not doing so now, so it is a good thing if the situation is made public if the crisis should become acute.

When the Opera does not manage (although Director Ranft has the luck of Caesar), and when the Dramatic Theater does not either, there will have to be a solution sooner or later. Then it will probably be discovered that the undertaking has been too ambitious for our small resources. Even if the Opera gets a subsidy, the company cannot play to empty walls, for that is depressing for the cast. The same is true for the Dramatic Theater.

So: reduction by the state! Originally the Opera had dramas as part of its program and therefore called itself, not the Opera, but the Royal Theater. With three evenings of opera and three of dramas, that theater ought to be filled with people, and that is the goal. That is how it was in Edholm's[24] day, and the finances were excellent (our encyclopedia, *Nordisk Familjebok*, says!). The arrangement was a little troublesome, but it always is on the stage. Great drama (*A Midsummer-Night's Dream*, *Egmont*, *Joan of Orleans*, etc.) would flourish up there in the world of music, where there are orchestras, choruses, and ballet dancers that are already available and paid.

But then the White House near Nybron[25] would be superfluous? Yes, if it is, it is — for that purpose! But the house can be very much needed for another and just as fine a purpose. Music! We need an academy of music and a concert hall.

Take a look at the ghastliest building in the country: the Academy of Music! A masterpiece of ugly proportions, a "two-sided triangle," in which music seems to have been included as an afterthought, an aloofness that does not become a public building, an entrance way that one cannot drive on, and a back entrance that is the main entrance. If a public building is frozen music, the Academy of Music is like something frozen after a thaw, but it is not music!

If the state sells the Academy to be used as a storehouse for coal or goods and expropriates the White House for nationally important purposes, or takes it over in escheat because it has no owner, that problem would be solved and at the same time Stockholm would get its concert hall.

The building is so beautiful it glows. It is a descendant of the Villa Borghese, but the marble resounds as if it were waiting for music.

If this were done, the Swedish Theater would get a breathing space for middle-class drama, the higher comedy, and children's plays, and no one would have been hurt.

The Östermalm Theater will close of itself—there is to be a square there.

Oscar's Theater will present operettas without competition.

The Vasa Theater probably will disappear as superfluous or will be closed by the university which needs it as a lecture hall.

The rest will take care of themselves!

*

But if the crisis becomes a crash, and there has to be an investigation, Parliament will first of all have to examine the Opera's records in detail, and explain to the public what is meant by a corporation without paid-up shares, without property, without capital, and the state will have to serve as the representative of the public, which has flattered itself as a partner in this incomprehensible corporation—the Opera and the Dramatic—flattered so they would buy lottery tickets.

It should also be investigated why the Opera had only four

and a half million crowns to operate with (*Nordisk Familje-bok*), while the Dramatic needs twenty million; then the Dramatic Theater's lottery affairs ought to be examined to find out how much the tickets brought in, how much was gain, how much remained, what the surplus was used for, whether the building actually cost six million, if the state has state money coming to it from Personne and Fredrikson for the rent that was illegally remitted (only Parliament and the government can spend state money), and if the same men as private citizens had the right to take funds from the Dramatic Theater's lottery.

That a review is needed is certain, for there is much talk about these institutions. If it is false, it ought to be disproved. I have aired this talk to get it tested, and I reserve the right to judge by the records. If I have been misled by having been given inaccurate information, I want to correct it.

The worst competitor of the theater still undoubtedly is the operetta. I was brought up in the golden age of the operetta when the archdemon Offenbach almost drove humanity mad [with delight?]. As an Aristophanes he foreshadowed the fall of a culture, and after Sedan his star set with the second empire. He could have lived during the Roman empire just as well, because he dissolved the Greek ideal of beauty so that we believed we could never read Homer or Vergil again. In my upper seventh year at school both teachers and pupils laughed when we ran across the names of Orpheus and Achilles, but after 1890, when Gluck's *Orpheus* took the opera in Paris by storm, the laughter had died away, and Gluck rose from the grave killing that which already was dead. And when in Boito's *Mephisto* Goethe's Helena reappeared, no one thought of the Beauty from *Bouffes* and *Gaité*. (Offenbach did leave a heritage in *Tales of Hoffman* where he leaves the negative and does something positively beautiful.)

There was a certain greatness in the master's denial, which was directed against the degenerate opera as well as against history, the state, and the community. As music it is an outrage, for the motifs were stolen from the greatest works from Sebastian Bach to Beethoven, but so skillfully transformed that only on hearing the masterpieces does one see Mephistopheles sticking out with his pointed ears. The epigons continued the work of destruction systematically, and, although I have not seen an opera for thirty years, it still happens when I hear Bach, Haydn, or Beethoven (I do not want to hear Mozart's distorted "adaptations" of Haydn!) that my enjoyment is disturbed by reminiscences from — operettas. I do not want to point out any particular places, for I do not want to destroy them for others. But they have even stolen Haydn's *Sieben Worte*, Beethoven's sonatas, and a certain song makes it impossible for me to listen to the last movement of the Ninth Symphony. The operetta picks up everything banal at the core of a tired human being; and a weary person is literally ambushed by these evil musical thoughts so that he is pursued by them, disturbed by them in his greatest moments, when they force their way into his seriousness and even his reverence.

Since Offenbach, the operetta composer and his fellow criminals are thoroughgoing professional thieves, and they play only on one motif: to make ridiculous what even by the most complete skeptic is considered somewhat sacred, a certain day in his life when he founds a home and a family and gives himself naïvely to an illusion, which all the same has something of the reality of eternity. One does not hear an operetta unpunished, because it is as suggestive as it is evil; and one goes like a medium to the unknown composer, feeling the dance steps in one's body when he pulls the strings; one becomes literally infected; and the one who wants to remain free, independent, untouched in his being watches out for the virus, especially if he goes with open wounds. It is not innocent, because it is concealed by expensive costumes and choice instrumentation; it is not witty, for it is idiotic to laugh at what in daily life one takes seriously, perhaps tragically. Rather, then, a movie or an innocent circus with handsome horses and hilariously funny clowns if one needs harmless entertainment! But the operetta producer feared the harmless circus and got it forbidden during the winter; it cannot be called sound competition to force poor taste on the public, a taste that all the same has enjoyed the encouragement of the very highest in the community—both the builder and the operetta producer were knighted, and the institute was named for the most recently constructed church.

This we found out, good friends of the Intimate Theater; when we tried to put on tragedies that had been rejected, we were treated as outcasts. The operetta prince was interviewed so that enlightened contemporaries would get his enlightened judgment of our tragedies, and, when he shook his head, the cultural elite in the community (and the press) wrinkled their noses—at us!

The operetta had become the criterion! It is time for us to watch out!

But, and finally: operating a theater in Stockholm is risky. Initiates see it like this. October and November are good months, December impossible, January–April best, May–September impossible. So there are only six months when it really pays. But then there is this, too: Monday is bad, Tuesday half-bad, Thursday and Friday pretty good. A theater should do nicely on Saturday and Sunday. So in order to be able to work half a year, with special holidays included, the personnel has to be paid for the whole year, and that is why, they say, tickets have to be so expensive. That sounds reasonable, but it is a dangerous situation.

In Copenhagen the Danes can put on both opera and drama in the same house. The people of Copenhagen are [not?] wealthier than we, but they are more sensible. Possibly we shall have to become sensible, too, but it will take us a long time!

In Christiania [Oslo] the Norwegians built a temple to the national muses (*Patriis Musis*). But, when it did not pay, the operetta had to be dragged in, and Offenbach's miserably poor *Brigands* is now a repertory play there.

We have seen the operetta standing watchfully waiting in the Opera foyer when there was talk about cooperation between Oscar's Theater and the Opera. If the Dramatic Theater is threatened by the same fate, we had better try to save the theater in good time! But the nation—which has the right, I take it, to tax itself—ought to see to it that the tax is not levied by corporations, councils, or ministers, but by Parliament and the government, which are the proper forum!

FOURTH LETTER

Introduction

As John Landquist says in his notes to Volume 50 of *Strindbergs Samlade Skrifter*, the fourth letter did not actually go to the company at the Intimate Theater. But the letter is obviously an extension of the sort of analysis of Shakespeare plays Strindberg had presented in the second and third letters. The fourth is, moreover, the one in which Strindberg reveals himself most fully as a student of Shakespeare and, while doing so, presents a fascinating example of something relatively unusual — one great artist's evaluation of a great predecessor's achievements.

If and when the forces that helped shape Strindberg as a dramatist are ever satisfactorily determined, it will probably be clear that Shakespeare had by far the greatest influence. These open letters are a logical point of departure for such a study or series of studies, for in them Strindberg has stated frankly how Shakespeare served him as a teacher and guide and has stated precisely what there is in Shakespeare's plays that attracted and inspired him.

The letters were written toward the end of Strindberg's second period of active engagement with Shakespeare's dramas. The first had come in his youth in the late 1860's and the 1870's when he had had to read certain Shakespeare plays in school and at the univer-

sity as texts and, to his amazement, had found them highly interesting in spite of what he considered their mutilation in the classroom.
Perhaps the most important bit of instruction in reading Shakespeare that he received was, as he suggests, Brandes' explanation and
interpretation of Shakespeare's realistic technique. His most important gains from his early exposure to Shakespeare, he admits, were
confirmation of the validity of his own objections to the contemporary Swedish historical drama and the courage to write a historical play (*Master Olof*, 1872) in his own fashion.

A generation later, in his fifties, Strindberg again turned to
Shakespeare, this time voluntarily, deliberately, and purposefully.
Not only did Strindberg turn back to literature as his primary professional interest in the late 1890's, but he renewed his interest in history
and the drama. In his opinion, no one had created greater
historical dramas and nonhistorical plays than Shakespeare. In this
second period of intense interest Strindberg studied his predecessor's plays to determine as precisely as possible just what Shakespeare had achieved and how he had done it, not in order to pay
Shakespeare the dubious compliment of merely imitating him, but
instead to regain the inspiration and the courage to write new plays,
historical and nonhistorical, in his own fashion.

During both of these Shakespearean periods, Strindberg had ac-
cess to plenty of material for his studies. In addition to Shakespeare's
own plays in the original, there were — fortunately, since Strindberg
never mastered English adequately — Carl August Hagberg's excellent Swedish translations in twelve volumes (1847-51). While Strindberg scholars will never admit that Strindberg was a scholar in an
academic sense, they can hardly deny that he was a librarian and a
very good one. His years on the staff of the Royal Library had made
him well acquainted with source materials without destroying his
sense of proportion.

One secondary source — Brandes' *Kritiker og Portraiter* (1870) —
had helped him to understand Shakespeare's dramas in the 1870's, so
he turned to other secondary sources for further help in the late

1890's and continued doing so in the following years. The problems that the Shakespeare scholars and critics dealt with, from textual criticism to interpretation of individual speeches, fascinated him, tempted him occasionally to indulge in textual criticism, but never caused him to lose sight of his primary objectives: to find out just what Shakespeare had done and how he had done it. In other words, Strindberg knew that secondary sources can at best only furnish leads and ideas; if one is to know Shakespeare's plays (and, by extension, any other works of art) one must go to the works of art themselves.

As one reads his open letters, one should remember that they were never intended to be scholarly papers but were written to help and instruct the members of the company at the Intimate Theater, in practical terms: to get them to read plays intelligently, analyze both the play as a whole and the individual actor's particular role, and participate creatively in the production of Strindberg plays. Strindberg's analysis of *Macbeth*, for example, may strike the academic reader as pretty much the sort of thing that pupils or young students indulge in, but a close reading of any one of his analyses, comments, interpretations, and judgments will reveal an awareness of the members of his particular audience and a successful effort to adapt what he had to say to their needs and interests. Great as his admiration for Shakespeare was, Strindberg was no blind hero-worshiper of Shakespeare or anyone else. He warns his audience repeatedly against admiring anything merely because it was created by Shakespeare. Aware that the texts of various plays are probably imperfect, however, he admits that some of the flaws may not actually be Shakespeare's.

It should be remembered that Strindberg believed that other creative writers use themselves, their imagination, and their experiences in much the same way as he himself did. It is for this reason that Strindberg read Shakespeare's plays as personal documents, which, if carefully examined, could give him reliable clues to Shakespeare's personality, life, and thinking about God, man, and the universe.

For example: "*The Tempest* is considered Shakespeare's last play: the aging man's need for peace, summing up, and coming to terms with life find their expression here." All the essays on the individual plays indicate clearly that Strindberg read Shakespeare's works in this fashion. Aware of the danger of reading into another man's work what one would like to find there, Strindberg does on several occasions qualify his conclusions. But all that he has to say not only reveals what he particularly liked in Shakespeare but also suggests what he himself was trying to do in his own plays.

He did not doubt that Shakespeare's major interest, like his own, was people: "Whatever he does his major interest is this: to depict human beings." What amazed and delighted Strindberg as he read the plays were Shakespeare's inclusion of almost every conceivable variety of humanity, his insight into the complexities of human character, and his ability to bring them alive within the limits imposed not only by the dramatic form but by human communication itself. Not that Strindberg insists that Shakespeare was always successful in his depiction of human beings, but he pays tribute to such superb characterization as that of Ophelia and to the little touches and details that give life to minor characters like the murderers in *Macbeth*.

Even if Brandes had not called for the discussion of problems in literature, Strindberg would undoubtedly have indulged in such discussions anyway. His very nature made him deeply conscious of the difficulties and conflicts he and his fellows had to contend with. When he read Shakespeare's plays, it seemed to Strindberg that Shakespeare had been aware of every conceivable human problem and had dealt with it effectively whether the problems concerned youngsters in love or an old man who did not know how to age gracefully. Strindberg believed that Shakespeare was as profoundly concerned with the problems of good and evil as he was himself. Strindberg read Shakespeare subjectively:

What bitter experiences Shakespeare had lived through one does not know, but he had daughters and was unhappily married. Most likely his competitors, too, made his life bitter, and I have begun to wonder if all the lost originals Shakespeare is supposed to have plagiarized aren't pure fabrications, lies spread by actors and theater directors for the most part. His own life was stormy and irregular, and various admissions in the sonnets imply that he had early in life learned the secrets of life and its joys.

Strindberg, one might say, was trying to find in Shakespeare the very sort of thing most Swedish Strindberg scholars have looked for in Strindberg's own works.

As attractive to Strindberg as Shakespeare's interest in and depiction of human beings and their problems was his thinking about the force behind the universe. Strindberg's faith in deity after his Inferno period was over in the late 1890's had been renewed, of course, and it is in light of that renewal that one needs to consider what he has to say about Shakespeare's religious faith. For example: "At forty Shakespeare was an enlightened believer, who behind things and phenomena had discovered the controlling powers that guide the destinies of human beings." Everything that Strindberg believed he had detected about Shakespeare's faith in God was congenial: Strindberg had become very much interested in Roman Catholicism, and he was delighted when he believed he had found evidence for concluding that Shakespeare was a Catholic; Strindberg was more than merely interested in the Powers, and he was sure that *The Tempest* and *Macbeth* contain evidence of Shakespeare's belief in superhuman and supernatural forces. In general, one may justifiably say that Strindberg believed he discovered evidence that Shakespeare's thinking about God, man, and the universe was much like his own.

Then there was Shakespeare's uncanny knack for telling a story well. In the second letter Strindberg had already explained a great deal of what he had discovered about Shakespeare's dramatic art:

> I was determined to study his method of constructing a drama. . . .
> I noticed that his structure was both formless and at the same time strictly pedantically formal. All his plays have the same cut: five acts, with four or five scenes, but one cannot really see how this is done. He

begins at a certain point; then the play develops in a straight line to the end. The technique does not show, no effect is calculated, the great strokes are there after a beautiful development, and then comes the peaceful settlement with drums and trumpets. Someone has said that it all seems like nature itself, and I agree.

It is this basic conclusion about Shakespeare's dramatic composition that Strindberg explores in the essays on the various plays, not merely to clarify his own understanding of the techniques but to accustom the members of the company at the Intimate Theater to a sane and sensible method of analyzing a play, a method that could and presumably should be applied to the Strindberg plays they were to appear in as well as to Shakespeare's. Strindberg obviously wanted his fellow workers at the theater to understand not only the elements of Shakespeare's technique but those of the strikingly different Scribean school; therefore, he presents a striking comparison between the two and suggests that both are effective in the theater. But running through almost everything he writes in these letters is an enthusiasm about Shakespearean form and substance, the like of which he never expressed in writing about any French dramatist or French dramaturgy.

In spite of his failure to master English, Strindberg was able to appreciate Shakespeare's verbal magic, unsurpassed imagery, and daring use of language. The last was the element that was to have a great influence on Strindberg:

> In this beautiful work of art [*The Tempest*] Shakespeare as usual has not excluded what is ugly but has on the contrary given it a major place. That is Shakespeare's philosophy and poetics — one that I have followed, in defiance of and with constant disapproval of those who were called idealists, and who permitted only polished, tidied up, colorless, and therefore false images from life.

To be sure, Strindberg in this passage has more than ugly words in mind, but time and again he makes the point that Shakespeare gave him the courage to use the right word in the right place in spite of Oscarian or Victorian objections.

As a man of his time and with his endowment, Strindberg could use all these matters in his own dramas only within certain limitations. Although he was an able poet and was to become a highly influential one, Strindberg undoubtedly could never have written blank verse that could begin to compare with Shakespeare's; but Shakespeare's lack of hesitancy about using the rich resources of English suggested that he could do the same in his own language — primarily in prose, however. Every one of the other matters could be used as guiding principles. What cannot be emphasized too strongly or too often, it seems to me, is that Strindberg's debt to Shakespeare is a matter of principles, not lines, scenes, or plots. It is the sort of debt that one writer who is essentially original can owe to another.

It has to be emphasized, too, that these letters were written by the aging Strindberg at the close of his second period of studying Shakespeare. Much of what he has to say about various Shakespeare plays is the result of deliberate analysis, not of the young Strindberg's racing through Shakespearean dramas because he found in them the inspiration and the courage to write original plays of his own in his own way for his own time — and the future. Strindberg's primary fascination with himself and his fellow human beings, his engagement with his personal problems and those of others, the evolution of his religious beliefs, his great gift for storytelling, and his own preference for the realistic techniques of dramatic composition throughout much of his career as a creative writer are all factors that will have to be taken into consideration by the scholars who may arrive eventually at the truth about Strindberg's debt to Shakespeare. [W.J.]

Macbeth

When I saw Josephson's production of *Macbeth* at the Swedish Theater about 1880, the play seemed decidedly boring. The play is well made: ambition causes the first murder (Duncan); the next logical step is the murder of the two pages; this makes it necessary to remove Banquo, the dangerous witness; but new witnesses come forward as avengers; Macduff does escape, but Macbeth strangles Macduff's wife and children.

This sequence of crude murders is entirely too elementary for us; it is crude, smacks of the picaresque, and plays on a lower level than we are used to; and Shakespeare has elsewhere, especially in *Othello*, worked with the higher equations of psychic or soul-murders.

Even the characters are too simple or unclear. Duncan is noble, honest, carefree; Banquo is also noble; Macduff is without flaws; and Malcolm, the heir to the throne, is a real paragon. They are abstract, hard to tell apart, what we call types, and are not personally interesting but interest us only as the tools of vengeance (justice).

But Macbeth himself and his lady have been too hastily put together. In Act I, scene 2, Macbeth is called a brave and faithful vassal and cousin of King Duncan. In the third scene he meets the witches, and upon their merely hinting about the crown (and the fulfillment of the first two prophecies), he has his murder plan ready. In the fifth scene of Act I, we meet Lady Macbeth; she has just received a letter from her husband explaining the situation, and she has her mind made up about the murder.

Then confusion sets in. The lady eggs her husband on, is abusive toward him, calls him cowardly and the like, and scene 5 ends with Macbeth's beginning "to reflect"; but his lady says, "You shall put this night's great business into my despatch," without our getting to know what the rest is.

The first act ends with a somewhat confused plan, which does not make it clear who has agreed to commit the murder. Lady Macbeth has hit upon the trick of putting to sleep the pages who are to bear the blame. Then she says:

> What cannot you and I perform upon
> The unguarded Duncan? . . .

Macbeth answers:

> . . . Will it not be receiv'd
> When we have mark'd with blood those sleepy two
> Of his own chamber and us'd their very daggers,
> That they have done't?

The husband and the wife seem to have decided to do the deed together.

In Act II, scene 1, Lady Macbeth appears alone saying that the pages are sleeping and that she has laid out the daggers for Macbeth, who can be heard crying out in the bedroom. Lady Macbeth now relates an important minor detail, which unfortunately has been put parenthetically: she had been in the bedroom ready to murder the king herself when she suddenly noticed the king resembled her father. What does this parenthetical remark say? Is it intended to show that Lady Macbeth has human feelings in spite of her having boasted about her so-called strength when she earlier declared she would have murdered her own infant-in-arms if it had meant getting the crown? The lady here shows herself an ordinary blusterer, who lacks the terrible qualities she has given herself. Then comes

Macbeth, conscience-stricken and with bloody hands. The play was written during the Hamlet period, and both Macbeth and his lady suffer thoroughly from the philosophy of indecision. But Macbeth has forgotten his role and comes out with the daggers, which he should have left in the bedroom. Now his lady is self-assured again after being so faint-hearted a little bit earlier that she could not kill the king; she calls Macbeth infirm of purpose when he cannot make himself go back. So Lady Macbeth returns the daggers herself and promises to "gild the faces of the grooms" with blood. After a while she returns, her hands bloody; but she has not murdered the pages. Schiller changed the scene with the porter, and others have wanted to eliminate it. Now that I have read that Shakespeare is considered innocent of perpetrating this unparalleled crudeness, I propose eliminating it, too. The scene is not true to life, for little people are not blasphemers, and when I heard it at the Swedish Theater I did not find it pleasant, although I was not at that time squeamish about a dirty story.

After the porter come Macduff and Lennox, then Macbeth. But Macduff enters the bedroom first and comes back right away to tell about the murder.

Macduff laments and says:

> . . . do not bid me speak;
> See, and then speak yourselves.

Then, according to the English text, Macbeth and Lennox enter the murder chamber. Hagberg has forgotten to put this in, so one does not understand what follows or that Macbeth enters and murders the pages, pretending fury about the horrible deed. His lady then pretends to faint, but nothing can dispel one's suspicions. Malcolm — the heir to the throne — and his brother Donalbain flee to England, and thereby become suspect, a situation that makes the play sound like a drama of intrigue.

Although Lady Macbeth has done nothing about the matter and has murdered no one, she all the same gets her big scene in Act V, scene 1, the scene which solo actresses who think of the sleepwalker as a mass murderess love. But Lady Macbeth now is tortured by pangs of conscience. If Shakespeare with his usual humaneness meant that the lady did have human feelings, she should not be played as a model of cruelty and inhumanity. Through her talk she has made herself worse than she is, and, when she has transferred her evil will to her husband, she regrets what she has done and ends by taking her own life. She did not have any part in the murder of Banquo, for he was murdered by hired assassins. Shakespeare has included an unusually enlightened doctor, who has not studied materialism or biology with Giordano Bruno because, when he has observed her sleepwalking, he does not prescribe a bromide but, explaining his helplessness, rejects playing any part in the matter:

> More needs she the divine than the physician.
> God, God forgive us all! . . .

Lady Macbeth is a beautiful and amiable woman (Duncan says so), a good and faithful wife, and has had children that she has nursed herself. Macbeth addresses her by the not too common words: *my dearest love.* He even uses the expression, *my dearest partner.* When Macbeth learns of her death, he is already beyond the limitations of our world and is waiting only to see Birnam's Wood come to Dunsinane; therefore, he becomes angry and says she died at an inconvenient time. But he need not mean that, because he has shown himself very affectionate toward his wife when even in the midst of getting ready for battle he consults the doctor about her illness. Never throughout the whole play does he utter [what would have been] a justified reprimand for her having inspired him to commit the murders. But this fact can have more profound explanations, as we shall see!

In this tragedy as in *Hamlet* there is a commutation of passion. Macbeth is not evil from the beginning but has in his veins the milk of human kindness, but Lady Macbeth is thoroughly evil and, by transfusion, transfers her evil will to her husband by the usual means: lying, poisonous words — you are no man(!), you do not love me, etc. When she has planted her evil in her husband, she seems to be freed from it, becomes weaker, gets pangs of conscience, and takes her life, while her husband takes up her passion, develops it until he is like a wild animal, a being filled with terrifying strength. Finally he can suffer no more but simply becomes evil. But behind all this evil (a problem Shakespeare frequently treats), he has shown beyond a perspective of the human passions something else, which the classical authors of tragedies always included and which they called the gods but we call evil powers. This signifies the witches. They are not a stage device designed to amuse the mob; appearing on four separate occasions, they direct the whole action, take care of the intrigue, one might say. Strangely enough Lady Macbeth never gets to see them and is never incited by them; only her husband's letter about his two first meetings with them on the heath gives her any information about their existence. It is therefore possible that Macbeth does not blame her for having egged him on.

When we introduce the concept of guilt into Shakespeare's tragedy, we never hear the murderers trying to whitewash themselves by means of [heredity], the modern cure-all or "Pear-soap," which we used in our childhood in dealing with inexplicable cases and then called inherited; the murderers do not blame others, do not deny facts, but suffer under the weight of their crimes. Lady Macbeth even becomes so sensitive that she punishes herself for sinful thoughts.

Macbeth considers guilt as being possessed by evil powers and acts almost without free will, almost always disapproving of his own behavior pattern. In the last act his remorse has become contempt for himself and fury against fate. In the last scene he says to Macduff:

> . . . my soul is too much charg'd
> With blood of thine already.
> . . . .
> I bear a charmed life . . .
> . . . .
> And be these juggling fiends [the witches] no more believed,
> That palter with us in a double sense.

Let us now pull the roots out of the witches and see what is left under the roots. The tragedy opens with the witches; that is significant. They do not say much, but they utter Macbeth's name and the formula for the nature of original evil:

> Fair is foul, and foul is fair.

This is the Bible's "Woe unto them who call evil good and good evil!" *

In the third scene the witches return. After listing some misdeeds that were still punishable according to the old national laws and the nature of which can be sought in demonology and not in Shakespeare's imagination, Macbeth's arrival is announced. He comes with Banquo, who is the first to *see* the witches, who resemble women, but have scarred fingers, withered lips, and beards.

* C. J. L. Almqvist, author of the *Törnrosen* books, bore this sign of the wild beast on his forehead. This is the whole secret about Almqvist and explains both the silence with which some people respond to his name and the jubilation which is raised from the depths of Hell in his unmerited praise.[1] [A.S.]

The witches make three prophecies: Macbeth will become thane of Glamis, thane of Cawdor, and king of Scotland. Banquo will become the father of kings.

Has Shakespeare fallen into notions from antiquity in this tragedy? Is this Oedipus' oracle pronouncing the will of the gods that Oedipus, while himself innocent, must according to the law of fate kill his father and marry his mother?

"No!" says one commentator. Macbeth is a Christian. He lived during the time of Edward the Confessor (about 1000); the witches are tempters who can be opposed and who should be resisted.

But the two first prophecies come to pass at once, and when the third one — the crown — does not, Macbeth goes to work to get it in illegal ways.

He has come so far that Banquo has been got out of the way, but the latter's son Fleance has fled and prophecy has said he would become king. There we have a new figure borrowed from music and which could be called "a rest or pause," since Macbeth's king's motif remains but in Fleance's person, forming then a transition to the resolution. Macbeth becomes uneasy and seeks out the witches to get certainty.

Now Hecate, goddess of the moon and queen of ghosts from Greek mythology, but decidedly Christianized, adopted by the enemy of man, God's adversary, Satan, appears. She says her work is the ruination of an immortal soul; she recommends the concoction of a witches' brew which will wake up satanic spirits in Macbeth's mind.

> He shall spurn fate, scorn death, and bear
> His hopes 'bove wisdom, grace and fear:
> And you all know, security
> Is mortal's chiefest enemy.

Macbeth does not come until the beginning of Act IV.

There is the witches' sabbath, and the drink has been brewed. When Macbeth asks, he gets answers, hellish ones and bad advice:

> Be bloody, bold, and resolute; laugh to scorn
> The power of man, for none of woman born
> Shall harm Macbeth.

Absolutely right, but Macbeth can be killed by Macduff, who was cut from his mother's womb.

> Be lion-mettled, proud; and take no care
> Who chafes, who frets, or where conspirers are:
> Macbeth shall never vanquish'd be until
> Great Birnam wood to high Dunsinane hill
> Shall come against him.

Then he is allowed to see Banquo's eight descendants wearing crowns, and he damns this day.

Well, this is more than soothsaying; it is more than temptation; it is impulse or obsession. Perhaps Shakespeare can have had the Calvinistic concept of predestination in mind, but his purely Catholic concept of Edward the Confessor's power to heal clashes with that possibility. The third scene in Act IV is set in England, not in Scotland, a fact that can easily be overlooked and can cause misunderstanding when Macduff and Malcolm begin to talk about the good king whose touch cures the evil (scrofula?). The king in question is Edward the Confessor.

What is related in Act IV about King Edward's power to cure the sick is something Shakespeare believed in; otherwise, he would have ridiculed it; and he could believe in it since his contemporary Elizabeth had the same miraculous power as Edward. Hagberg says that it was generally believed the queen healed nine people on a visit to Kenilworth.

At forty Shakespeare was an enlightened believer, who had

discovered the controlling powers behind things and phenomena that guide the destinies of human beings. If one assumes that the witches are allegorical figures, one has to conclude that for Shakespeare they are the representations of the positively evil, the existence of which he never denied. The horrors he must have lived through at forty show up in Hamlet, Julius Caesar, and Macbeth, whose last outburst in Act V after his wife's death is a cry of despair over all existence and probably a confession since it does not quite fit in in the play:

SEYTON: The queen, my lord, is dead.
MACBETH: She should have died hereafter;
There would have been a time for such a word.
To-morrow, and to-morrow, and to-morrow,
Creeps in this petty pace from day to day
To the last syllable of recorded time,
And all our yesterdays have lighted fools
The way to dusty death. Out, out, brief candle!
Life's but a walking shadow, a poor player
That struts and frets his hour upon the stage,
And then is heard no more: it is a tale
Told by an idiot, full of sound and fury,
Signifying nothing.

Macbeth is no monster; like Hamlet and Brutus he is a brooder and a believing skeptic. He has complete conviction about God, the life after this, and retribution.

His enemies do give another portrait of Macbeth which does not resemble the original. Macduff sketches him like this: "Not in the legions of horrid hell can come a devil more damn'd in evils to top Macbeth." Malcolm gives the amazing information that Macbeth is bloody, ostentatious, avaricious, false, deceitful, sullen, and malicious. When one gets such assertions and the text does not demonstrate them, one is somewhat lost because in the play Macbeth never acts as if he were pretentious or avaricious. I have made the same comment about Horatio, who

Hamlet says has "a merry spirit" but that is never shown in the play. Casca in *Julius Caesar* is also given long characterizations which do not fit in with the text. Is this sort of thing inadvertent slips or carelessness, or has Shakespeare gone so deeply into wanting to depict man as he is and he is believed to be, differently by friend and enemy? Or are these matters what I call unfinished intentions or abortive details?

An example out of my own experience opened my eyes to this sort of ellipsis in writing. The German translator[2] of *Easter* asked me if it were a mistake or had a special significance. Eleonora asks Benjamin, who has failed in Latin, who his instructor in Latin was. He answers, "Algren!" Eleonora: "I'll remember that." — Later she does recall the name, and I believe the author had intended to let Algren appear as Providence later on. I say "I believe," for the process of literary creation is just as mysterious to me now as it was forty years ago, even if it has to do with fully conscious cold calculation or not. Well, I told the translator it probably was an oversight. When he then suggested eliminating it, I was not able to. I got the impression that it should remain, and then I began to wonder why it should and what it signified. I found I missed it if it was not there, that it gave an appearance of reality to the whole play because it recalled the common human way of tossing out a thousand projects, of which only some are carried through. I let it remain and called it an unfinished intention. It is possible that Laertes' revolution, which is never carried through in *Hamlet*, is such a discordant note which ends with a dead stop against all rules but is effective. See the principles of harmony.

The scene in Act IV in *Macbeth*, in which Malcolm lies about himself to Macduff in order to test the latter's loyalty, has a strange effect. He accuses himself of having all the vices, and one does not know what is what; for a long while one feels lost—until the surprise in the form of the sealed packet appears. It is an hors d'oeuvre or an entremets, like Brutus' and Cassius' typical squabbling, which can be eliminated but would be missed. It is this sort of thing one calls "Shakespeare."

In *Macbeth* one also gets "Shakespeare" in a few lines. There are two professional murderers who do not have a high enough rank to possess any personal, individual characteristics or qualities that make them human or unlike each other. So that they will not merely be extras or supers, Shakespeare lets them at least motivate their choice of such a horrible calling:

> SECOND MURDERER: I am one, my liege,
> Whom the vile blows and buffets of the world
> Have so incens'd that I am reckless what
> I do to spite the world.
> FIRST MURDERER: And I another
> So weary with disasters, tugg'd with fortune,
> That I would set my life on any chance,
> To mend it, or be rid on't.

They do not have time to narrate their biographies, only to hint that there are factors that do not excuse, but explain. This is what we call "Shakespeare," without my being able to say precisely what it is.

There is another scene (Act IV, scene 2) that is somewhat unclear. Gollancz says that none of Shakespeare's texts is as corrupt as that of *Macbeth*. Possibly this scene has been ruined, although it is beautifully conceived but not successful.

Macduff has fled, too, first to Fife, then to England, to get help from King Edward against Scotland's new tyrant Macbeth. Now Lady Macduff, her little son, and Lord Ross appear at Fife.*

---

* Note Lady Macbeth's monologue in which she says: "The thane of Fife [Macduff?] had a wife. Where is she now?" [A.S.]

The lady is furious because her husband has fled without saying goodbye. Ross tries to calm her and then leaves. The ensuing conversation between the mother and her little boy begins beautifully:

> LADY MACDUFF: Sirrah, your father's dead:
>   And what will you do now? How will you live?
> SON: As birds do, mother.
> LADY MACDUFF: What, with worms and flies?
> SON: With what I get, I mean; and so do they.

The mother wants to test the boy, I suppose, for his father is not dead, and the boy objects, "My father is not dead, for all your saying." The mother continues the poor joke, which stamps her as a foolish person: "How wilt thou do for a father?" Here the bubble bursts and stinks. The little boy ceases to be a child and, one-two-three, speaks like Froth in *Measure for Measure*: "Nay, how will you do for a husband?" The mother answers like a fishwife: "Why, I can buy me twenty at any market." It may be she is a coarse woman, but now the boy begins to drop witticisms as if he were one of the clowns and speaks so precociously and cynically it becomes absurd.

A messenger enters and asks the lady to flee with the child. Then she becomes sensible:

> Whither should I fly?
> I have done no harm. But I remember now
> I am in this earthly world; where to do harm
> Is often laudable, to do good sometime
> Accounted dangerous folly. . . .

The murderers come: "Where is your husband?" Lady Macduff: "I hope, in no place so unsanctified / Where such as thou mayst find him." The murderer: "He's a traitor." The son: "Thou liest, thou shag-hair'd villain!" Murderer: "What, you egg! [*Stabbing him.*] Young fry of treachery!" The son: "He

The final action in a performance of *The Father*

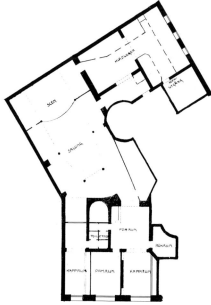

Plan of the Intimate Theater. *Scen*=stage, *salong*=auditorium, *klädloger*=dressing rooms; *scenutgång*=stage exit, *förrum*=lobby; *rökrum*=smoking room, *kapprum*=cloakroom, *damrum*=ladies' lounge

Etching of Strindberg by Anders Zorn (1910)

has kill'd me, mother: / Run away, I pray you!" The boy's last thought is of the mother. The mother actually runs away from her child and makes herself guilty of the same flaw she had just accused her husband of having—precisely the same thing that happened to Lady Macbeth. They are both garrulous, but Lady Macduff is unbelievably shabby and low.

The scene is not successful, and I do not believe that Shakespeare put these words into the child's mouth, for he knows how to depict children. Hagberg says that on page seventeen Hunter[3] has assigned the speeches differently between Macbeth and the lady in such a way that the meaning is considerably changed. Such an error in assignment may have happened here, too, so that the mother originally uttered the cynicisms and not the child. But that is only a guess.

I want merely to warn against blind admiration of everything in Shakespeare, for one can be fooled into admiring stupidities committed by others. And warn as well against reading a Shakespeare play too hastily, for it is so unbelievably rich that an endless leafing back and forth is required to get hold of all the threads. For example: I read in one commentary that Lady Macbeth kills Duncan—she does not. In the Swedish book, *Shakspere och hans dramatiska arbeten*[4] [*Shakespeare and His Dramas*], based primarily on a work by Eduard Hülsmann, I read that Macbeth strangles Macduff's wife and children. In the play, murderers stab a little son, whereupon the mother flees. In an earlier scene, Macbeth has declared that he intends to conquer Fife and kill Macduff's wife and children. In Act IV, scene 3, Ross tells Macduff that Macbeth has captured his castle (Fife) and murdered his wife and children. But nothing is said there about strangling or about the separate murder of the little boy. Where the commentator got the strangling I do not know; I have searched but cannot find it. Still there is a possibility it is in the text, for I know that on every reading new details stand out and the old ones hide as if to mock the wanderer and lead him astray.

One should not waste praise on Shakespeare for sharply delineating *all* minor characters. He does not, but his not doing so does not matter, for the major characters stand out against the others' faint background. Donalbain, Lennox, Ross, Menteith, Angus, Cathness, Fleance, Siward, and Seyton are weak sketches, schematic mouthpieces; that is how it has to be, but one should not insist they are individualized when they are not.

There is an old standing criticism of Shakespeare, which nowadays is no longer used: the reproach that his use of motivation is inadequate. The accusation is both right and wrong. For a person who thinks quickly motivation carried through in detail can be wearisome, is called pointers, while a mere hint is a form of politeness toward the members of the audience, a confidence directed to his intelligence. Macbeth's change in character from brave and loyal, Bellona's bridegroom, with a temperament full of the milk of human kindness — "What thou wouldst highly, that wouldst thou holily" to a mass murderer is motivated by the witches' promptings, conceived as evil thoughts or powers and by his wife's inciting words. Lady Macbeth's change in character from a conscienceless murderess to the pitiable woman who, sick with pangs of conscience, commits suicide is less motivated or, more accurately, not at all. Probably some scenes are missing, or Shakespeare has thought of her as a boastful but weak woman, who is able to sin in her thoughts but shrinks back when the act has been committed. If so, the motivation lies within her.

Macbeth belongs to Shakespeare's third period (1601–10) during which epoch his characters, which had been static before, began to develop. That can be a good thing for actors to remember, and these plays belong to this period: *Julius Caesar, Hamlet, All's Well That Ends Well, Othello, Measure for Measure, King Lear, Macbeth, Antony and Cleopatra, Timon,* and *Coriolanus.*

Othello

Othello is not likely to become a repertory play — the subject is too painful. Seeing innocent people suffer is not edifying, because one is then tempted to doubt the existence of a just God. Shakespeare himself is Providence in this case, of course, and does mete out justice to the point that the villain is condemned to torture, but that cannot restore Desdemona's life, and there remains something unreconciled in her death.

The matter becomes even worse when they cut out several important bits of minor action, which show that the innocent persons do have a measure of guilt and that even the villain has motives for his acts.

Iago, whom Shakespeare depicts with an inner pleasure and whose cynical philosophy of life seems to be an aspect of Shakespeare's own complex nature or a momentary point of view at one stage of his development, is no out-and-out villain, who gets pleasure out of evil for its own sake, but he resembles the motivated murderer in *Macbeth*, "So weary with disaster, tagg'd with fortune." He has participated in military expeditions, commanded troops on Rhodes, Cyprus, and other places, but he remains a subordinate officer, passed over by a seamstress, a bookkeeper, who lacks experience but pursues girls. But hoping for and expecting promotion, he has to supress his resentment and play up to his commander just as other people have to do. Sick with brooding like Hamlet, Brutus, and Macbeth, he speculates about himself: "I am not what I am." Rather honest by nature he maligns himself, and when he admits that "In following him I follow but myself," he is no worse than people generally are. He wants to become a lieutenant first and take Cassio's place, so he sees to it that Cassio gets drunk — an underling can permit himself to do that, of course. But as a noncommissioned officer he hates his commander Othello in his capacity as commander; this general is, moreover, a black or colored man, and, as a white man, Iago sees something unjust in Othello's position — that is another motive! Then comes Iago's greatest source of suffering — he is married to a slattern, whom he suspects of having had illicit relations with both Othello and Cassio. As a soldier and a man, Iago is not anxious to reveal his dishonor, so that important point remains somewhat unclear. If Shakespeare had made it clear that Iago's jealousy was justified, Iago would be Othello and would be acting with the latter's passion. The text (Act I, scene 3) has Iago say:

> . . . I hate the Moor;
> And it is thought abroad, that 'twixt my sheets
> He has done my office: I know not if't be true;
> But I, for mere suspicion in that kind,
> Will do as if for surety. . . .

In Act II, scene 1, Iago says again:

> . . . Now, I do love her too;
> Not out of absolute lust . . .
> . . . .
>
> But partly led to diet my revenge,
> For that I do suspect the lusty Moor
> Hath leap'd into my seat; the thought whereof
> Doth, like a poisonous mineral, gnaw my inwards;

And nothing can or shall content my soul
Till I am even'd with him, wife for wife. . . .

So there has been gossip, and Iago is being eaten inwardly
just as Othello is. The actor should emphasize this to help the
author make the motivation clear. In the same monologue
Iago says that Cassio, too, has deceived him.

In Act IV, scene 2, Emilia says that Iago unjustly suspects
her and Othello, but Emilia is a slattern and does not have to
be believed; her philosophy (Act IV, scene 3) is, moreover, of
a feminine variety when she impudently asserts, "But I do
think it is their husbands' faults / If wives do fall . . . ," and,
"The ills we do, their ills instruct us so." Even Iago in his evil
has more beautiful thoughts of love when he says (Act II,
scene 1) that "base men being in love have then a nobility in
their natures more than is native to them." He means that
when a man loves a woman he teaches her nothing evil.

Emilia is a wonder, but typical in her indescribable sloven-
liness. One becomes absolutely amazed by her chatter so that
one does not fathom her: who she is, what she is, how she is.
One does not know, for she is nothing. Is one to take seriously
what she says? One cannot, for one cannot take hold of it. She
is certainly agreeable to anything — probably in her thoughts
mainly, but her words reveal the pattern of her thinking. For
example: in Act IV, scene 3, where as the maid she helps Desdemona get to bed. The scene in itself is as vivid as if it were
being seen:

EMILIA: Shall I go fetch your night-gown?
DESDEMONA: No, unpin me here. —
   This Lodovico is a proper man.
EMILIA: A very handsome man.

Desdemona relives with this innocent little comment about
Lodovico the unpleasant preceding scene when Othello struck

her, and her relative Lodovico came to her defense; in a word, one gets to know in that line what she was thinking of just then but did not want to talk about. Emilia has seen Lodovico merely as a handsome man.

Desdemona corrects her: "He speaks well." Emilia continues her line of thought: "I know a lady in Venice would have walked barefoot to Palestine for a touch of his nether lip." Does she mean herself, Desdemona, or someone else? I do not know! For she herself does not know.

Then Desdemona interrupts her by singing the "willow song," and then she asks somewhat bluntly, "Dost thou in conscience think . . . / That there be women do abuse their husbands / In such gross kind?" — Emilia answers at once: "There be some such, no question." Desdemona continues, "Wouldst thou do such a deed for all the world?" Emilia answers indirectly in this way, "Why, would not you?" Desdemona: "No, by this heavenly light!" — Then Emilia shifts without taking anything back, "Nor neither I by this heavenly light: I might do it as well i' the dark." This is a confession of her way of thinking about the subject, and in the following scene Emilia becomes the emancipated woman who preaches equality in vice, after she has said ghastly things about her own sex. Then she blames all immorality on the man — as usual. But Desdemona is quite different, and she explains in her last speech that if she saw her husband do something bad, the example would frighten her away and make her not bad but good! That is the basic difference between the two women!

Yet, when Iago kills Emilia in the last scene, she can still arouse [my] sympathy, because Shakespeare pities the creature and puts a few attractive words in her mouth.

Iago is driven by the same affliction as Othello even if Emilia has been no more unfaithful to him than Desdemona has been to the Moor. Gossip has poisoned Iago, and now he poisons the Moor with gossip. "Wife against wife!" If Shakespeare had wanted to acquit the Moor of this guilt, he could have had the Moor swear he was innocent, and he would have been believed. Now it is an open question.

Then Desdemona comes! She is depicted as gentle, tender, faithful — even if Emilia's hymn of praise is worthless, for as a woman she feels loyal to other women and as a fellow sinner loyal to every one of her sex.

But Desdemona is careless and something of a chatterbox; she calls herself outspoken. She kisses Cassio or lets herself be kissed twice. Even if that were the custom in her country (comparison: Romeo kisses Juliet when they meet for the first time), Iago notices it and finds it unusual. Desdemona has even toyed with Cassio's hand.

In Act II, scene 1, Desdemona speaks too long with Iago, whose noncommissioned officer's witticisms she encourages and is apparently amused by. Shakespeare does let her explain in an aside that she was pretending, but in the same breath she encourages Iago to continue his "profane and liberal" talk.

Desdemona's careless way with Cassio is depicted by Iago in a soliloquy and is therefore not slander:

> He takes her by the palm: ay, well said, whisper: with as little a web as this will I ensnare as great a fly as Cassio. . . . Very good; well kiss'd! an excellent courtesy! 'tis so indeed. Yet again your fingers to your lips? would they were clyster-pipes for your sake!

As the general's wife, she should not have permitted herself such conduct with a lieutenant and woman chaser! Desdemona is innocent, but not absolutely free of responsibility, as a judge would say.

In the provinces Desdemona is usually played by a "sweet" operetta diva. But in the text Desdemona is not quite that sweet.

Cassio does call her divine, but one later learns that the general's wife is now the general — that is, has begun to show her will to power. And in Act III, scene 3, when Emilia acts as the go-between for Cassio, Desdemona boasts about her power over the Moor, although it is he who through his love has given her that power. Desdemona says to Cassio:

> His bed shall seem a school, his board a shrift;
> I'll intermingle everything he does
> With Cassio's suit: therefore be merry, Cassio. . . .

These are bedroom tactics; besides, the method of using the wife's influence on her husband is a poor method that leads to damnation. They cannot manage Othello, but, when they use his wife as a lever, they can lift him out of the saddle. This is the most dangerous element in Iago's tactics — his irritating Othello through Desdemona's influence, because then the Moor senses how he is beginning to be controlled by underlings through her.

That relationship between Desdemona and Othello has not been perfect is clear from Desdemona's remark to Othello (Act III, scene 3):

> . . . What! Michael Cassio,
> That came a-wooing with you; and so many a time,
> When I have spoke of you dispraisingly,
> Hath ta'en your part. . . .

That Cassio served as a lightning rod or friend of the house is also an important minor factor just as is the fact that husband and wife have been angry. If one eliminates this, Desdemona becomes an abstract woman who is sweet, but that is absolutely contrary to Shakespeare's method of depicting weak people with flaws, and surely Iago's famous "For I am nothing if not critical" is a translation of Shakespeare's own way of looking at people and life. [In Swedish] translate "critical" by *kritisk*, and one reads a confession by Shakespeare, who in Iago has given one of his incarnations, without doubt a Mephistopheles, whom he does liquidate in the last act. Hagberg has been careless with the text — to Iago's disadvantage for in the text "critical," according to Gollancz' dictionary, means "censorious." Swedish *häckla* [Hagberg's word] means "slander," "defame," or "misrepresent."

The arranged scene, *qui pro quo*, in which Iago has Othello listen to Cassio and Bianca, under the impression that the latter is Desdemona, strikes me as unbelievable, belongs to high comedy, and is not successful, since it is not in keeping with the tragedy.

Without wanting to condemn Desdemona, I — as examiner — want to recall Act II, scene 1, in which Desdemona shows herself in a light quite different from the divine.

There Cassio kisses Emilia, Iago's slattern, on the mouth. But he explains to Iago first that as he is a native of Florence, he has this custom:

> . . . Welcome, mistress:
> Let it not gall your patience, good Iago,
> That I extend my manners; 'tis my breeding
> That gives me this bold show of courtesy.

Iago is too proud to *show* his disapproval, but gives them a little dig anyway:

> Sir, would she give you so much of her lips
> As of her tongue she oft bestows on me,
> You'd have enough.

Desdemona answers, immediately supporting her sex:

> Alas, she has no speech.

This is false, for Emilia is very talkative. So Iago answers:

> In faith, too much;
> I find it still, when I have list to sleep:
> Marry, before your ladyship, I grant,
> She puts her tongue a little in her heart,
> And chides with thinking.

Emilia answers somewhat dully:

> You have little cause to say so.
> IAGO: Come on, come on; you are pictures out of doors,
> Bells in your parlours, wild-cats in your kitchens,
> Saints in your injuries, devils being offended,
> Players in your housewifery, and housewives in your beds.
> DESDEMONA: O, fie upon thee, slanderer!

Here Hagberg has added onions to Iago's salmon, because "slanderer" is simply "gossip" (from *skandalon* = indignation [*förargelse*]), and "gossip" is not "defamation" but "telling about" what can certainly be true, but this need not be pointed out here.

Paul was called "a gossip" by the philosophers in Athens, because he "told about" the corruption of pagandom and the birth of Christ, all of which was true, but aroused indignation (*skandalon*). Still indignation must come — sometimes!

Emilia interjects: "You shall not write my praise!"

Iago answers: "No, let me not!"

As a respectable lady, Desdemona should have let the subject be dropped, but she is eager to hear Iago's wisecracks so she spurs him on: "What wouldst thou write of me if thou shouldst praise me?" It is then Iago answers: "For I am nothing if not critical." That means: "I'm too skeptically inclined and have seen too much of Emilia to write unqualified praise of you!" Desdemona insists: "Come on, assay! There's one gone to the harbour?" This little question, "There's one gone to the harbour?" can mean a little pang of conscience (about standing talking nonsense to a noncommissioned officer while her husband, the general, is expected on the ship), or does Shakespeare want to apologize to the audience for this intermezzo, or does he also want to show that he has not dropped the thread though he has dropped a stitch (he is always aware of what he is doing! Almost always!).

Iago answers: "Ay, madam." (Cassio had sent a nobleman to the harbor earlier to see if Othello's ship had arrived.)

But now Desdemona says in an aside: "I am not merry; but I do beguile / The thing I am, by seeming otherwise." Why is she not happy? Because a storm has separated Cassio's ship from Othello's, and she is uneasy about her husband's fate. Perhaps Shakespeare has used this seemingly indifferent scene with its small talk to show that Desdemona wants to kill time and uneasiness by talk! Shakespeare can be unbelievably subtle on occasion, and he means something definite by almost everything he includes. These two pages prepare both for Othello's arrival and for Cassio's coming entanglement in the Moor's marriage, for it is in this scene that the flirting (he takes her hand; whispers, "well kissed"; fingers to his mouth, etc.) is observed by Iago and is interrupted by the trumpet blasts, which signal the Moor's return.

The talk itself is somewhat questionable, but ought to have been stopped by Desdemona, when Iago lets slip this insult against her:

> If she be black, and thereto have a wit,
> She'll find a white that shall her blackness fit.

But Desdemona wants to hear more and gets to, too.

It is clear that, in their lack of common sense, they have been toying with what is sacred, and Iago's unusually sensible words (Act III, scene 3) can be applied to Desdemona:

> . . . Why, say they are vile and false;
> As where's that palace whereinto foul things
> Sometimes intrude not? who has a breast so pure,

> But some uncleanly apprehensions
> Keep leets and law-days, and in session sit
> With meditations lawful?

In spite of Iago's evil purpose in this speech — to poison the Moor — it is either unlikely that he could say anything so fine ("uncleanly apprehensions"), which is a direct defense of Desdemona (and all other mortals who in their better moments rise above themselves and in their worse moments sink below themselves), or Shakespeare sticks his head out through the window of the role and talks to the audience.

But, if one assumes Iago, too, has his better moments, Shakespeare has probably unintentionally made the traditional theater villain sympathetic in Act III, scene 3, when Iago first admits he has flaws:

> As, I confess, it is my nature's plague
> To spy into abuses, and of my jealousy
> Shapes faults that are not. . . .

This sounds too honest to be the hypocrisy by means of which he wants to trap the Moor.

Immediately afterward the same Iago gives a description of jealousy, which supports my earlier suspicion that Iago secretly has the same burden of jealousy as Othello and that he has borne in silence all the pangs Othello has:

> O, beware, my lord, of jealousy;
> It is the green-eyed monster which doth mock
> The meat it feeds on. . . .

And then he adds, as if from experience, the observation that the deceived husband, who knows his lot, is happy "if he does not love his false wife."

> But, O, what damned minutes tells he o'er
> Who dotes, yet doubts, suspects, yet strongly loves!

This is a complete confession about Iago's and Emilia's relationship, and, when Iago finally bursts forth:

> Good heaven, the souls of all my tribe defend
> From jealousy!

he has forgotten his murderous undertaking and is simply shouting aloud his justified pity for himself as a human being and as his own [Shakespeare's?] fellow human being! Then comes the poisoner pure and unmasked!

However, it often happens in Shakespeare that a jewel is attached to his answer which is more than adequate; then the answer ceases to exist, but one can rejoice over the jewel. Iago's little expressions of humanity are diamonds. And the actor must not play them in the manner of Tartuffe but as so-called weak moments; otherwise, Iago is merely a stage villain or an abstraction.

Why Shakespeare does not clear up the confusion and let the audience have certainty about Othello's and Cassio's relationship to Iago's wife can depend on this: either he wants the question kept open ("when one does not know something") or he feels it resembles life more in that uncertainties are seldom cleared up but end in catastrophe.

The older concept of justified jealousy as a variant of common envy is too perverse for us; and to conceive of jealousy as a mental sickness without factual or sufficient grounds is biology!

During the period when *Othello* was written, Shakespeare was profoundly serious, even strict: Nemesis controls man's actions; everything that is sown must be reaped. Does he mean that her father's curse affects Desdemona's marriage since she without his approval or knowledge had married Othello and run away from home: "She did deceive her father, marrying you" [and can deceive you]? Her father Brabantio dies of grief, we learn in Act V. One does not have time to consider all this when misfortune strikes; and when pity is aroused in even the worst of people, all concepts of guilt or *who* is guilty disappear. Through suffering the matter has undergone a shift in level so that it cannot be got at through one's opinions but only through a feeling of fear and friendly pity, so that when Iago kills his slattern, one weeps over her fate, too; and when Iago is escorted to the torture chamber, one hardly believes in that or does not care. But, before this, one has become so hardened that when Roderigo is struck down, one does not observe it although Iago has stripped him earlier. A soldier, a noncommissioned officer used to plundering, Cassio is also a parasite thief. Cassio may be left unjustified. Emilia has a brief but wonderful exchange with Bianca:

> EMILIA: Fie, fie upon thee, strumpet! [typical!]
> BIANCA: I am no strumpet; but of life as honest
> As you that thus abuse me.

There we learn who Emilia is, for her own information cannot be depended on.

Othello is not jealous by nature; he never spies, and he is not little-minded, but has the manly feeling for purity that makes him shudder at illicit sexual intercourse with a woman, and his nature makes him vomit up the poisoned food he thinks he has swallowed. Shakespeare most likely uses Othello to expectorate, and, not happily married himself, he has no exalted thoughts about matrimony and woman:

> . . . O curse of marriage,
> That we can call these delicate creatures ours,
> And not their appetites! . . .

That is what Othello says, but Iago makes still uglier remarks! But even in *Othello*, as in *Macbeth*, these matters are something other than intrigues and bad people's notions; there are evil powers involved in all this, and *one* situation is thoroughly satanic.

In Act III, scene 3, Othello bursts forth and declares in a soliloquy that all women are strumpets and that even in their mothers' wombs horns begin to grow on men's foreheads. Then comes Desdemona, happy in her innocence, and sees that the Moor is angry. "Are you not well?" Othello answers in an attack of gallows humor: "I have a pain upon my forehead here." Desdemona does not understand the witticism, but answers naïvely, meaning well. " 'Faith, that's with watching; 'twill away again: / Let me but bind it hard" [with the handkerchief]. Then Othello becomes furious, thinking she is mocking him! That is the sort of thing one can call a satanic misunderstanding. Desdemona, who has taken out her handkerchief, drops it when she is going to run after Othello, hurt by his rejection of her good intention. This is the start of the handkerchief matter and its fatal consequences. But it was not Iago who started the intrigue; it was a black hand that reached out from the dark void! ("And an evil spirit from the Lord tormented Saul." "May God send an evil will between Abi-Melech and the men of Sichem." It is this that base men call chance.)

Cassio's drunkenness is a detail, depicted convincingly, with expert knowledge that one can expect of Shakespeare, who most likely knew his liquor. But the hangover scene contains the best temperance sermon, too: "O thou invisible spirit of wine, if thou hast no name to be known by, let us call thee devil!"

Iago, who *can* drink, has a different opinion. "Come, come, good wine is a good familiar creature if it be well used; exclaim no more against it."

Othello's fool is neglected; he does not say anything worth thinking about or amusing.

The opening of the play—Shakespeare is famous for his opening scenes—is not successful this time. Iago stands for a long time defaming "him" without mentioning Othello's name. That is a minor error, and it can be a scribe's. It hurts the play when the opening scene is not interesting and when something essential has been omitted.

After I jotted down this objection, I have tried to meet it myself. I have wondered, what if Roderigo or Iago mentioned Othello at once; and then I wonder if the liveliness of the scene would not be disturbed. The purpose would be noticed; it would sound like a billboard or an announcement. As it is, one is thrown headlong into the situation. Iago rages about the Moor's unfairness in not having him a lieutenant; he is so angry with the Moor he does not want to mention his name. Probably that is Shakespeare's point, and my criticism is unwarranted.

My comment on Shakespeare's neglect of the clown is probably wrong, too. Perhaps Shakespeare felt that joking is silenced in the presence of boundless suffering. Perhaps the clown in talking to Desdemona wants to hint at the rumor about her. His talk is vague, and when Desdemona asks the clown if he knows where Lieutenant Cassio is housed, the fool answers:

> CLOWN: He's a soldier; and for one to say a soldier lies is stabbing.
> . . . To tell you where he lodges is to tell you where I lie.
> DESDEMONA: Can any thing be made of this?
> CLOWN: I know not where he lodges, and for me to devise a lodging
> and say he lies here or he lies there, were to lie in mine own throat.

Desdemona does not understand what he means, because she is innocent. Is that what Shakespeare intended? Did he intend that the fool's chatter should be an ugly allusion to the nasty rumor? Bianca has not appeared yet. I cannot believe it is the clown's usual quibbling, for Shakespeare always means something. The scene ends with Desdemona's sending the clown to fetch Cassio.

With these comments I end my consideration of *Othello*, for it is so richly composed that one would never finish if one were to unwind all the yarn that went into that weaving. Iago particularly has been created so thoroughly and from so many points of view that the actor ought to study that role, not merely memorize it.

What I have learned on this brief excursion is mainly this: one has to be careful in associating with Shakespeare, and, if one wants to get something from him, one should approach him with the preconceived idea that he can give one something of his unlimited abundance and that he will give with open hands if one places oneself receptively and a little below [him].

*

When I recently returned to *Romeo and Juliet* and rediscovered its beauty, I lost every desire to pick that precious flower to pieces. I did begin, though, by answering some older criticism I and others had made. In the first place critics have complained about the introduction of Rosaline, Romeo's first love. She belongs to the same enemy family as Juliet and apparently is Juliet's cousin since she is Capulet's brother's daughter. But she is a Diana, "she'll not be hit with Cupid's arrow" — in other words, she does not want to get married. She has not responded to Romeo's love, so his [love] is something that concerns him alone, a desire for something, almost nothing then, for love is something mutual. Two have to be involved; otherwise it is nothing and remains nothing. Rosaline seems to have been sketched earlier in *Measure for Measure*, where she is called Diana Capulet and acts almost like a suffragette. Shakespeare sometimes is amused by masquerading as a woman and speaking with a woman's voice, tossing out all of woman's stupid accusations against men, which amounts only to throwing her guilt on him (compare Emilia's emancipation chatter in *Othello*).

Romeo Montague goes to the Capulet ball to see Rosaline, but instead sees Juliet—and that is that!—It is as if they recognized each other and are bound for life. Rosaline is immediately blotted out of his memory! This is properly conceived and executed! The Rosaline motif is merely the prologue of the overture which then swings over into the melody Juliet.

Who is Juliet? She is Romeo's Juliet and nothing else, his fair maiden, his bride, his love that has taken form. But she is not abstract but complex. The nurse presents *her* Juliet or her aspect of Juliet which she has seen; her parents call her a whining mammet, a proud minion, and a young baggage; we outsiders would say: a girl with a mind of her own; Father Lorenzo observes that she has an easy walk; Prince Paris has seen her beauty. Juliet can pretend when she wants to conceal her grief over Romeo's flight into exile, pretends sorrow over Tybalt's death, and there plays a whole little comedy. She has her sides, but that she is, as one commentator says, merely the embodiment of sensual love is false; for she wants Romeo only as her mate, and the first balcony scene is merely courtship. Even as his wife she speaks like a young girl about their relationship:

> . . . Come, civil night,
> Thou sober-suited matron, all in black,
> And learn me how to lose a winning match,
> Play'd for a pair of stainless maidenhoods:
> Hood my unmann'd blood, bating in my cheeks,
> With thy black mantle; till strange love, grown bold,
> Think true love acted simple modesty.

Actresses have always wondered about the meaning of the first vague words Romeo and Juliet exchange: the commentators have discovered profound meaning in them. I have thought about them, too, but I now believe they are a finesse of Shakespeare's: the young people are bewildered upon seeing each other, but they have to say something to conceal their feelings; it is a conversation suitable for a ball, where the one picks up the other's words and weaves a web that catches both; they are conceits in keeping with the taste of the time; they are "words, words," beautiful sounds by means of which they caress each other, artificially, because they are embarrassed, so embarrassed they say stupid things. Juliet's letting him kiss her on the mouth right away has been interpreted by some as immodest, but doing so was the Italian custom; in her response to his second kiss her passionate nature has been revealed. In the Swedish translation, she says: *"Ni förstår er på!"* In English she says, "You kiss by the book!"—This probably means (but I am not sure): "You know courtly customs well," or something like that, and can be translated, *"Ni förstår er på!"* But when Englishmen themselves are uncertain about the meaning, we must not be absolutely certain!

Besides their whole little exchange is highly decent without any innuendoes of the kind that frequently appear in our lieutenants' conversations at balls and in Shakespeare's comedies. After that exchange their conversation is on its way to taking a definite direction; therefore Shakespeare brings it to an abrupt end and has the nurse interrupt them.

How old is Juliet? Hardly fourteen, which as is known is not too young in southern countries, but on the stage she can be older, since theater time is something else again (see Hagberg)[5] and theater age, too!

Some bright soul engaging in the perennial quarrel about Hamlet's age has discovered that he ought to be thirty since the drunken gravedigger says that Hamlet was born the same day the old king defeated the older Fortinbras. But the grave-digger's memory must have slipped because Horatio says in Act I that the older Hamlet, who died two months ago, had defeated old Fortinbras and that young Fortinbras is rebelling. If one assumes that young Fortinbras rebelled soon afterward, which the text seems to indicate, Hamlet is hardly a couple of years old. So the gravedigger is talking nonsense, and his next bit of information that the clown Yorick, who had carried Hamlet on his shoulders, has been in his grave for twenty-three years is not reliable. When Claudius does not want to send Hamlet back to school in Wittenberg, Hamlet cannot be twenty for at that time one became a student at twelve. All this point-less quibbling about bagatelles is the sum of the would-be critics' Shakespeare research. Anyone who has not written a drama should not write about Shakespeare.* Nowadays it is a requirement in all fields that a man should know his profession before he is appointed judge in the committee.

People have even criticized Shakespeare's use of ugly words and tasteless images. In the love scenes, the language is marvel-ously beautiful and the images flash like diamonds. Only in one place I have been annoyed—when Juliet says in Act III, scene 5:

> Some say the lark and loathed toad change eyes;
> O, now I would they had chang'd voices too!

The Swedish translation:

> *Det sägs att lärkan ögon bytt med paddan;*
> *O, att de också hade röster bytt!*

The Swedish *padda* is ugly. "Loathed toad" is like a gentle kiss, while "*äcklig padda*" is despicable.

---

* Hamlet's thirty years were motivated the other day by the queen's calling herself matron and by the assumption that a woman becomes a matron at forty-seven. The queen may have been joking to calm Hamlet. And a woman may become a matron just as well at thirty-five, as I have suggested. Let Hamlet be thirty, then! But not forty, for then his mother will be sixty! [A.S.]

The criticism is invalid; and the image, resting on an observation made in England — the toad has beautiful eyes, but the lark ugly ones—becomes for the initiated striking in its antithesis.

In *Othello* one notices what the play *could* gain by the absence of scenery. This lack sometimes reinforces nature descriptions and the like. See Act II, scene 1, and compare that to the prologue to *The Tempest*.

The Tempest

It seems to me sometimes that a literary work does not have a completely individual independent life but that its existence depends on cooperation with a circle or has to get its power from a dynamo of minds or a storage battery of sympathy. One sees reruns of masterpieces that fail. This means that people were not in the proper mood for them just then. In the same way a good play can fail in its première because it lacks topical or immediate interest. Another season a new wind is blowing, and then the limp sails are filled and the ship sails full speed ahead.

Shakespeare's *The Tempest* has never been a repertory play; we knew it, of course, but we did not like it. At the beginning of this century it was rediscovered and became popular; I read it and heard it read. The gentle, conciliatory tone; the innocent love affair in which the young people are tested and resist temptation; a life on an island reminiscent of *Robinson Crusoe*; Shakespeare's farewell to his public, in which he thanks them and ends with a prayer— all have a calming effect and fore-shadow a new time at the end of a period of decadence, the parallel of which can be found in imperial Rome and during the French Revolution. Why *The Tempest* was not produced in Stockholm before depended, I suppose, on the theater direc-tors' continuing with decadence, their fear of changing public taste so that fin-de-siècle repertory might be kept from becoming out of date or being driven off the stage.

They did not dare to put on *The Tempest*, for it would have destroyed friends and enemies alike.

But *The Tempest* went like a cyclone throughout the whole country; August Lindberg[6] brought it without costumes, scen-ery, and actors—as a monodrama. And it cleared the air, dis-persed Ibsen fog, and melted ice. It appealed to what was good in people, what had been buried under Norwegian avalanches and French glaciers; it mentioned the expression "the golden age," and it taunted the Nora-man [Ibsen]: "No marriages among your subjects?—None at all! All loose and available, prostitutes and scoundrels."

But there was another factor at the beginning of the century which made *The Tempest* understandable and interesting. The inclusion of the spiritual world, the renewal of acquaintance with magic, which had hitherto been considered delusion and superstition or, in Shakespeare, poetic ornament. That is how most of the scholars had disposed of Shakespeare's occult knowl-edge, precisely knowledge, based on his own experiences. Even Professor Schück,[7] who was not particularly profound, ex-plained with conviction, when he came to the witches in *Mac-beth*, that Shakespeare believed in them just as Ben Jonson and Middleton did. When such an enlightened man as Shakespeare ("the Renaissance man") believed that evil has a terrifying power, he must have had his reasons for doing so. During the

"Protestant" Elizabeth's time, the stakes for witches were lighted frequently, and the reason was that a great many people, women in particular, had misused their natural powers of suggestion for evil purposes so that even Elizabeth had a witch condemned for having caused the queen to become ill.

Oh well, at the end of the century we got the witches' trials again through the misuse of hypnotism. There were trials in which the defense was that there was no motive for the crime but that he (or she) felt himself acting in accordance with someone else's will and at a distance (*actio in distans*). In Paris, where I associated with occultists and theosophists, demonstrated cases were cited in which people had been made ill and even murders had been committed.

If Shakespeare experienced anything like that and had seen it practiced, he would have been an ass if he had not "believed" in it!

At the end of the century important men like Lombroso and Crookes,[8] who at first had not believed in their own or other people's experiences, had had their eyes opened to the natural powers at the bottom of the human soul, and both of them had to believe when they had seen and heard. They became believers on the grounds that they knew! And those who had not dared to believe their own experiences because they had not understood, believed now, absolutely logically.

So the ground was well prepared when *The Tempest* came, and there was not any discussion about it any longer, but it was just understood and accepted!

The content of *The Tempest* is known, of course, but may have been forgotten, so I shall review it in order to have a point of departure. A ship is at sea in a tempest. On board are King Alonso of Naples, his brother Antonio (the usurper on the throne of Milan), and others. The shipwreck — on two printed pages — is a masterpiece, but must be *read* slowly so that one will notice both the maneuvers at sea and the presentation of the characters; one finds that Gonzalo is an honorable wag, Antonio a brawler, and the boatswain a gallowsbird. Then they are on the island. Prospero is the duke of Milan exiled by his brother Antonio; Prospero has been living on the island for twelve years with his daughter Miranda. Prospero signifies about the same as Faust, the favorite of fortune, and there is something of Faust in Prospero. He is a philosopher, who had lived in his library instead of ruling; he is a raiser of spirits and has two demons in his service — the good Ariel and the evil Caliban. But there is also a weak echo of *Hamlet*, in that Prospero like Hamlet's father has been replaced by his brother. Through Ariel, Prospero has arranged for the shipwreck, not for revenge, because he is a good man, but for reconciliation and setting everything right. *The Tempest* is considered Shakespeare's last play: the aging man's need for peace, summing up, and coming to terms with existence after a rather difficult life find their expression here. It is almost as if he had begun living on the other side [of death], and has tried to depict a better world as man has conceived it in his dreams. The plot is, briefly, that Ferdinand meets Miranda and, after tests, gets her. Ferdinand is not the son of the usurper (brother), but the son of King Alonso, who has helped Antonio overthrow Prospero.

The play ends in a general settlement, everyone is forgiven, even Caliban the human monster, who probably was modeled on Shakespeare's worst enemy. Prospero (Shakespeare) even forgives Caliban, who has accused him of the worst possible deeds and who has tried to kill him. Shakespeare's last farewell to humanity is undeniably more attractive than Ibsen's, who in his last play[9] sticks out his tongue at the public and contemptuously says that by means of his grimaces he has gained much "money" from them, and, in the words of his hero, who now wants to climb "upward," only tosses a taunt at them.

Someone has said that in Shakespeare's plays it is neither the action nor the characters that are most interesting — it is what is said! Yes, one can say that; and I do not want to see *The Tempest* performed; I want to read it and make my own setting of only air and light.

The play says so much that is beautiful and that one wants to hear silently; the play is Shakespeare's final confession, view of life, farewell, thanks, and prayer.

He buries his book and his magic wand, in which he has created a world of people and landscapes, presented philosophy and tavern talk, conjured up the shadows of heroes from English and world history. He feels the end approaching; he is about to wake from the instructive dream that is called life:

> Our revels now are ended. These our actors,
> As I foretold you, were all spirits and
> Are melted into air, into thin air:
> And, like the baseless fabric of this vision,
> The cloud-capp'd towers, the gorgeous palaces,
> The solemn temples, the great globe itself,
> Yea, all which it inherit, shall dissolve
> And, like this insubstantial pageant faded,
> Leave not a rack behind. We are such stuff
> As dreams are made on, and our little life
> Is rounded with a sleep. . . .

That is really how it is when one gets on in life; if one looks back at what one has lived through, it is so terrible one hardly believes it is real, and the best that had a sort of reality slowly dissolves as if it were smoke. Is it strange if one begins to doubt the reality of reality?

In *The Tempest*, Shakespeare has in several places emphasized that life is a dream and has tried to dramatize this Buddhist idea, partly when he has Prospero put Miranda to sleep, partly when he has the shipwrecked people overcome with the desire to sleep, partly also when he summons up dream images (Ceres, Iris, Juno).

[Note] in one place:

> SEBASTIAN: What, are thou waking?
> ANTONIO: Do you not hear me speak?
> SEBASTIAN: I do; and surely
> It is a sleepy language and thou speak'st
> Out of thy sleep. What is it thou didst say?
> This is a strange repose, to be asleep
> With eyes wide open; standing, speaking, moving,
> And yet so fast asleep.

And Antonio in another place:

> Say, this were death that now hath seized them. . . .

Even Caliban becomes moved when he touches on the subject:

> Sometimes a thousand twangling instruments
> Will hum about mine ears, and sometimes voices
> That, if I then had waked after long sleep,
> Will make me sleep again: and then, in dreaming,
> The clouds methought would open and show riches
> Ready to drop upon me, that, when I waked,
> I cried to dream again.

This outburst of Caliban's despair reminds me of our Swedish river sprite's[10] sorrow over not being able to attain salvation. But at the end even Caliban's sense of guilt is awakened, and, when he promises to improve, he is forgiven and freed from the curse by Prospero whose motto is this:

> . . . the rare action is
> In virtue than in vengeance: they being penitent,
> The sole drift of my purpose doth extend
> Not a frown further. . . .

Miranda's love came at the end of the century as a discovery when Ibsen's epigoni had recently proclaimed the fury and the busybody as the only "true women." Let's listen to Miranda:

FERDINAND: Wherefore weep you?
MIRANDA: At mine unworthiness that dare not offer
What I desire to give, and much less take
What I shall die to want. . . .
. . . .
. . . Hence, bashful
And prompt me, plain and holy innocence!
I am your wife, if you will marry me;
If not, I'll die your maid. . . .

A kind of melody quite different from that of the shrews from 1880!

Then comes the epilogue, spoken by Prospero, but created in Shakespeare's name, and expressing the aging poet's hope for mercy and reconciliation:

And my ending is despair,
Unless I be relieved by prayer,
Which pierces so that it assaults
Mercy itself and frees all faults.
As you from crimes would pardon'd be,
Let your indulgence set me free.

That is religion, and it is Christianity; and Shakespeare like Goethe (*Faust*, II) ends his career with a regained certainty about the highest matters — that is faith!

*

In this beautiful work of art Shakespeare as usual has not excluded what is ugly but on the contrary has given it a major place. That is Shakespeare's philosophy and poetics — one that I have followed, in defiance of and with constant disapproval of those who were called idealists, and who permitted only polished, tidied up, colorless, and therefore false images from life. The *ugly* has to be along; otherwise, one is cheating. Caliban, Trinculo, and Stefano are horribly ugly and talk coarsely, but it is stylized for us, either because aging has veiled it or because he has really touched it up a little. Caliban in particular has an unusual way of expressing his ugly thoughts, aside from his lying without blushing, but in such a way one passes it up and does not believe him. When he has discovered the secret of the bottle, he wants to worship Stefano as a god:

> Hast thou not dropp'd from heaven?

Stefano says he has and persuades him that he (Stefano) is the man in the moon. Notice how stiffly Caliban expresses himself in spite of being drunk:

> I have seen thee, in her [the moon] and I do adore thee:
> My mistress show'd me thee and thy dog and thy bush.
> [The man in the moon's dog and bush, according to the English notion.]

Stefano asks him to swear on the Bible. Then Caliban answers in verse, almost nobly considering he is drunk:

> I'll show thee every fertile inch o' th' island;
> And I will kiss thy foot: I prithee, be my god.
> . . . .
> I'll kiss thy foot; I'll swear myself thy subject.

The scene compares favorably with Cassio's "intoxication" scene in *Othello*.

And further on Caliban says:

> I'll bear him no more sticks, but follow thee,
> Thou wondrous man.

(He wants to serve, for he knows his place, but not serve just anyone.) He then becomes lyrical and noble, and he speaks in

verse. He wants Stefano to become king and offers his services
so naïvely that it seems innocent when compared to Iago's conscious cruelty:

> Yea, yea, my lord: I'll yield him thee asleep,
> Where thou mayst knock a nail into his head.

Murder is a natural, simple matter for him!

King Lear

Just after having read *King Lear* in one sitting recently I
thought: Does one have the right to criticize this play? Can one
compare the author's visions with reality? Why, that is his way
of looking at the matter. How then should we want him to see
in our fashion? That is quite simply insolent.

In *Lear* Shakespeare has selected his motifs and characters
only with the intention of saying just what he means. He has
tired of what is either grand or common and of depicting human
beings; he has discarded all conventional scruples about his
fellow men, love of his neighbor, sympathy. The fool is almost
the central character and speaks more sensibly than anyone else;
Kent pretends to be mad, Edgar behaves as if he were mad;
Lear becomes mad; Regan and Goneril are, morally, feeble-
minded; Gloucester praises the sin of adultery; Edmund speaks
well of bastardy and ridicules the marital bed as boring, in
which a crowd of fools are conceived between sleep and waking.
The poet has placed himself far above all this, with an almost
religious contempt for the world, but only for a moment, in a
mood, for when the resolution approaches he metes out dra-

matic justice extremely strictly in such a Nemesis fashion that Gloucester is blinded in the same room where his bastard was conceived.

To express what he wants to say, he [Shakespeare] uses his characters as his mouthpieces, but he confuses the mouthpieces occasionally so that Lear in spite of his strong character begins to preach immorality in Act IV with a zeal that cannot be irony. "The wren goes to't, and the small gilded fly / does lecher in my sight. / Let copulation thrive. . . ." This is a certain temperament's way of looking at things, but is not an expression of a definite point of view on the part of the poet. He observes from various points of view; he assumes postures when doubt of everything prevents him from *being* this or that. Time and again he assumes Hamlet's way of playing mad. Sometimes he sympathizes with Lear when the latter does not deserve it; sometimes he has the fool ridicule him [Lear] when he deserves sympathy alone.

Lear is played in the pagan world, an eye for an eye, a tooth for a tooth; they call upon the gods and swear by Zeus, and finally the executioners execute each other.

Lear is relatively innocent, but not without blame because of his unruliness and his demands. Kent, Albany, Edgar, and Cordelia are unselfish or good people, one might say Christians; they return good for evil, suffer instead of torture.

Gloucester is enigmatic, but is punished for his faithfulness to the king.

Goneril and Regan are right to a certain extent, when their father brings crude fellows into their homes; but afterward they reveal themselves as merely degenerate wild beasts, mad as dogs. Cornwall is a wild man, Edmund an Iago.

There are just as many good people as bad, and Shakespeare

can sharply distinguish between the two kinds. There is not a good word about Regan and Goneril:

> See thyself, devil!
> Proper deformity seems not in the fiend
> So horrid as in woman.
>
> . . . .
>
> . . . howe'er thou art a fiend,
> A woman's shape doth shield thee.

This passage (and Lear's monologue as well: "Down from the waist they are centaurs, / Though women all above.") is the same observation that has sometimes given Shakespeare the false reputation of being a woman hater.

Nevertheless the dying villain Edmund reveals that he still has sympathy for others when he wants to send a messenger to rescue Cordelia, and with these significant words: "some good I mean to do, / Despite of mine own nature." This "Despite of mine own nature" is an admission and, at the same time, an apology. Why, it is almost the repentant thief (we suffer according to our deeds).

I have always been unable to understand the scene in Act I in which Lear becomes angry with Cordelia. And now I find that Goethe himself found it absurd. But it is possible, of course, that Shakespeare meant precisely that Lear is abnormal, and that seems to be the general opinion in the play itself. Lear had expected to hear the finest compliments from Cordelia, and, when he does not get them, he is disappointed; that is how little it takes to make him shift to cursing her. Lear is one of those people who become angry because of nothing, and because of everything. At his son-in-law's home he fights and behaves atrociously. That he was finally shut out on the stormy night should have been shown (on stage); as it is, that matter is only talked about, and in Hagberg's translation the typography is faulty, because everything important — entrances and exits, *jeu de théâtre* — is printed in entirely too fine a type and can easily be overlooked.

The old man is not pleasant and is hard to deal with. But he has been blameless in his relationship with his children, and this fact gives him the right to burst forth:

> . . . I am a man
> More sinn'd against than sinning.

This is not a Pharisee's self-praise, it is justified self-respect; but for morally corrupt people whose sympathies are always with the villain, self-defense is not permitted. The villain is right [they feel] — the injured party must remain silent, and the person who has been robbed is always wrong, since he himself has stolen apples as a child. That is the morality of villains! The witch morality in *Macbeth*: "Fair is foul, and foul is fair." Briefly: the morality based on what is done! And in *King Lear* it is represented by Albany's Goneril, this Messalina who commits adultery with the courtier, ridicules her husband because of his piety, sense of justice, and humaneness. Lear admits that he has sinned, but not in this case, and in general less than the others! And the others' behavior becomes the scale on which he weighs himself! For that reason he has the right to hold up to the wild beasts their despicable behavior, his own irritability being disregarded.

That Cordelia is strangled in prison has been considered cruel in terms of dramatic justice; for that reason the ending has been changed even in English editions so that Cordelia gets Edgar. But Shakespeare does not need to be made responsible for man's cruelty which one often sees strike the innocent while people elevate the criminal to honor.

Cordelia's death is perfectly natural for Shakespeare, who in this period of his life seems to have seen through the whole mess, and to have lain on the rack of torture.

> LEAR: . . . The usurer hangs the cozener.
>   Through tatter'd clothes small vices do appear;
>   Robes and furr'd gowns hide all. Plate sin with gold,
>   And the strong lance of justice hurtless breaks;
>
>   . . . .
>
>   . . . Get thee glass eyes;
>   And, like a scurvy politician, seem
>   To see the things thou dost not. . . .
>
>   . . . .
>
>   . . . we came crying hither:
>   Thou know'st, the first time that we smell the air,
>   We wawl and cry. . . .
>
>   . . . .
>
>   When we are born, we cry that we are come
>   To this great stage of fools. . . .

There you have the sketch of Timon, who hated man. What bitter experiences Shakespeare had lived through one does not know, but he had daughters and was not happily married. Most likely his competitors, too, made his life bitter, and I have begun wondering if all the lost originals Shakespeare is supposed to have plagiarized aren't pure fabrications, lies spread by actors and theater directors for the most part! His own life was stormy and irregular, and various admissions in the sonnets imply that he had early in life learned the secrets of life and its joys. About lust he writes:

> Mad in pursuit and in possession so;
> Had, having, and in quest to have, extreme;
> A bliss in proof, and proved, a very woe;
> Before, a joy proposed; behind, a dream.
>   All this the world well knows; yet none knows well
>   To shun the heaven that leads men to this hell.

When a human being despairs, he first of all doubts God's goodness, and that is close to blasphemy. Shakespeare blasphemes ("the gods") in *King Lear*:

> Oh heavens,
> If you do love old men, if your sweet sway
> Allow obedience, if yourselves are old,
> Make it your cause; send down, and take my part!

Henry VIII

No other Shakespeare play is as dangerous to touch as *Henry VIII*. No matter how one approaches it, one burns one's fingers. I heard it interpreted in English (read in English) by Adjunkt Edman[11] at the University of Uppsala about 1870. We got it in fragments, and it did not interest us, but we listened in order to learn English pronunciation. We felt that there was too much history and too little of the purely human in the play; but when one reads it through at one sitting, it is obvious the play is decidedly human; and the major motif—the breaking up of a marriage—is so painful that Shakespeare, who depicted many separations but only this one divorce, himself seems to have suffered when he wrote it. But every other adverse criticism of the play upon closer scrutiny seems to be answered in the text, even this: that Shakespeare is not its author but that Fletcher or Ben Jonson wrote it; but it is the aging Shakespeare's great and gentle philosophy (*The Tempest*), it is his manner and it is his pen [we find in the play], though not his light white pen from the comedies. Instead we find his raven-dark and black

banners, infinite suffering and great crimes, and also atonement
and reconciliation in abundance.

Anyone who wants to understand what I mean should first
read the play, slowly and with pencil in hand, because it is hard
to grasp the whole of the play and to keep it intact in one's
memory.

In the prologue criticism is directed at Shakespeare: scholars
have been inclined to the conclusion that Ben Jonson wrote it
as a representative of good (i.e., academic) taste.

The prologue contains among other things:

> . . . Only they
> That come to hear a merry bawdy play,
> A noise of targets, or to see a fellow
> In a long motley coat guarded with yellow,
> Will be deceived; for, gentle hearers, know
> To rank our chosen truth with such a show
> As fool and fight is, beside forfeiting
> Our own brains, and the opinion that we bring,
> To make that only true we now intend,
> Will leave us never an understanding friend.

Why, that is like a spear hurled at all of Shakespeare's
dramas, in which the fool is indispensable to say what those
bound by the laws of convention have not dared to say. But I
do want to make one objection: the aging Shakespeare had left
his clown's cape behind him; the terrifying seriousness of life
had forced him to his knees; he had probably acquired better
taste and did not approve of joking about what is holy and
sacred; the clown's absolute skepticism had given way to a
dearly purchased faith in the "ideal forces" in life.

The whole play including the language is unusually tidied
up, almost too much so, until the third scene of Act V, where
in a scene with the porter, the old (i.e., the young) Shakespeare

opens up in his unembarrassed way in a manner directly contrary to the good intentions and fine promises about taste and good tone in the prologue. "So what?" one might ask. The old Adam was not dead, and — so what? This "contradiction" is just as natural as it is agreeable; it contains talk that is nonsense, but no one learns any evil from it.

Gervinus [12] and others have criticized the structure of the play as loose, and people have called this play an occasional play. Maybe so: but the masterpieces *A Midsummer Night's Dream* and *The Tempest* were written on order; yet they are among the best of Shakespeare's dramas. *Henry VIII* seems to me to be too tragic to be a play written for a coronation, and I rather believe it was written for its own sake but was later used for certain purposes and with changes and adjustments.

But the structure is not loose, although the motifs are many and supersede each other; the play is extremely complex and artistic.

Buckingham tries to overthrow Wolsey, but is overthrown himself. Wolsey wants to separate the king and Katharine with the object of getting the king to marry the sister of the king of France; Henry is divorced but marries Anne Bullen; then Wolsey falls; and a new man Cranmer emerges. But woven into all this is the thoroughly tragic motif: Katharine's divorce.

In that Shakespeare has proceeded in a manner that can be called flawless. The play was written during the reign of James I — after Elizabeth was dead. Notice this about history: the way Providence goes to work; since Elizabeth did not want to marry, she left no heir to the throne, and James, the son of Mary Stuart — whom Elizabeth had had executed, became her successor. James I, who reigned when *Henry VIII* was written, hated the House of Tudor, so Shakespeare, on the one hand, did not need to be embarrassed if he wanted to hit out at Henry *and*

Elizabeth; on the other hand, he had no reason for flattering Elizabeth, who was dead.

In the difficult divorce case, in which guilt and innocence had to be carefully weighed by the court, the poet has certainly expressed sympathy for and acquitted Katharine, but, on the other hand, he has also acquitted Henry of the charge of having sought the divorce on the false grounds of scruples of conscience (which Suffolk mentions by name: Anne Bullen). Henry VIII was married six times and has acquired a certain reputation as a Bluebeard because he had to execute two wives because of "treason against the crown." We are concerned only with his relationship to the best of the six, Katharine of Aragon.

She had been married for only a few months to Henry's brother Arthur, when the latter died. Then they wanted to force twelve-year-old Henry to marry the widow, but he refused to do so for several reasons. Finally he did marry her eight years later when he was twenty; and he lived with her for twenty years. She bore children, but the sons were stillborn, which disturbed the strictly religious king's conscience so that, long before Anne Bullen appeared, he began to believe that the marriage was not blessed, probably incestuous. Besides there was what Shakespeare has him say in his defense. His daughter Mary (the Catholic) was to be married to a duke of Orléans when the latter began to question if the bride was "legitimate," since her parents' marriage was questionable. But even Charles V, who had had his eye on Mary, withdrew his suit, since the Spanish Cortes (States of Castile) opposed the match on the basis of her illegitimate birth. All this disturbed King Henry, and other more private matters which Hume tells about but which Shakespeare omits out of consideration for Katharine though they were a credit to Henry.

First, after six years of investigation and the promised dispensation of the pope — Anne Bullen appears on the scene, and she really gave the last blow to his qualms, but only the last. The fact that the courtiers (in the play) blame Anne Bullen alone is a means of cutting bother short, a means certainly used in ordinary daily life, in which for the sake of convenience one hits on what is closest at hand and most entertaining as suitable for dialogue.

There are in the drama no guilt and no accusations, but Katharine's fate is just as cruel [all the same], and her suffering arouses one's deepest sympathy.

For those who have forgotten, I want to recall the marvelous little song, with glorious music by O. Lindblad,[13] which we still sang twenty years ago and which opens Act III and is sung for Katharine:

> Song.
> Orpheus with his lute made trees,
> And the mountain tops that freeze,
>   Bow themselves when he did sing:
> To his music plants and flowers
> Ever sprung; as sun and showers
>   There had made a lasting spring.
>
> Every thing that heard him play,
> Even the billows of the sea,
>   Hung their heads, and then lay by.
> In sweet music is such art,
> Killing care and grief of heart
>   Fall asleep, or hearing, die.

Katharine dies, after having had a vision of the message of the white-robed messengers of heavenly mercy, stripped of all earthly glory, with thoughts about her children, her servants, and her — husband, who is now remarried! Without bitterness, without regret.

Henry VIII is considered Shakespeare's very last play, later

than *The Tempest.* I believe that he feels the end approaching
when he simply laments without complaining, judges without
condemning, lets each and every one who leaves the stage do
so with resignation and a gentle contempt for the world. Buckingham goes (in Act II) to the block with words like these:

> As I would be forgiven: I forgive all;
> There cannot be those numberless offences
> 'Gainst me, that I cannot take peace with: no black envy
> Shall make my grave. Commend me to his grace. . . .

Cardinal Wolsey, the archvillain of the play, makes his departure from life, after his fall, with out-and-out self-accusations,
warnings:

> Cromwell, I charge thee, fling away ambition:
> By that sin fell the angels. . . .
>
> . . . .
>
> . . . Be just, and fear not:
> Let all the ends thou aim'st at be thy country's,
> Thy God's and truth's. . . .

And when he is dead, the deposed Katharine's own marshal
Griffith dares to speak well of Wolsey before the queen whom
he has overthrown. Griffith does not deny flaws, but insists on
all his merits, and this in such a way that Katharine can become
reconciled in her own mind with the dead archvillain and is
forced to honor her worst enemy.

From all this it seems to me apparent that *Henry VIII,* the
supposed festival play, is just as personal as any other, but there
is another "dog" hidden in this rich drama, too. Gervinus says
that this play was produced in 1613 under the title *All Is True*;
the prologue hints at that, too: "Such as give / Their money
out of hope they may believe, / May here find truth too." etc.

How is one to find any meaning in that? Were Henry VIII
and the others maligned in their day so that Shakespeare needed

to whitewash their reputations? No, so much the less as Shakespeare makes a false accusation against Wolsey—the one about the inventory of the spoils, which happened to Ruthall according to Wolsey's arrangements. That Henry played cards and was miserly, as it says in the play, may or may not be true. I don't know.

If "the truth" about Elizabeth were to come out (she was always flattered), there is no exposè in the drama; on the contrary, for she is both a virgin and everything [else usually said in her favor].

Then all that remains, it seems to me, is to consider it a so-called drama of ideas or à thèse, in which the author drives home a point, defends a thesis, or illustrates a proverb.

"All Is True" would then be either an expression of absolute skepticism (which is not the case) or a formula of Jakob Böhme's[14] mystic oneness, which may be used only on a higher plane. In everyday middle-class life people go about with their passbooks keeping account of their own claims and other people's debts, where it will not do to say before any court that a single fact is both true and false or persuade the judge that a human being is both good and evil; the sword of justice cleaves such two-edged matters, and double-tongued confessions are there not at all valid, all this for practical considerations, because life is short and things must be done summarily to bring them to an end. In the world of the poet, when he raises himself above the everyday plane, in which before a higher court one can plead both-innocent-and-guilty, there it can be true *and* false without the wicked becoming attractive and black becoming white. It is human to err, but divine to forgive. Fine! Shakespeare was in a mood to forgive when he wrote *Henry VIII*—he was in the midst of settling his own accounts; but in *Macbeth*, *Othello*, and *King Lear*, he does not forgive but punishes uncompromisingly and cruelly, for the reason, however, that in those plays the characters are moving in a completely ordinary life. I suspect that, facing the terrible drama of an innocent sufferer (Katharine), he was gripped by a universally great divine sympathy, which extended even to the intrigant Wolsey. When he says that Wolsey is an archvillain, he is immediately seized by a longing to be able to say: Wolsey has great merits, however.

This is, then, only a point of view that Shakespeare has assumed for the time being, and I compared his point of view with Jakob Böhme's *oneness* expressed in the formula: Everything consists of its opposites; everything contains a yes and a no. But this dangerous philosophy, which in the hands of evil men can lead to damnation, was developed by Hegel in his famous: Everything is born of its opposite, and the truth, the absolute, is the synthesis of thesis and antithesis. Shakespeare has probably intuitively touched on the problem, or tried to solve it by means of religious resignation: because only through that can one see the truth about the heights of honor, human greatness, wealth, and all vanity, and come away from all that with a blessing as Buckingham, Wolsey, and Katharine do.

That Shakespeare meant anything so banal in his title as an assurance that this play is a true story (printed this year), I do not believe, because he always has striking sonorous titles, which are not happily translated into Swedish. But that by *All Is True* he meant what I think, I am not sure.

Anne Bullen is depicted as an attractive lady whose only merits are that she shows no malicious joy over the overthrow of the queen and that she becomes the mother of Elizabeth.

That she was to end on the block, Shakespeare knew, but there is not the slightest hint of that, not in the play; on the contrary, she is depicted as very sensitive, intellectually honest, and modest. Possibly Shakespeare wanted thereby to acquit her of all guilt, because he found her punishment for her carelessness too severe. She did receive young lords in her chambers and spoke with them frivolously about her king and husband. (See Hume's *History of England*.) The king's love for Anne is beautifully depicted in D'Aubigné's *The History of the Reformation*.

Cranmer, who plays Fortinbras, got a pitiful end, too — on the stake, during the reign of Mary the Catholic. He was a swindler, and his overestimated merit in *Henry VIII* consisted of talking *for* the king's divorce.

One can imagine Parts II and III of *Henry VIII* as developments of Anne Bullen's and Cranmer's stories; even Cromwell, Wolsey's "servant," who becomes a state secretary and is beheaded, could be used; then it would have become, along with the king's new marriage, a mighty tragedy of fate, in which one great person trampled down his predecessor and was trampled down by his successor. But that was not in the plan, and Elizabeth had already received her apotheosis.

The one who would like to know who Elizabeth really was should read David Hume's *History of England*;* and one gets a certainly tidied-up but quite repulsive view of her character in Walter Scott's *Kenilworth*. The novel has this very revealing motto: "No scandals about Elizabeth, I hope?"

---

* Schück has revealed Elizabeth's controversial "secret" in his book about Shakespear, p. 265. [A.S.]

A Midsummer-Night's Dream

I have seen this beautiful poem presented several times — with Mendelssohn's music;[15] but the glorious music has captured my ears and drowned out the voices of the actors so that the play never fully came into its own. I have heard it presented by the best of actors, but that did not help.

As a director I shall make a few comments and consider the possibility of improving the situation, because I am by no means the only one who has missed out on the undivided enjoyment of the play in performance that one looks forward to when reading the play.

One comes to the theater feeling that one knows the content of the play; but one does not in detail, because one has forgotten some of the details since the last time. In order that a tired person may be able to enjoy a drama comfortably, the plot should be simple, the characters not too many, and the language a little elevated but not too rich in symbolism. It takes real effort to solve puzzles.

The composition in *A Midsummer-Night's Dream* is polyphonic, extremely artistic with these five motifs:

Theseus = Hippolyta; Oberon = Titania; Lysander = Hermia; Demetrius = Helena; the craftsmen's play.

When the motifs of Hermia and Helena cross because of Puck's intrigues and mistakes and are developed contrapuntally, the unraveling becomes tiring. I can hardly keep it straight while reading the play even if there is only one misprint. The director ought to select actors and actresses decidedly different in appearance and voice, dress them in contrasting colors, and not have changes in costumes.

It has been said that Shakespeare selected names without good taste. Hermia and Helena sound too much alike, and that is [probably] why Hagberg's translation has interchanged them in one place. (Compare Cassius and Casca in *Julius Caesar.*)

It is stated that one girl is tall and the other short. That helps.

But the language in the play is like filigree work, the imagery as rich as in the finest Italian lyrics, and in our large theaters all this portraiture in miniature is lost. It goes by half-understood, and this makes the audience uneasy and uncomfortable. Then there is the music, which I think measures up to the text, if such things can be measured.

The overture opens one's ear and mind in a special way; one is ready for music. The curtain goes up; Theseus begins to talk. What he says sounds false since it is not in harmony with the music; it grates because the ear is already adjusted [to the music]; but what he says sounds uninspired, empty, banal simply because — it is not music.

The poet's imagery has already been profaned by the written word; the written drama is profaned in a way when it is put into material form through performance. One notices this first and most plainly when one's ear has caught the music; that is *why* music during intermissions has been eliminated at newer theaters.

Any attempt at harmonizing the actor's speeches with the music, as in melodramas, is impossible because they are incommensurable. In some melodramas the clashing of the voice with the music does not matter too much.

A drama with music can also go if the plot is simple so that while one is enjoying the music one does not need to exert oneself to keep what is happening clear.

But it does happen that the actor has caught the music and loses control of his own voice so that he varies his register and gets into strange keys.

Music can then be the reason why the play is not effective. But when one does not want to lose one word of the text and not one note of the music, the problem cannot be solved unless one should experiment by giving the play without music or having the play performed by opera singers, who can "speak in harmony" with the music and phrase in their stylized manner.

If Mendelssohn had composed an opera with a simplified text, Shakespeare would have been saved, and then we would have had the opera and the play intact as well. But the play by itself is complex. Puck, who is not a figure of light but one of evil, since he rejoices over the suffering of innocent people, muddles the intrigue through his mistakes so that the action finally becomes nightmarishly twisted, and one sees before one a drama of intrigue. I have never liked that kind of drama because it calls for effort, and, when I am looking for entertainment, I do not want to work, but relax. When I was young, I once saw a drama of intrigue called *Who Is She?* When we came to the end, I was so weary of the whole thing (it had to do with family difficulties) that I left without finding out who she was.

When I now reread *A Midsummer-Night's Dream*, I discovered details I had never noticed before. Thus I discovered that Hippolyta is an Amazon whom Theseus has courted "with force." Furthermore, that Hermia is ordered to marry Demetrius or lose her life. So she should appear in the forest as a person condemned to death because she has defied the laws of the country. Theseus does give her another alternative: to enter a cloister.

But there is also a thread of dark pessimism in the thirty-year-old poet. For him love is certainly a pleasant fact, but it is very fragile. "The course of love never runs smoothly." There were such matters as differences in birth and age, relatives' choices, and the like.

> LYSANDER: Or, if there were a sympathy in choice,
>   War, death, or sickness, did lay siege to it,
>   Making it momentary as a sound,
>   Swift as a shadow, short as any dream;
>   Brief as the lightning in the collied night,
>   That, in a spleen, unfolds both heaven and earth,
>   And ere a man hath power to say "Behold!"
>   The jaws of darkness do devour it up:
>   So quick bright things come to confusion.
> HERMIA: If then true lovers have been ever cross'd,
>   It stands as an edict in destiny:
>   Then let us teach our trial patience,
>   Because it is a customary cross,
>   As due to love as thoughts and dreams and sighs,
>   Wishes and tears, poor fancy's followers.

This, however, is a wedding play, written by a thirty-year-old who could, of course, have "believed in love" as our women say.

A fairy calls Puck "thou lob of spirits"; that is something quite different from the one who as a spirit of the air dances about on an aerial machine in Germany. Eysoldt[16] in Berlin must have seized upon that expression, because she has accoutered herself as a devil of the forest. Other descriptions in the text correspond to those of a *tomte* or elf, which must be the right thing.

An attractive, surely unnoticed feature is Titania's declaration that all imperfections in nature, illnesses included, and all the offspring of torments are the fruit of her and Oberon's dissension:

> And this same progeny of evils comes
> From our debate, from our dissension;
> We are their parents and original.

Whoever has seen what havoc an unhappy marriage or the dissension between husband and wife can cause about them — the ruination of the home, the neglect of the children, cheerlessness, illnesses ("They hate each other so they get cancer") — understands that what Titania says is more than a poetic expression. It is also moving when the two couples, poisoned by Puck, pour epithets over each other (vile thing, cat, serpent), and that is close to the limits of the permissible in a wedding play, because it is tragic. But Puck, that half-Satan, explains that "this their jangling I esteem a sport."

In Act V I notice that the poet speculates on whether these ocular illusions had any reality. Theseus (that smug soul) states emphatically:

> The lunatic, the lover, and the poet
> Are of imagination all compact:
> One sees more devils than vast hell can hold,
> That is, the madman: the lover, all as frantic,
> Sees Helen's beauty in a brow of Egypt:
> The poet's eye, in a fine frenzy rolling,
> Doth glance from heaven to earth, from earth to heaven. . . .

Hippolyta, however, considers

> But all the story of the night told over,
> And all their minds transfigured so together,
> More witnesseth than fancy's images
> And grows to something of great constancy;
> But, howsoever, strange and admirable.

I suspect Shakespeare agreed with her!

Directors apparently used to cut *A Midsummer-Night's Dream* mercilessly, because one never became intimately acquainted with its characters from seeing them on stage. In the text itself, one learns Helena and Hermia have been brought up together and have been friends.

Their relationship is depicted extremely attractively by Helena, but I had not noticed that until now:

> Injurious Hermia! most ungrateful maid!
> Have you conspired, have you with these contrived
> To bait me with this foul derision?
> Is all the counsel that we two have shared,
> The sisters' vows, the hours we have spent,
> When we have chid the hasty-footed time
> For parting us, — O, is all forgot?
> All school-days' friendship, childhood innocence?
> We, Hermia, like two artificial gods,
> Have with our needles created both one flower,
> Both on one sampler, sitting on one cushion,
> Both warbling of one song, both in one key,
> As if our hands, our sides, voices and minds,
> Had been incorporate. So we grew together,
> Like to a double cherry, seeming parted,
> But yet a union in partition;
> Two lovely berries moulded on one stem;
> So, with two seeming bodies, but one heart;
> Two of the first, like coats in heraldry,
> Due but to one, and crowned with one crest.

Those are beautiful, glowing, innocent images — "double cherry," "one crest" — and now one becomes interested in the young people, who after the cuts are like two skeletons.

I want to interject a comment about Shakespeare's diction in the plays.

There is sometimes a wealth that is excessive and gives one too much; the one image pursues the other, and much in a great scene is lost because the metaphor is a word puzzle which it takes time to solve. Sometimes the metaphor is extended through several verses but then has a didactic effect as in Vergil or Dante; a figure of speech should illuminate the context, a correspondence or relationship as Swedenborg[17] would say; it should combine ideas from different planes: two young girls, two cherries; an idea from human life with one form from the world of plants, both equally beautiful in their different ways. When commentary is supplied in time, the point becomes clearer, but the circumstantial reduces the effect just as when one restates a witticism.

But there is beauty of sound in Shakespeare's best verses, music that cannot be reproduced in translation, depending partly on the freedom of versification in English, where the iambs are not always iambs in our sense, partly on the language itself. Shakespeare does not always count to five; often he has four; and, when he is particularly stirred up, he does not count at all. Sometimes he omits the iamb and opens with a trochee. Furthermore, the words do not have a definite stress, and, finally, Shakespeare is just as great a self-indulgent careless soul as Lord Byron, who years later wrote the poorest verse in English (Ruskin's [?] statement). For example, Juliet's soliloquy, Act II, scene 5:

> Which ten times faster glide thăn thē sŭn's bēams.

Here he stresses the article *the* making it long and makes the noun *sun's* short.

> Is three long hours, yet she is not come.

We would not approve of *thrēē lŏng hoūrs* and not *nōt cŏme* either; in English it will do. Besides the line contains only four iambs, which would be considered a crime by our verse-writing bookkeepers, and even by the few members of the Swedish Academy [18] who can write.

We may surely consider it carelessness when the poet in two consecutive lines stresses the same word differently. In Juliet's same soliloquy is this:

> Therefore do nimble-pinion'd doves draw love,
> And therefore hath the wind-swift Cupid wings.

In the first line the word is pronounced *thĕrefōre*, and in the next *thērefŏre* if one insists on iambs; otherwise it is a spondee: *thērefōre*.

On the other hand, the effect of "a standstill" is deliberate when Juliet says:

> My words would bandy her to my sweet love,
> And his to me: [*Notice!*]
> But old folks, many feign as they were dead. . . .

This ellipse: *And his to me* has an amazingly fine effect.

As we know, French counts only syllables and does not stress them as iambs or trochees. For that reason we consider French verse as unmusical, but it is not. There is a delightful but free music in Musset's verses; Verlaine on the other hand, like Belgare, has borrowed Heine's rhythms and introduced alliteration and assonance, so that French has acquired a Germanic music. The great Peladan has written metrical verse (which centuries ago had already been done by some Frenchmen).

English like French has a shifting accent, probably more so than French, but has a somewhat stricter rhythm. This lack [of fixed accent] provides an opportunity for music; and all languages are beautiful when they are used by a musical poet. Shakespeare is thoroughly musical, although we in our prejudice against English have a hard time hearing it.

Even the person who knows only a little English should read Helena's verses cited above. But he should read them until he knows them so well that they flow off his tongue and do not get stuck. (That is, he should get the pronunciation absolutely down pat first and mark where final *e* is pronounced and where it is not! Then he should probably learn it all by heart so that he can enjoy the sounds even if he does not understand every word!) Helena's lines are beautifully musical, so I wonder if

Mendelssohn was not simply directly inspired by the poet's harmonies.

Mendelssohn's overture, which opens with the wonderful motif of the fairies, was probably inspired by the fairy's stanza in the first scene of Act II:

> Over hill, over dale,
>   Thorough bush, thorough brier,
> Over park, over pale,
>   Thorough flood, thorough fire,
> I do wander every where,
> Swifter than the moon's sphere;
> And I serve the fairy queen,
> To dew her orbs upon the green.
> The cowslips tall her pensioners be:
> In their gold coats spots you see;
> Those be rubies, fairy favours,
> In those freckles live their savours. . . .

The anapests ($\cup\cup$—) "over hill, over dale" are those of the overture so one could sing them according to the notes.

Our prejudice against the English language is a result of our common inability to pronounce it! But English is both gentle and strong; gentle through the Germanic, strong through its Romance sounds. In "Swifter than the moon's sphere" the Anglo-Saxon sounds steal up to "sphere," where the Romance languages take over.

In "Crowned with one crest," *corona* and *crista* are decidedly Latin; in

> *Injurious* Hermia! most *ungrateful* maid!
> Have you *conspired*, have you with these *contrived*
> To bait me with this foul *derision?*

appears much Latin, and that can be heard, too.

But to return to *A Midsummer-Night's Dream* and the fairy's song! What a nice sharp observation of the flower (cowslip =

cow's lip). "In their gold coats spots you see; / Those be rubies, fairy favours, / In those freckles live their savours." School botanists in England knew the flower resembled a cow's lips; they knew about "flowers pale yellow in drooping umbels," too, but they had not seen the red "freckles" (Marshall Vatts's *A School Flora*). That is the lightninglike figure Shakespeare excels in: "freckles." Or when he talks about the ivy's wedding rings (*vines*) that she places on the elm's fingers (*branches*): "The female ivy so enrings the barky fingers of the elm." Or this: "the green corn hath rotted ere his youth attain'd a beard." "Hoary-headed frosts." Or in a line without an image making an abstract time concrete and vivid: "When wheat is green, when hawthorn buds appear." But this is the English landscape in a verse; I saw it in Gravesend one May day: there were fields and hedges, wheat and hawthorn, and it's in Dickens' novels!

At the risk of boring you, I shall quote Romeo and Juliet's first exchange at the ball to complement what I have already said. The reader should above all notice the beauty of the sounds in English. Romeo, dressed as a pilgrim, begins with a rhymed quatrain, which probably is something he has memorized — as young gentlemen of that time rehearsed for conversations at balls.

> If I profane with my unworthiest hand
> This holy shrine, the gentle fine is this:
> My lips, two blushing pilgrims, ready stand
> To smooth that rough touch with a tender kiss.

Juliet answers with another quatrain and picks up Romeo's *this* and *kiss*:

> Good pilgrim, you do wrong your hand too much,
> Which mannerly devotion shows in this;
> For saints have hands that pilgrims' hands do touch,
> And palm to palm is holy palmers' kiss.

As I have said before, this conceit is neither witty nor happy; it is forced and artificial, but has been concocted to cover up their feelings. They are "words," but caressing ones; they are shuttle-cocks thrown, returned, and thrown again. As carelessly as a child, Juliet takes Romeo's words (and rhyme) into her mouth, and then he is in, too.

They continue the dangerous game, are caught in the glue, and would not come apart if the nurse did not enter and cut the scene:

> ROMEO: Have not saints lips, and holy palmers too?
> JULIET: Ay, pilgrim, lips that they must use in prayer.
> ROMEO: O, then, dear saint, let lips do what hands do;
> They pray, grant thou, lest faith turn to despair.
> JULIET: Saints do not move, though grant for prayers' sake.
> ROMEO: Then move not, while my prayer's effect I take.
> Thus from my lips, by yours, my sin is purged.
> JULIET: Then have my lips the sin that they have took.
> ROMEO: Sin from my lips? O trespass sweetly urged!
> Give me my sin again.
> JULIET: You kiss by the book.

Before I stop, I should say a few words about Hagberg's translation. We used it as an aid in our interpretations [of the original], and it was always reliable. I have not examined it [with care] since then, but have only had occasion to admire it and to make a few minor criticisms.

There are translations in which the translator really has excelled the original. Strandberg[19] in his translation of Byron's *Don Juan*, for Byron had been careless and written miserable verses and Strandberg replaced them with masterly ones. I will go that far, even if in general the translation of a literary work is impossible, for the spirit of the poem is in every word of the language.

Without being a poet, Hagberg has devoted his whole life to

this task, and for that reason no other Swede has known his Shakespeare as he did. But Hagberg, too, was an artist in the use of words and could be inventive in Shakespeare's spirit and manner. Sometimes where Shakespeare is weary and has taken colorless words, Hagberg comes with a more pregnant term that is indescribably delightful but always in Shakespeare's style. One example! In Cassio's famous hangover scene in which he curses strong drinks, Iago answers like this: "Come, come, good wine is a good familiar creature, if it be well used; exclaim no more against it." Hagberg says: "*Se så, se så; ett gott vin är ett beskedligt och trevligt kräk, om man rätt umgås med det; trät inte på vinet.*"

"A good familiar creature" is translated inimitably by "*ett beskedligt och trevligt kräk* (I would have eliminated "*beskedligt*" as a watered-down epithet). But Hagberg has put more punch into the expression "*trät inte på vinet,*" in which the abstract, colorless "exclaim" has been changed into "*trät,*" and the toneless "it" into "*vinet.*"

I find Hagberg's translation of "Orpheus' song" more beautiful in diction than the original in *Henry VIII*:

> Orpheus with his lute made trees,
> And the mountain-tops that freeze,
>   Bow themselves, when he did sing:
> To his music plants and flowers
> Ever sprung; as sun and showers
>   There had made a lasting spring.

> *Orfeus sjöng; vid lutans toner*
> *Fjällens snöbetäckta zoner*
>   *Sänkte sig för skaldens sång;*
> *Blommans kalk och trädens toppar,*
> *Solens ljus och daggens droppar*
>   *Följde tjusta toners gång.*

Shakespeare's original sounds like dry prose; "that freeze" is a slap in the face.

> Everything that heard him play,
> Even the billows of the sea,
>   Hung their heads and then lay by.
> In sweet music is such art:
> Killing care and grief of heart
> Fall asleep, or, hearing, die.

> *Allt hvad lif och anda hade,*
> *Hafvet själft sig stilla lade*
>   *För att lyss som spegelsjö;*
> *Så musiken döfvar smärtan;*
> *Kvalda sinnen, brustna hjärtan*
>   *Somna eller stilla dö.*

Hagberg's verses are better, but Otto Lindblad's music is the best of all.

Hagberg committed a minor but fatal mistake when in *Twelfth Night* he translated "There dwelt a man in Babylon" by *"Joakim uti Babylon"*[20] and "O, the twelfth day of December" with *"November den 15:de dagen."*

To be transported in a flash from Illyria to Par Bricole[21] or Gustav III's age through Bellman is a blunder that can, of course, do no great harm to the boring and poor comedy *Twelfth Night*, in which the amusing is not amusing and the lyrical is decidedly dull, but it does make the play still flabbier. The play is a rehash of *The Comedy of Errors* (Plautus' *Menaechmi*), and its theme is *A Midsummer Night's Dream's qui pro quo*. *Twelfth Night* wearies without interesting me.

People should not admire a great writer's inferior works: if they do, they develop poor taste. I want to state that once more. Holberg has written much more entertaining and better plays [than *Twelfth Night*].

FIFTH LETTER

Introduction

WHILE the fifth letter deals with many interesting subjects, the most important matter in it is Strindberg's frank discussion of his own theory of historical drama and his application of that theory in several of his major plays. His comments on *Julius Caesar*, his analysis of *Antony and Cleopatra*, and his brief note on *Richard II* supplement what he had said about Shakespeare in earlier letters. The long section on Goethe's *Faust* includes a consideration of that masterpiece which leads to an informative discussion of Strindberg's thinking about translating and various translations; then comes an intensely interesting discussion of stage design and staging, the major ideas of which are applied to productions of his own plays either at the Intimate Theater or elsewhere; and the whole section ends with praise for August Falck's successful experiments with stage design and production. The final section considers not only the concept of stylizing but such topics as the dramatization of other writers' prose fiction, the adaptation (or Swedishing) of foreign plays, his own use of Walter Scott's novels, plagiarism, and a dramatist's justified use of certain literature (the folk ballads, for example). But what he has to say about his theory and practice in writing historical dramas overshadows all the other matters since

234

he is the greatest modern author of historical plays. His discussion of the genre at some length in terms of his own efforts and achievements deserves extended consideration.

Strindberg thought of the historical drama as a work of art designed to entertain and interest audiences in theaters. Such a work of art should, he felt, be as human a document as any play about either himself or his contemporaries. It should, moreover, not be a mere dramatization of episodes out of the past arranged in bare chronicle form and playing up to traditional, idealized notions of the historic dead. Such a concept of the historical drama involves many things, among them the sources of historical materials, Strindberg's attitude toward the sources, his use of the material, his concepts of the particular historic dead, his way of bringing them alive in plays that would be entertaining and interesting for modern people, his views on the structure of such plays and the kind of dialogue to be used in them, and the relationship between his concept and those of his predecessors within the genre. Strindberg dealt very frankly with every one of these matters.

He had no hesitancy about revealing exactly, though not in footnotes, to what books, manuscripts, letters, articles, and other sources he went when he was preparing to write a historical drama. He says:

> History and the folk ballads have always and rightly been considered common property, which the writer has had the right to use and exploit. Fryxell, Afzelius, and Starbäck have been used for the purpose most advantageously since they have included more little human details than the dry chronicles and official histories. Fryxell narrates in a lively fashion with a flowing style, but rather colorlessly. Starbäck (and Bäckström) have amassed an amazing amount of material, badly worked up and not well arranged, so that one has to go at it with a drill and pickax to get at its jewels.

The three histories he mentions are popular histories. They are not carefully footnoted and scrupulously qualified accounts of Swedish history; they are instead filled with extremely detailed accounts of the prominent people of the past and their very human involve-

ments not only in affairs of state but also in personal dilemmas. The
vast amount of material based on standard histories, popular traditions, and gossip probably accounts for the fact that the three histories were widely read wherever Swedish was the first language
back in the nineteenth century and even at the beginning of the
twentieth. Anyone who has read the three sets in whole or part must
surely agree with Strindberg that they contain material about historic individuals, the like of which cannot be found in any academic
history or in "official" biographies.

Strindberg's assumption that theater audiences are made up of
people intensely and primarily interested in themselves and their
fellows, a fact that Fryxell, Afzelius and Starbäck (and Bäckström)
had successfully exploited, did not restrict him to the use of popular
histories as sources of his material. He used all kinds of material that
concerned history. He knew the academically acceptable sources as
well as the popular sources, and his use of scholarly history was extensive. By way of illustration, one might cite his references in merely one source to indicate the scope of his preparatory reading: in the
section "The Historical Drama" he refers to his acquaintance with
both the unabridged and the abridged versions of Odhner's *History
of Sweden* (a standard text in the schools), Geijer's histories of
Sweden, Schiller's *History of the Thirty Years War*, the official
Swedish archives, and other official documents. That he used more
specialized academic studies is also clear. But Strindberg said frankly that he preferred the popular histories because they were more
human in their appeal, and in a historic drama the human factors
were most important.

In using history primarily as background, however, Strindberg
was keenly aware of the fact that, if he were to write historical
dramas that would go in the modern theater, he had to distinguish
carefully between history and historical drama. The distinction obviously involves compromises in the use of history on the part of
the dramatist. What these compromises were for Strindberg he made
crystal clear. Aside from such matters as judging the accuracy and

psychological validity of the sources' interpretation of the historic dead for himself and rejecting the idealization or traditional apotheosis of any of them, Strindberg insisted on his right to fill gaps when the historical facts were not known, to disregard chronological order of events when absolutely necessary for dramatic purposes, and to arrive at his own interpretations of the great and not-so-great men and women of the past.

Surely there can be no sound objection to an author's arriving at his own concepts of the historic dead. Even scholarly historians must do that. Furthermore, there never have been universally accepted concepts of such historical figures as Göran Persson, Queen Christina, Charles XII, and Gustav III; they have been objects of controversy among professional historians and even laymen over the years. Nor can there be any serious objections to supplying — for dramatic purposes — material when the facts are not to be found in the historical accounts, providing, as Strindberg says, one does not distort established facts. Note this excerpt from what he says about filling gaps in the records about Engelbrekt:

> History does not make clear the motive for the murder. Engelbrekt had had a quarrel with the murderer's father, but they had been reconciled. Since no one knows what the quarrel was about, I had the right to make Måns Natt-och-Dag the envious man in whose way Engelbrekt was unfortunate enough to get. . . .
>
> But, to increase the suspense, I had to introduce still more intimate conflicts, so I let him suffer in his marriage all the horrors of disunity. And since no one knows with whom Engelbrekt was married, I had the right to make his wife a Dane, which I thought was a very fine device for making the disunity concrete.

Strindberg's conviction that he did not have the right to distort the *facts* of history probably accounts for the extended explanation in his prefatory note on *Earl Birger of Bjälbo* of why it was necessary for him as a dramatist to disregard the chronological order of events and even the specific times when some events occurred. After insisting that he has not distorted well-known facts, he goes on to say that like his great predecessors within the genre he found it necessary and justified for dramatic purposes to compress historical events in a remote period:

> I have never committed such an unnecessary crime against historical accuracy when it has concerned universally known matters, since I do not approve of that manner of concocting historical data and facts. Compressing historical events in a remote period I have, however, always permitted myself in keeping with the great models, and still do, for the drama is an art form by means of which I must give illusion and an art form in which everything is illusory — language, dress, time above all. . . . The compression of events and the related resultant liberties demand more care so that one does not violate generally known matters but restricts oneself to areas about which people have to go home to consult a book to find the deceptive trick.

Strindberg then distinguishes between dramatic time and ordinary time as Shakespeare and other predecessors had done; he deliberately avoids having the audience's attention directed toward dates simply by not mentioning them. His plays are theater and literature, not history textbooks.

As a result of reading many varied sources, and of his own creative insight, Strindberg gained personal understanding of the well-known historic dead who were to become the central characters in his major historical dramas. His intense interest in and curiosity about himself and his fellow human beings, and his conviction that the people of the past were very much like those in his own day, made him view not only Earl Birger of Bjälbo, King Magnus, Engelbrekt, Sten Sture, Gustav Vasa, Olaus Petri, Erik XIV and Göran Persson, Gustav II Adolf, Queen Christina, Charles XII, and Gustav III, but also a host of others of secondary or even minor importance, as human beings — that is, individuals, not types. His central characters and such people as the court fool at King Valdemar's court, the woman who was to become St. Birgitta, the notorious if not infamous archbishop Gustav Trolle, young Queen Karin, Axel Oxenstjerna, Swedenborg, and that perennial object of Swedish gossip, Munck, had lived long ago; some of them had accomplished great things, some of them not; none of them had been paragons of virtue, none of them outright evil; but every last one of them had been a person of flesh and blood sharing in the human condition. To arrive at an understanding of any one of them Strindberg used his historic sources for what they had to say or to suggest about the individual's life and personality in terms of his various roles in his day.

Theoretically, anyone who writes about a historical figure must present an interpretation of that figure within the frame of time, place, and position, and, even though the scholar attempts to base his interpretation on established facts, evaluating and relating those facts to one another in order to arrive at a reliable account, there must obviously be a goodly measure of subjectivity involved. Strindberg was very much aware of the validity of this general assumption, which helps explain, for example, the highly differing interpretations by both historians and nonhistorians of Charles XII. No other writer, academic or nonacademic, could ever be franker than Strindberg in admitting that he was subjective in his interpretation of the historic dead.

His admission concerns not only the very personal way in which he weighed and assessed established facts, but also the way in which he complemented those facts in order to make the historic dead come alive for the sensitive and imaginative reader, and even more for an audience in a theater: "I made the major characters live by taking blood and nerves out of my own life." Such a frank and concise statement needs only one qualification, it seems to me: the word "major" should be eliminated, for in his *Open Letters* Strindberg makes it clear that he did not restrict his practice to central characters alone. But his statement suggests that he was doing what creative writers must do. If one keeps in mind Strindberg's conviction that human beings share in varied degrees the whole range of intellectual, emotional, and physical experience, it follows that Strindberg believed that in interpreting others one must guess and imagine, and fill in from one's own experience.

Strindberg was admittedly at least partially to blame for the Swedish notion that his characters are nothing but versions of Strindberg himself. Some of his statements can easily be misinterpreted, particularly if taken out of context. Take, for example, the frequently quoted statement about characters in *Master Olof*:

> As far as the characters go, he [Strindberg] had depicted himself as he wished he were in the man of action (King Gustav Vasa) and his half-shadow the sensible marshal; in Gert as he was in his moments of fervor; and finally in Master Olof as the sort of person he found he was after years of self-examination.

Such statements have helped nourish the myth that the characters in the historical dramas are *merely* lightly disguised versions of himself. The truth is far more clearly expressed in his confession in *Ensam*:

> I live and I live in manifold ways all the lives of the people I depict, am happy with the happy, evil with the evil, good with the good; I creep out of my person and speak through the mouths of children, of women, of old men; I am king and beggar; I am the man at the top and the man most despised of all, the oppressed hater of tyrants; I have all points of view and confess all religions; I live in all periods of time and have ceased to exist myself. This is a state that gives me indescribable joy.

The two statements do not contradict each other, but the second one is a clearcut expression of Strindberg's use of his imagination, a faculty every creative writer must exploit.

Although he has a great deal to say about his idea of human character and the technique of characterization in almost every one of the "open letters," the finest statement of both appears in the preface to *Lady Julie* (1888). There he protests against the tendency on the part of many of his predecessors in dramatic composition to look upon human character as something fixed and set. He suggests instead a concept that he thought Shakespeare had sensed and applied, the concept of what Strindberg calls "the characterless character." Far from implying that the human individual lacks notable traits of moral or intellectual behavior, Strindberg is merely emphasizing that human beings are individuals, that they are not forever the same, that there are all sorts of possibilities of development of the human individual, and that such factors as heredity, environment, time, and chance shape him and continue to shape him. In other words, "characterless character" implies that the human individual (and hence the character in a play) is essentially not a static type but a dynamic and complex living person.

Strindberg insists again and again that, in presenting the historic dead, he had no intention either to elevate them above the human condition or to denigrate them. He had, for example, no particular admiration for Birgitta; in his fairly lengthy discussion of what he had discovered about her in the sources, he says: "Of this unsympathetic woman I made — based on the sources — the unmanageable fool you will find in the drama although in her honor I let her wake up to a clear understanding of her foolishness and pride." And, in presenting his explanation of his Göran Persson: "Göran Persson's history has been written by his enemies; I had to take him as a man of principle, and I have not concealed the evil man's good little qualities, which is the poet's duty when he writes a drama and not a satire or a memorial volume."

Gustav Adolf is Strindberg's only historical drama in which there is an apotheosis, and, even before he ultimately rejected and removed the final scene, he supplied that play with characterization in keeping with his basic principle that the historic dead were as human as modern people are in their varying combinations of degrees of greatness and littleness. For even a folk hero like Gustav Adolf had had his frailties. Without the inclusion of these, too, a modern audience or a modern reader could hardly get what Strindberg wanted to give — a conception of the historic dead that is understandable and interesting, and that gives the modern man the feeling that the heroes and the villains and the people in between are as much creatures of flesh and blood as he is.

Strindberg believed that an effective way to throw light on the central character and some of the others was to let the character be seen in action in his various roles in life. Thus, Gustav Vasa would be much more fully revealed if he appeared not only as a heroic leader but as a husband, a father, a friend, an opponent, a ruler, a man with his own religious faith, the object of hero worship, and an executive. Furthermore, Strindberg believed that a character could be revealed by making use of what Strindberg considered one of his greatest strengths—the use of parallel actions, as in the parallel stories of the royal marriage and that of the Schröderheims in *Gustav III*. What was most important from Strindberg's point of view in the characterization of a central figure was to make it as complete and natural and psychologically sound as possible.

Fundamental to a drama about such a central character were, Strindberg insisted, a simple plot, a limited number of characters, and a language that was not encumbered with excessive imagery. He did not like any element of plot structure that involved intrigue for the sake of intrigue, errors in identity, or the essential confusion of either the story line or the essential mood. He made it quite clear in the open letters that he preferred the clarity of plot which is "a straight line with flourishes"; that the playwright should avoid causing the spectator (or reader) any difficulty in keeping the characters clearly identified; that any dramatist writing a historical drama in his day had to provide exposition and preparation when needed—as much so as if he were writing a realistic or naturalistic play about living people.

Strindberg saw little or no point in making the historic dead speak either in archaic language or in verse in plays designed for modern people. His basic assumption that human beings in the past had the same basic problems, inner conflicts, and interests as modern people, and his understanding of the example of Shakespeare, made him decide that, except on extremely rare occasions when an archaism might serve to give the patina of a remote time, the characters in his historical dramas would speak a modern Swedish not restricted to any one level of style and deliberately suited to the person and the occasion. He also assumed that, since the great ones of the past were human, they spoke in ways parallel to those of human beings in his own time. As he says in various places, he had no intention of avoiding the right word or of indulging in false squeamishness. That he indulged in the use of verse only in one version (that of the *Master Olof* of 1876) of one major historical play is in keeping with this basic assumption. His ideal was to produce dialogue that would be understood, that would be alive, and that would in no way hinder the audience's enjoyment and understanding of the play.

As amazing as anything about Strindberg is his virtuosity in adapting the form of his play to suit his concept of the central character. What he had learned from his predecessors and his inability to be an imitator merely help account for his skill in using a wide range of approach to the problem of constructing plays. *Master Olof*, which is probably the most Shakespearean of all the major dramas, was designed to be structurally "artlessness in art," a combination of strict form and formlessness of the kind Strindberg found in *Hamlet*, for example. Strindberg found variety as well as similarity among his central characters; the striking differences between a crowned actor like Gustav III and a self-confident, dominant Gustav Vasa called, Strindberg believed, for two strikingly different structures, the one somewhat reminiscent of the artificial well-made or Scribean play, the other structurally recalling some of the best realistic plays of the 1880's. Strindberg believed in fitting the form to his concept of the central character, and that is precisely what he did.

It is no coincidence that Strindberg wrote no historical dramas during the period when he tried desperately to accept determinism and its implications. Not only had the historic dead he was particularly interested in lived in periods when faith in a higher being was vital, but for a historical drama in which the tragic experience must be generally significant the setting must be one of a moral order.

One may assume that every writer within any genre owes a debt of gratitude to various predecessors. No other dramatist has more generously acknowledged his literary debts than Strindberg has:

scattered throughout his correspondence, the autobiographical volumes, and the open letters are listings of what he read and generally clear indications of what he gained from his reading. As I have already noted in introductions to preceding letters, his accounts of his reading and study of Shakespeare are particularly important, even though Strindberg knew well the rest of Western drama from the Greeks to his contemporaries. But the influence of his predecessors and his contemporaries on Strindberg's theory and practice has yet to be definitively determined.

Strindberg provided, moreover, a great deal of information about the creative process by which his historical dramas took form. What he has to say in the open letters, supplemented by the unpublished notes and other material now in the manuscript division of the Royal Library, indicates that he planned each major play with great care. The information he gives is such that one can quite safely outline his procedure: reading popular and other histories to refresh his memory, to give him the historical background, and to permit him to arrive at his own understanding of the central character and the figures about him; supplementing from his own experience the information given in his sources about the conflicts, internal and external, with which the characters were involved; determining on a structure that would fit his central character; and reading Walter Scott:

> But in order to "capture a mood and atmosphere" and to move back into a remote time, I did as I usually do in my historical dramas: I read Walter Scott. There was no Earl Birger [in Scott], but there were ingredients, decorations, and stage properties for the Middle Ages, tournaments and inspections of weapons, because Walter Scott was a great antiquarian and *Ivanhoe* is particularly rich in antiquities.

Finally, of course, there was the creative act itself. There he gives one striking bit of information: he began with the last act and then wrote the others, done with remarkable speed in a state he himself could not quite explain, in a sort of delirium or trance of creative activity as he explained:

It begins with a sort of ferment or a kind of pleasant fever, which becomes ecstasy or intoxication. Sometimes it's like a seed that sprouts, attracts all interest to itself, consumes everything ever experienced, but still selects and rejects. Sometimes I believe I am some kind of medium, because the writing goes so easily, half unconsciously, [is] only slightly calculated! But it lasts at most three hours (9–12 o'clock usually). And when it's over, "everything's as dull as usual again!" until next time. But it doesn't come on demand and not when *I* please. When *it* pleases, it comes. But best and most powerfully after big general failures!

The result, he believed, was a work of art, not history in a conventional classroom or academic sense. It is easy to sympathize with his sharply worded defense when one recalls how petty the reviewers and the critics had been about minor details and even about his interpretations of the historic dead:

> Even in the historical drama the purely human is of major interest, and history the background; souls' inner struggles awaken more sympathy than the combat of soldiers or the storming of walls; love and hate, torn family ties, more than treaties and speeches from the throne.
> Whoever believes anything else can try to write a historical drama in absolute keeping with the written records or the Swedish archives; then we shall go and take a look at him if he succeeds in interesting [anyone].

How right he was, was demonstrated in his own lifetime when audiences — according to available accounts — responded with enthusiasm to performances of his plays which leading critics belittled and ridiculed; it has been demonstrated since 1912, too, when not only have the audiences responded enthusiastically but even some of the critics have admitted that several of his major historical plays are highly effective theater, and have largely refrained from pedantic small-minded emphasis on occasional anachronisms or excessive effort to equate each central character with Strindberg himself. [W.J.]

From Some Prefaces to the Historical Plays

Alle Poesie verkehre in Anachronismen. Die Ilias, wie die Odyssee, die sämtlichen Tragiker und was uns von wahrer Poesie übrig geblieben ist, lebt und athmet nur in Anachronismen.

—GOETHE

Master Olof, written in 1871–72, came into being under the influence particularly of Shakespeare's *Julius Caesar*. I had very early been amazed by Shakespeare's manner of depicting in his play one of the greatest men in the world: a hero, a conqueror, a statesman, a lawgiver, a scholar, a historian, and a poet. Caesar was to Shakespeare merely a human being, and as such he is almost a minor character in that bit of world history that has been given the name *Julius Caesar*. The play in Swedish translation covers seventy-nine pages, and Caesar dies on page thirty-eight, that is, in the first scene of Act III. This in spite of all dramatic rules, dramatic economy, and everything that arbitrariness and the whims of the moment have made into rules. How does the greatest dramatist the world has ever had depict the greatest hero, who says about himself:

> . . . danger knows full well
> That Caesar is more dangerous than he. . . .

Caesar appears in only four short scenes. The first is a street scene. Caesar is on his way to the races. He says a few words to his barren wife, telling her to place herself in Antony's way when he runs, and he asks Antony to touch Calpurnia, because:

> . . . for our elders say,
> The barren, touched in this holy chase,
> Shake off their sterile curse.

This is quite simply a husband's desire for children, who would not only make their home life more pleasant but continue the family. Then a soothsayer comes and warns him about the fatal ides of March. Caesar goes away, after one short printed page. In the second scene of Act I he comes back. On one new page, but not more, he expresses to Antony his fears of the strange company he sees about him; he is particularly disturbed by the thin Cassius, whom he considers dangerous. Still, he adds, in his capacity as a hero:

> I rather tell thee what is to be fear'd
> Than what I fear; for always I am Caesar.

This latest addition is more boastful than heroic, but that does not matter:—Caesar lives again!

In the second scene of Act II we find him in his nightclothes in a room next to the bedroom. He has had a bad night: his wife has screamed in her sleep, it is thundering, and now the hero is literally afraid, for he sends a servant to the priests so that they will arrange prophetic sacrifices. Calpurnia, too, comes in in her night apparel. She tells him about various signs as well as a dream and begs Caesar to stay home because something evil will happen at the Capitol the following day. Caesar refuses at first, and continues to refuse when the servant returns from the priests with renewed warnings. Finally he gives in to his wife's pleas.

> Mark Antony shall say I am not well;
> And, for thy humour, I will stay at home.

That's nice of the husband, no doubt, but the hero surely suffers a bit.

Then Decius comes and gives Caesar a flattering interpretation of Calpurnia's dream, and the hero changes his mind immediately, in spite of his firmness of character as stated in world history.

After this bedroom scene Caesar goes out to drink wine and to forget his wife's good advice.

In the first scene of Act III the Capitol can be seen. After yet another warning — in an anonymous letter — and after some blustering talk, Caesar is struck down on page 3 by Brutus. And thereby Caesar is out of the play.

Hagberg calls this play a dramatic masterpiece and one of Shakespeare's most theatrical plays.

A beginner who knows all the answers would naturally criticize Shakespeare for not showing the hero on the battlefields, would from his little mind suggest improvements in the plan such as the introduction of panoramas from the captured citadels of Germania and Gaul; he would eliminate the bedroom scene as belittling for a great man, and above all insist that the writer not permit Caesar to be influenced by other people's whims, pleas, or flattery.

I, on the contrary, in 1870, in my youthful ignorance found Shakespeare's *Julius Caesar*, with its good and bad qualities, with its great and little elements, on the right path in spite of my doubts concerning the hero's weaknesses and the looseness in the dramatic structure. My inborn desire to go beyond what I had learned, to develop and perfect, made me examine and criticize [the play]. I said to myself that for our skeptical and experimental time, with our ideas of human rights and human dignity, it would not do to make any external difference between "better" and "lower" people, so that princes, courtiers, and their equals spoke beautifully in verse, while ordinary people spoke the language of the streets and were ridiculed in comic situations. As a result I cut down the heels on the high-ranking characters and raised those on the lower-ranking a bit.

In that way the manuscript of *Master Olof* was prepared.

*

When I returned after twenty-five years to the historical drama, I did not have to bother with my scruples of 1872 when I wanted to depict historical men and women, so I went back to my dramatic technique from the first *Master Olof*. My purpose was, as it was my teacher Shakespeare's, to depict human beings both in their greatness and their triviality; not to avoid the right word; to let history be the background and to compress historical periods to fit the demands of the theater of our time by avoiding the undramatic form of the chronicle or the narrative.

*

The Saga of the Folkungs.[1] To represent the bloody saga of the Folkungs which very much resembles the War of the Roses in England and the struggles of the Sköldungs in Denmark in the thirteenth century was my object in *The Saga of the Folkungs*. Magnus Eriksson, the last reigning Folkung, who in my schooldays still had an ugly nickname, has been washed clean by more recent historical research. In his textbook Odhner has eliminated the nickname *Smek* and recalled that the Norwegians called him Magnus the Good. He supposedly got the nickname because he let Scania slip out of his hands, even though the king — lacking money or troops — was in no position to defend a country without means of defense against superior enemies. According to all that I can learn from history,

Magnus was really a good man who had learned to bear his fate with humility and for that reason was despised by evil people in an evil age. It was easy for the author to consider him [Magnus] a sacrifice for the guilt of others, which was to place the question on a classical and Christian foundation. And thereby the basic idea of the tragedy was obvious.

*

The indispensable Birgitta belonged to Magnus Eriksson's court, of course. That person, who has lately become a sort of Lutheran saint in Sweden, at least arranged matters so that there are definite accounts of her achievements and her deeds — a woman anxious to rule and to gain honors who consciously strove for canonization and for power over "the other sex." To that end she first tried to get a cloister of her own, not a cloister for women but a joint cloister, in which the men were to be *subordinated* to the women. The cloister rules were those of the Augustinian Order, and Fontévrault's in France served as a model. Nevertheless Birgitta says that her cloister rules "were directly and without exception dictated by Christ, while all preceding monastic rules had been composed by human beings. . . ." She condemned "worldly rulers who avoid the simple word and cause confusion, raise doubts about whether or not men will want to be ruled by an abbess, and cause opposition to the rules." That was directed to King Magnus, who in his capacity as a man did not want to be a woman's underling. For that reason the saint graded him as follows:

1. The vilest conduct. (When his reputation has been destroyed through lies and he has been made to seem infamous, his conduct is vile.) 2. Magnus attended mass although he had been excommunicated. (That Magnus dared to show that he had a more religious spirit when he broke the canonical law;

Birgitta did not dare to.) 3. Robbed the crown of both land and goods. (Absolutely false.) Etc. (See Emil Hildebrand's *The History of Sweden*, in which Magnus is completely acquitted.)

Birgitta was not fortunate in her prophecies. She had advised the war against Russia and had prophesied a sure victory, but when defeat came she became angry with Magnus. Another time she prophesied that the successor to the throne had been born a native within the kingdom. But he was in Mecklenburg, and his name was Albrekt.

She ordered Magnus to make peace between the kings of England and France, to carry on a crusade against Livonia, to convert the Greek Catholics to the Roman faith, and to go to Palestine and capture Jerusalem. He couldn't, of course!

To Avignon she sent Bishop Hemming of Åbo, "who *had to* talk about Birgitta's miraculous gift of grace before Clement VI."

She settled at Alvastra among the Franciscan monks, contrary to the regulations. Master Mathias warned her: "The devil can transform himself into an angel of light."

Birgitta lacked all political understanding when she opposed Håkon's marriage to Margaret [of Denmark]; and she was suspected of trying to get one of her own sons made successor to the throne.

At court she was called a witch because of her maliciousness, and she was often the butt of ridicule when her prophecies failed.

She herself has made the following contributions to her own characterization:

She was often spanked as a child because she was proud. She warns [others] to beware of the sins "which have tempted her more than others." These sins were; "Pride, loose living, vain words, excess in food and drink, joy in living, and frivolity."

(After her husband's death she was advised to remarry.) In Rome she lives in "*galanterie spirituelle*" with the Spaniard Alfons, who got the job of changing her revelations "*ad normam Catholicam.*" (Most likely with an eye to her canonization).

Her temptations in Rome increased to such a degree that she yielded even to going to parties, balls, and hunting.

Of this unsympathetic woman I made — based on the sources — the unmanageable fool you will find in the drama although in her honor I let her wake up to a clear understanding of her foolishness and pride.

*

Since the historians nowadays do not consider themselves able to label Queen Blanche a poisoner, I very carefully let the question remain open. The accusation that she was guilty of adultery is equally not established; for that reason I had to keep that point uncertain.

Finally, a couple of words about the nasty expressions. Disqualified as a witness, I would have had the right — as the accused — to defend myself, but I will let the prosecutors' expert authorities answer for me. Professor Hagberg of the Swedish Academy (!) taught me in my student days never to avoid the right word, even if it is coarse. Hagberg's translation of Shakespeare is not the book to put on the parlor table — at least for those who place parlor literature above all other. Falstaff's language in *Henry IV* is such that the translator feels called upon — not to apologize for himself but to defend the author. "If any reader should be offended by the Falstaff (brothel) scenes as well as the blunt language used in them, I should point out that Shakespeare, far from being the author of reading for children, is rather an author who tests the whole sharpness of a masculine and well-trained judgment. . . ."

In the matter of my *Saga of the Folkungs* the judgment of a certain gentleman seems to have been anything but masculine, and his laments over the nasty words stem from squeamishness or conventional hypocrisy.

In our time, when the Swedish language has been strengthened by our dialects, I did not consider it unsuitable to use strong words, current and well known in the spoken language in all circles. So I did not avoid the splendid word *hor* [*whoredom*], a word that our teachers — through the catechism — teach the pure lips of children to pronounce in the early grades.[2]

The other coarse words are taken from contemporary speech and are therefore justified.

*

Engelbrekt is one of Sweden's most beautiful memories, and I felt I should keep his character as high and as pure as Schiller had kept his William Tell. Johannes Magnus says that he [Engelbrekt] was illegitimate. I disregarded that, since it did not concern me and since there still are people who consider illegitimacy disgraceful to the child. I even had a vague memory of a statement in *The Foreign Archives* [*Utländskt Arkiv*] about an illicit love affair that supposedly played a part in Engelbrekt's life. I disregarded that, too, because it did not interest me!

Since I begin with the last act in constructing a drama, I proceeded from Engelbrekt's murder, which is a fact. History does not make clear the motive for the murder. Engelbrekt had had a quarrel with the murderer's father, but they had been reconciled. Since no one knows what the quarrel was about, I had the right to make Måns Natt-och-Dag the envious man in whose way Engelbrekt was unfortunate enough to get. It certainly is true that ingratitude is often, though not always, the reward of the world, of course, but a person probably does not have the right to toss out one-sidedly such a comfortless and half-true idea, so I tried to give the great man something of an appearance of tragic guilt. In the manner of the Greek tragedies, I took the liberty of foisting upon him the very human sin that almost regularly follows great success, that is arrogance, *hubris*, which the gods hate above everything else. When the hero has, then, come as far as the election of a regent and considers himself the obvious and only possibility, it is not at all strange that he becomes emotionally intoxicated, particularly since he is ill enough to run a temperature. And, in the intoxication of victory, he sees the prospect of both the royal crown and the power — the power to oppress enemies, to trample under foot, to humiliate. Then come his reverses, when he is rejected in the election, and everything collapses!

This final scene is tragic and could be called Swedenborgian. My *Engelbrekt* is a tragedy, and as such it should be judged, without regard to the latest fashions in literary journals.

But strong inner conflicts also belong to tragedy. The first conflict is that he had made the idea of the union one of his youthful ideals and has made his son accept it as well. When he now like the prophet Jonah does not want to step forward to prophesy, a man is sent to him, and that man takes him by the ears and pulls him forward. That is Erik Puke. But now the hero stands between the vow of his youth and his oppressed country. He finally breaks his vow, comes into disharmony with himself, and goes to pieces when his own son, representing his former "I," rises against him as he is *now* imbued with a new ideal. That is tragic conflict.

But, to increase the suspense, I had to introduce still more intimate conflicts, so I let him suffer in his marriage all the horrors of disunity. And since no one knows with whom Engelbrekt was married, I had the right to make his wife a Dane, which I thought was a very fine device for making the disunity concrete.

When Engelbrekt is forced to imprison his own son, the tragedy has reached its highest point. That is Brutus the Elder, but with a plus, since the Swedish Brutus thereby passes judgment on himself as having deserted the idea of his youth, but for a higher goal, one more than equally justified for the time being.

The tragedy therefore has no points of contact with Blanche's play, which was based on inadequate knowledge. Since 1846 new information about Erik XIII has appeared, and Erslev in his study *Erik of Pomerania* (1901) presents three motives for the Swedes' dissatisfaction with the Danish union king, who was not so bad as he has been pictured. First is emphasized Erik's unforgivable way of forcing bad bishops upon the Swedes. Then he is accused, and rightly so, of using and ruining Swedish servicemen in the pointless war against Slesvig.

Last comes the matter of the bailiffs. The king had accepted complaints and removed Danish bailiffs, but, when complaints continued against the Swedish bailiffs, he got weary and did not find time to straighten out that matter. Since he was least defendable on the matter of bishops, I made that the major item, and I was right.

When they murdered *my Engelbrekt* during the fall of 1901,[3] they seemed to have been led by the same stupid motive that Måns Natt-och-Dag had when he murdered his. I have forgiven that crime, but I have not forgotten it!

*

The destiny of Gustav Vasa begins like a legend or a miracle story, develops into an epic, and is impossible to survey completely. To get this gigantic saga into one drama is impossible, of course. Therefore the only answer was to find an episode. That was the one centering in the rebellion led by Dacke. The king was then in his second marriage with children by two wives, and at the height of his power. But Providence wanted to test him and temper its man, to whom the building of the kingdom was entrusted, and for that reason it [Providence] struck him with all the misfortunes of Job. That time of despair gives one the best opportunity to depict the great human being Gustav Vasa with all his human weaknesses.

Academically trained people, born during a time when memorial volumes were the only form in which to write history, have found that I reduced the stature of our greatest historical character. May they answer for that! The future will judge between them and me.

As far as the technique in the play goes, I do not need these gentlemen's judgment. The actors and I have tested it sufficiently with the curtain raised, and it passed the test.

*

Erik XIV. A characterization of a characterless human being: that is my *Erik XIV.* Certain critics speaking in terms of the past miss having the murders committed on stage. We others and the actors, who do not like to look at slaughters, were more pleased by my discreet arrangement, but one cannot argue about taste, of course.

I have made Karin Månsdotter better than she was, because Karin was not so angelic, according to [Karin's biographer] Ahlqvist's discoveries. But that's not to be wondered at, either.

Göran Persson's history has been written by his enemies; I had to take him as a man of principle, and I have not concealed the evil man's good little qualities, which is the poet's duty when he writes a drama and not a satire or a memorial volume.

That the Stures were not absolutely blameless in their relationship with the Vasas has been proved. For that reason I have hinted at their relative guilt as revealed by their sympathy for the traitor John, the king's enemy.

The person who insists on the observation of the chronological order of events in the construction of a historical drama has no idea of what a drama is and should not be permitted to express himself with any claims to being heard. He can learn something about "theater time" in Hagberg's notes in his Shakespeare translation. Fifteen minutes on stage can be grasped as a whole forenoon, for example, and the period between acts can be felt to be many years, depending on the author's skill at concealing dates, which can be done most simply by not mentioning any dates. That is what I have done.

*

Gustav Adolf. A Lutheran saint, who has almost become a school text, had no attraction for me, but then came the tercentennial of 1894 and with it the memorials. In an unpretentious little [booklet] I happened to read that Gustav Adolf, who had begun his career by torturing Catholics (see Cornelius' *Church History*), had finally come so far that he hanged his own men for disturbing a Catholic service in Augsburg (or Regensburg?). Then I saw at once his whole character and the whole drama, and I called it my *Nathan the Wise.*

The blond man with the gentle spirit, who always had a joke on hand even in dark moments, very much a statesman and a little of the musketeer, the dreamer about a universal kingdom, our "Henri Quatre" who likes beautiful women as much as a good battle, half Swedish and half German, with a mother from Holstein and a wife from Brandenburg, related to Pfalz, Prussia, Hesse, Poland, Hungary, Bohemia, and even Austria, sufficiently sinful to be a human being, who has inner conflicts that make a drama rich and interesting. Supplied by Cardinal Richelieu with 400,000 a year on condition that he not disturb the Catholic League, he participates for [over] two years in the Thirty Years' War against the House of Hapsburg and involves himself — as a dramatic character, that is — in unsolvable difficulties since it is a matter of distinguishing friend from enemy, and only his death on the battlefield can restore the harmony and cut the tangled threads.

*

Christina. A woman reared to be a man, fighting for her self-existence against her feminine nature and succumbing to it. The favorites — translated lovers, frankly speaking — but with forebearance for the daughter of the great Gustav Adolf. Stjernhjelm includes among her lovers even Holm, the tailor, but I did not want to do that. Charge that to my credit, *Quiriter*!

Christina was so genuine that she was a woman hater. In her memoirs she says frankly that women should never be permitted to rule. That she did not want to get married I think natural, and that she who had played with love was caught in her own net is, of course, highly dramatic.

*

Gustav III. The enlightened despot, who carries through the French Revolution at home in Sweden — that is to say, crushes the aristocrats with the help of the third estate. That is a paradox that is hard to deal with. And as a character he is full of contradictions, a tragedian who plays comedy in life, a hero and a dancing master, an absolute monarch who is a friend of liberty, a man who strives for humanitarian [reforms], a disciple of Frederick the Great, Joseph II, and Voltaire. Almost sympathetic, he, the Revolutionist, falls at the hand of the Revolutionists. Anckarström [the assassin of Gustav III] was, namely, a man of the Revolution who has had his story written by the Swedish court of appeals [*Svea Hovrätt*].

*

Charles XII, the man who ruined Sweden, the great criminal, the champion fighter, the idol of the ruffians, and the counterfeiter, was the one I was going to present on the stage to my countrymen.

Well, everyone does have motives for his actions, every criminal has the right to defend himself, so I decided to plan my drama as a classical tragedy of fate and catastrophe. The end of a life that was a big mistake. A strong will that struggles against the course of historical development, forgivable because he did not understand what he was doing. Charles XII did not understand that Czar Peter of Russia was right when he wanted to Europeanize his country, just freed from the two-hundred-year domination by the Mongols; he did not understand that Europe needed Russia to defend its borders against the Turks and other Asiatics now that Poland had collapsed of itself. Charles XII is the barbarian when he stirs up the Turks against Czar Peter; he is the betrayer of Europe when he allies himself with Asiatics; Charles XII is a "*gengångare*," a ghost who walks the earth, who is given form by the smoke of powder, and who fades away as soon as the cannons are nailed down, the cannons with which he intended to keep world history from taking its course. Ruined even then by the revelation of his inner disharmonies and awakened doubt, he falls in his struggle against the powers. The problem of the bullet at Fredrikshald has not yet been solved; I let it come from "above," which Swedenborg, Charles XII's last friend, interprets in his elevated fashion, while the public believes it came from the fortress. Let that be as it may. It came when it should — and places the period after the last act of the tragedy.

The other day a fairly well-informed man told me that my *Charles XII* is not a drama, but merely [a series of] scenes. I am going to answer that [charge] in writing now.

My *Charles XII* is a drama of character and catastrophe, the last acts of a long story, and in that it follows somewhat [the model of] the classic tragedies, in which everything has happened, and it even resembles the admired Dovre-dramas [i.e., Ibsen's], which are only the resolutions of dramas that have already taken place. In my *Charles XII* I begin with his return; show in vivid images the miserable condition of the country; present the half-insane despot, who does not condescend to say a word and does not receive the representatives of the four estates. In the second act, he "lies" in Lund doing nothing; is ashamed to return to Stockholm; seeks a war, no matter where, in order to regain his lost honor or — die." The problem becomes then to find an army. The inner conflicts of the tyrant when he seeks support from a well-known adventurer (Görtz), who during his [the king's] absence had tried to dethrone him, are highly dramatic; and at the end of Act II he succumbs to the Tempter, who promises to make gold — out of brass.

In Act III, you see the *results* of the despot's reckless behavior. His victims seek a hearing, but the king is closeted with Görtz, "working." So the drama has gone forward the whole time and thereby fulfills the requirements of drama, for only a drama that stands still is undramatic. But something else happens here, too. Horn and Gyllenborg, the men of the future, the men of the Age of Liberty have—after passive presentation in Act II—entered into active service and being to sketch the perspective. Then something of world significance—historically—happens, symbolized by lowering the flag to half-mast: Louis XIV is dead. This signified the fall of Absolutism—and Charles XII's impending end.

That this act was eliminated [from the production at] the Royal Theater was a big mistake, which thinned out my play, which was intentionally thin to start with, as a drama of catastrophe should be (compare *Antigone*, in which almost nothing happens, but most is narrated).

In the fourth act the suspense is sustained by [watchful] waiting. Waiting for Görtz, who has been away. In the meanwhile Swedenborg and his Emerentia are brought in. This as a contribution to the characterization of Charles XII, for my drama was a drama of character, *too*. Charles XII's relationship with women (the girl and his sister) had to be included, of course.

Görtz returns from his mission. The adventurer was a good financier and a careful one, but Charles XII ruined everything for him because of his own indifference in selecting means. Görtz believed that the country could bear two million emergency coins, but the king on his own released more than twenty million. The kingdom is ruined, and only an honorable suicide remains. So—to Norway! This is dramatic, and it is the end of the act, too!

In the fifth act the bullet (at Fredrikshald) is foreshadowed. The suspense is sustained here, too, by waiting: waiting for the storming or "the bullet."

The little device of the return of the dwarf serves as a reminder of better times and gives the king an opportunity to defend himself, at least from unjust accusations, and he did have human qualities, of course. Horn and Gyllenborg open completely a perspective of a new and better future even if that, too, was to be accompanied by new conflicts. Swedenborg interprets the enigmatic character Charles XII; and, when the shot has been fired, everything is dissolved—and with that the drama itself is over.

The one who has written and had printed that my *Charles XII* is not a drama does not know what a drama of catastrophe and character is; and he has released a false evaluation, which in this case cannot be punished by public law, but ought to be corrected by public opinion.

The Historical Drama

When Schiller wrote *The Maid of Orleans*, he had been a professor of history at Jena for a long time. So we must assume that he knew that Joan of Arc was burned at the stake in Rouen. In his play, as is probably well known, he has his heroine mortally wounded on the battlefield and die in the arms of the French king and the Duke of Burgundy. Contemporary authorities criticized Schiller for having taken such a liberty [with historical fact]; I am convinced that Schiller's janitor when he saw the play was amazed by the poet's "ignorance."

When I saw *The Maid of Orleans* at the Royal Theater, I was neither amazed nor annoyed by the unheard-of liberty the poet had taken. I yielded to illusion and did not think about the stake at Rouen; in a word, that crime against historical truth did not disturb me. The poet undoubtedly felt that a long trial in the fifth act would counteract his poetic purposes, and so clipped the web, though he could have ended the play with [the stage direction], "Joan is taken away as a prisoner by the watch."

When we read Schiller's *Wallenstein*, we did not know that Octavio Piccolomini died childless and that his son Max never existed. The teacher did not say anything, probably did not know anything [about that], so everything was fine. Wallenstein's Thekla never existed as such but is pure fiction, for the daughter of Wallenstein and Isabella Katharina, Countess Harrach, had the name Marie Elisabeth.

Professor Schiller, who wrote the *History of the Thirty Years' War*, must have known that, but it suited his purposes better to present the conflicting pair Max and Thekla, so that is what he did. But requirements have become higher, and I have never committed such an unnecessary crime against historical accuracy when it has concerned universally known matters, since I do not approve of that manner of concocting historical data and facts. Compressing historical events in a remote period I have, however, always permitted myself in keeping with the great models, and still do, for the drama is an art form by means of which I must give illusion and an art form in which everything is illusory, language, dress, time above all. You can read about theater-time as compared to ordinary time in Hagberg's notes on Shakespeare's *Cymbeline*; I do not need to tarry with that, at least not for those who have so much imagination they can see a play in the theater without looking at the clock or the calendar.

To give the illusion of a long time dramatists have used changes of scene and intermissions, a major plot and subplots, and avoiding talking as much as possible about time. All these are elementary matters, which I have always practiced, but the compression of events and the related resultant liberties demand more care so that one does not violate generally known matters but restricts oneself to areas about which people have to go home to consult a book to find the deceptive trick.

When I began to plan and consider the subject of Earl Birger[4] about ten years ago, I discovered immediately that the material was unmanageable. His long life, with his crusades, disappointments, penance, two marriages, and the children who caused him trouble, was suitable for an epic and not for a drama, if I did not break off a piece that had dramatic force.

At first I thought of taking the whole story and using the chronicle style in Shakespeare's way, beginning with the earl's relationship to Erik XI, called the Lisping and the Lame, whose death could have been ascribed to the earl's lack of prejudice as demonstrated later at Herrevad's Bridge where he got rid of the pretenders to the throne in the manner of Richard III. But the story of the murder did not interest me, and I did not want to saddle the earl with any act that was not hinted at in the chronicles. Afterward I thought of beginning with Herrevad's Bridge, but then I would have had to deal with the Finnish Crusade, which was not tempting. As I went ahead, I noticed that the strongest motifs came at the end of his career, and that the motifs of Jutta and Mechtild extended beyond his lifetime. People generally remember 1266 as the year when the earl died, but people have not learned the date of the Jutta scandal by heart, so I took the liberty of moving this motif back and combining it with Valdemar's pilgrimage of penance to Rome and Magnus' regency. But it took me seven years to overcome my misgivings, and during that time I wrote a story as a sketch (in *Nya svenska öden*, "New Swedish Destinies"). But before that I had written *The Saga of the Folkungs*, which was the last act of the War between Brothers. Our Magnus

Folkung became the Christian who goes under before the lack of principle of the pagans, and he arose again recently in Sten Sture the Younger in *The Last of the Knights*.

So I knew what liberties I was taking; I knew what the drama was gaining; and since the Jutta motif strictly interpreted does not belong to history but to memoirs or family traditions, no injury was really done to "royal Swedish history" (as Geijer called his history of the nation).

The earl's unconsidered marriage to Mechtild, the widow of the murderer Abel, is kept out of the big Odhner history, and for good reason, but in a drama it is a major motif. When in my story [mentioned above] I permitted myself to confront the stepmother with his children by his first marriage, I understood that this scene would not do for the theater, and I spared both the earl and the children. In Denmark, Mechtild is considered at least fully aware of the murder of Queen Sophia's father; no one knows if she had taken the vows of the cloister, so I acquitted the earl of having committed a new unpardonable sin: getting married to a nun.

Abel declared on oath that he was innocent of fratricide but was not believed. Ingemann,[5] who was a well-informed man (lector at Sorö Academy) takes it completely for granted that Abel was a murderer, and as such he lives in the memory of the Danish people.

As usual in my historical dramas I have placed Swedish history within the frame of world history; for that reason the fool's listing of the foreign guests and ambassadors is not insignificant, and may not be omitted. The fool is a voluntary slave who glorifies the earl's great achievement as a humane lawgiver, but he is also the *raisonneur*, as in Shakespeare, who says bluntly what all the rest think; he is the People (*vox populi*), too, or the Greek chorus, which comments on the action of the drama, warns, advises. That I have borrowed his collar from Walter Scott's Wamba, since I needed it as an ornament, I have already admitted, and I insist on my right to borrow stage properties, especially out of novels, which are considered part of the common property of drama. The great power of the pope is motivated through the absence of emperors, since there was just then an interregnum after the fall of the last of the Hohenstaufens. The Saracen represents the crusades (St. Louis' last one was under way at the time); the celibacy motive was timely for the church council of Skänninge (1248) had taken place during the first year of the earl's period of power.

And I end the drama with a perspective, or with the beginning of something new: the struggles between brothers which were to go on for a century; so I had to move Magnus' regency back, although this first began when Valdemar set out on his pilgrimage to Rome.

Even in the historical drama the purely human is of major interest, and history the background; souls' inner struggles awaken more sympathy than the combat of soldiers or the storming of walls; love and hate, torn family ties, more than treaties and speeches from the throne.

Whoever believes anything else can try to write a historical drama in absolute keeping with the written records or the Swedish archives; then we shall go and take a look at him if he succeeds in interesting [anyone].

Antony and Cleopatra

Antony is Julius Caesar's friend, the one who made the beautiful funeral oration about him and afterward defeated Brutus and Cassius at Philippi. Octavius Caesar is the man who will become Emperor Augustus. These two and Lepidus have formed the second triumvirate.

Antony is married to Fulvia in her third marriage (first with Clodius Pulcher, second with Curio), but having been sent to the Orient he has been caught in Cleopatra's web, and is now sitting with her like a Hercules with Omphale. Cleopatra, who has been Julius Caesar's mistress, has visited Rome and has plans for dominion over the Romans. So she seeks out Antony in Tarsus and arouses his passions. Cleopatra, member of a collateral branch of the Ptolemies, is a Messalina; she has a lot of bastards about her; and one handbook says she had been married to her brother, the coregent; but I can't verify that.

Now we'll see how Shakespeare depicts this famous woman. The depiction is thorough and seems to have attracted the author, because right away in the first scene of Act I he has Philo, one of Antony's followers, present a portrait [of her]. Philo says she has a golden-brown forehead and calls her a gypsy. He says, "Antony is a whore's court fool." Immediately after that (on page 1) Cleopatra and Antony enter.

Cleopatra is furious. "If it be love, indeed, tell me how much?" She *talks* about love, a fact that can mean it's about over. She reveals her jealousy of Antony's wife by mentioning Fulvia's name five times in this scene. According to some authorities Cleopatra is thirty-six years old, according to others, forty, when the play ends after the battle of Actium (31 B.C.). So she is aging, but Antony is no youngster either — there is gray in his brown hair.

Shakespeare characterizes her by having her always speak in fury, slapping the people about her (exactly as Queen Elizabeth did), kicking servants out, swearing, and cursing (exactly as Queen Elizabeth did). In reality she was charming, witty, gay, imaginative, and gifted (in conversation). As Shakespeare has depicted her, one has to consider her ability to fascinate as something purely sensual; her love for Antony resembles hate, lust, and self-interest; he is the means by which she tries to seize power; but he seems to have some qualities, too, which attract her. He likes to celebrate and is brave and handsome (though one bust makes him resemble the swine Vitellius).

In the second scene of Act I, Cleopatra again comes on stage, raging as usual and still talking about Fulvia, who has started a little war in Antony's absence.* Antony seems to suffer guilt feelings from a permanent hangover: "O, then we bring forth weeds, / When our quick minds lie still. . . ." And: "These strong Egyptian fetters I must break, / Or lose myself in dotage."

Then comes the news that Fulvia is dead. Antony is ready at once to deliver the apotheosis. "There's a great spirit gone!" (She wasn't, of course, but it was nice of him to say so). ". . . She's good, being gone" (Exactly!) And he intends to flee from the temptress, calls on his "hanger-on" Enobarbus and tells him he has decided to leave. Enobarbus first states his ideas of wom-

---

* The Perusine War, which ended with the sacrifice of three hundred distinguished burghers — they were slaughtered on an altar in honor of Julius Caesar. (Compare *Den glada hedendomen* or the "happy" heathendom.) [A.S.] What Strindberg probably had in mind was the notion that the pagan world, unlike the Christian, was an essentially happy world. [W.J.]

an's position in general and shows that he is not an emancipator at least: "Under a compelling occasion, let women die . . . though, between them and a great cause, they should be esteemed nothing." Then he ridicules Cleopatra's peculiarities of conduct: "Cleopatra, catching but the least noise of this, dies instantly; I have seen her die twenty times upon far poorer moment. . . ."

Antony says in a moment of awareness: "She is cunning past man's thought." And immediately afterward: "Would I had never seen her!" And then: "Fulvia is dead." Enobarbus is courageous enough to congratulate him instead of offering his condolences. ". . . Your old smock brings forth a new petticoat," and a widower's tears are called forth just as well by smelling an onion.

Antony sticks to his decision to go home, for the reason, too, that Sextus Pompey is on the move and now controls the seas.

In scene 3 of Act I, Cleopatra enters, raging as usual. "Where is he?" (She does not know that her rival Fulvia is dead.) Charmian, her maid, is sent to "him."

> . . . if you find him sad,
> Say I am dancing; if in mirth, report
> That I am sudden sick. . . .

Charmian advises against this poor method of trying to punish [Cleopatra's] lover:

> Tempt him not so too far; I wish, forbear:
> In time we hate that which we often fear.

Antony comes. Cleopatra tries what is apparently the age-old trick of fainting. And then she brings up his wife Fulvia again. Antony wants to tell her that Fulvia is dead, but he does not get a word in edgewise. Finally he can tell her the news: "Fulvia is dead!"—"Can Fulvia die?" shouts Cleopatra in joy; but, immediately Antony gets a shower of abuse because he is not mourning for his wife, whom Cleopatra has replaced. And he gets an extra salvo for wanting to go home. This whole allegro furioso confirms Antony's decision to leave, and one really congratulates him for this decision, since one has yet to see one charming quality in his mistress that could captivate him or anyone else.

Act I, scene 4. Caesar (Augustus) speaks of the absent Antony as "A man who is the abstract of all faults / That all men follow." Lepidus says a good word [for him] as usual but in vain. But Antony is expected in Pompeii, and Caesar praises Antony as Antony was before Cleopatra got him in her power.

Act I, scene 5. Cleopatra rages because she misses her lover. She knows, though, how badly he talks about her, but she still loves him. "He's speaking now, / or murmuring 'Where's my serpent of old Nile?' / For so he calls me." Then she recalls Julius Caesar and indulges in comparisons, threatens to strike her maid who praises the dead Caesar, and demands writing utensils so she can write to Antony.

Act II, scene 1. Pompey reveals the situation, shows how false the members of the triumvirate are to each other, and how he is counting on their impending disunity.

Scene 2. Caesar is expecting Antony. The latter enters. They start quarreling; Lepidus arbitrates; Enobarbus plays the third opponent or fool. Enobarbus: "Or, if you borrow one another's love for the instant, you may, when you hear no more words of Pompey, return it again." (Iago's philosophy.) Agrippa, Caesar's (Augustus') follower, now proposes the radical solution of having Antony marry Caesar's sister Octavia. The proposal is accepted after some discussion, and now one thinks Antony is "saved."

Enobarbus does have time, though, to give Agrippa a miniature of Cleopatra which shows that her personal charm was such that everything was becoming to her:

> I saw her once
> Hop forty paces through the public street;
> And having lost her breath, she spoke, and panted,
> That she did make defect perfection. . . .

It is a shame one never gets to see this in her role, though. It would be the motivation of Antony's love for this fury.

Octavia, the bride-to-be, is, on the other hand, said by Maecenas to be endowed with "beauty, wisdom, modesty."

Scene 3. Only a few words are exchanged by Antony and Octavia. Antony has reformed: "I have not kept my square; but that to come / Shall all be done by the rule."

A soothsayer tells Antony that Caesar's good luck is greater than Antony's, and that Caesar will win the game. Then Antony is seized by a longing to flee back to Egypt sooner or later.

Scene 5. Cleopatra is in Alexandria being bored; she plays billiards with her eunuch. Then comes the message in which Antony after much circumlocution tells her that he has married Octavia. Cleopatra strikes the messenger, pulls his hair, and finally lifts her dagger. The messenger flees! Cleopatra rages: "Call the slave again: / Though I am mad, I will not bite him."

The messenger returns: Cleopatra regrets that she has belittled Caesar and praised Antony; she wants to faint but does not manage to; insists on knowing the color of Octavia's hair and the like.

One asks how Shakespeare hit upon the idea of always showing the irresistible Cleopatra as jealous. Is it because she has reached a certain age, or is the author punishing [woman] for his own sake?

Scene 6. Menas implies that the marriage of Antony and Octavia was politically motivated.

ENOBARBUS: . . . Octavia is of a holy, cold, and still conversation.
MENAS: Who would not have his wife so?
ENOBARBUS: Not he that himself is not so; which is Mark Antony.
He will to his Egyptian dish again.

So one got to know that.

Scene 7, in which all the heroes, Caesar, Antony, and Pompey, etc., get drunk and dance like fools, seems superfluous to us and probably can be cut completely.

Act III, scene 3. Cleopatra is boisterous in her usual unpleasant fashion, insisting on knowing what Octavia looks like; nothing [else] in particular.

In the following scenes, which are too numerous and too detailed [in taking us] back-and-forth, Antony has finally gone to Egypt, and in Scene 7 he meets his dear fury. Now she is most interested in the war and "as the president of my kingdom, will appear there for a man." But the scene is somewhat loose.

Scene 11, after the battle of Actium, where Antony has fled after Cleopatra. The leaders are lackadaisical; Cleopatra no longer rages but begs for forgiveness. The scene ends with Antony's begging for a kiss and calling for wine and food.

Scene 13. Antony leaves Cleopatra with the information that Caesar will pardon her if she will give up Antony. Cleopatra protests but apparently begins to consider the offer.

Enobarbus plans to desert. Ambassadors from Caesar are well received and without blows from Cleopatra, who seems to have the treachery well in mind. Antony comes back and speaks frankly after his eyes have finally been opened; he sees the ambassador Thyreus kiss Cleopatra's hand, an act which is rather innocent, but probably improper according to Roman notions. Antony: "You were half blasted ere I knew you."

Antony, taking over Cleopatra's tactics, rages; that has the same effect as on the shrew [in *The Taming of the Shrew*]: she submits. Antony says:

> You have been a boggler ever:
> But when we in our viciousness grow hard —
> O misery on't! — the wise gods seal our eyes;
> In our own filth drop our clear judgements; make us
> Adore our errors; laugh at's, while we strut
> To our confusion.

After still another reprimand which Cleopatra accepts submissively, they agree on reconciliation: a midnight feast in Antony's usual style. And now Act III finally ends.

Act IV, scene 2. Antony in Alexandria is sentimental, presumably senses his death, presses his servants' hands, after he has related how Caesar has refused to fight a duel with him. Cleopatra is present but is absent-minded and natural. "Let's to supper, come, / and drown consideration."

Scene 3. Subterranean music is heard by the soldiers, who interpret it to mean that the god Hercules is now deserting Antony just when the latter is going to be set free from his Omphale, in whose company he has actually once sat dressed as a woman.

In Act II, scene 5, Cleopatra says: "That time, — O times! / . . . and next morn, / ere the ninth hour, I drunk him to his bed; / Then put my tires and mantles on him, whilst / I wore his sword Philippan."

Act IV, scene 4. Cleopatra wants to help Antony put on his armor; she is still gentle, but Antony instead rages and leaves, after [giving her] a soldier's kiss.

Scene 5. Antony learns that Enobarbus has fled. He becomes sad and sends his [Enobarbus'] things to him.

Scene 6. Enobarbus suffers from pangs of conscience and wants to commit suicide.

Scene 8. Antony has won a temporary victory under the walls of Alexandria; he meets Cleopatra, still submissive and enigmatic, watching to see what the result will be.

Scene 9. Enobarbus dies suffering from pangs of conscience.

Scene 12. Antony is beside himself because Cleopatra has betrayed him. He curses her, wants to kill her, but forecasts her fate: to be led as a strange barbaric animal in Caesar's procession of victory.

Scene 13. Cleopatra sends a servant to Antony with the false message that she has committed suicide.

Thereby the Romeo-and-Juliet motif (Pyramus and Thisbe) is introduced. In the next scene Antony gets the message, whereupon he tries to kill himself, does not succeed right away but is brought to Cleopatra, in whose arms he draws his last breath.

We have a feeling the drama could end here, and we would have been satisfied with hearing about Cleopatra's decision to kill herself, since we know that from history and we know how she took her life. But Shakespeare adds a whole fifth act in which Cleopatra fools Caesar out of part of the booty of war and commits suicide by means of the serpents, which she buys from a farmer who talks a little nonsense. In keeping with Shakespeare's attractive custom, a few kinds words are said about the two dead — in the last scene.

If the play were to be produced now, it would have to be cut, for we could never stand the long monotonous anecdotes, which in the author's time could be enjoyed when one showed up at 5:30 o'clock and brought one's food and pipe along, and when no changes of scene delayed the progress of the performance. It is Cleopatra who interests us, of course, and her strange love relationship with Antony, if one can call this powerful attraction love. Antony the lover knows who she is, "a serpent of old Nile"; he maligns her out loud, "a morsel cold upon / Dead Caesar's trencher; nay, you were a fragment / Of Cneius Pompey's; besides what hotter hours, / Unregister'd in vulgar fame, you have / Luxuriously pick'd out"; and all the same he "loves" her. He marries Octavia; that does not help. Cleopatra only becomes gentler, and after their reunion the love flames sky high. Cleopatra betrays Antony to the enemy; that makes no difference; he loves her just as much, even more, though in the process he does curse her. Cleopatra pretends to die; Antony follows her into death, hurries to meet her on the Elysian Fields. "I come, my queen: — Eros! — Stay for me: / Where souls do couch on flowers, we'll hand in hand, / And with our sprightly sport make the ghost gaze: / Dido and her Aeneas shall want troops, / And all the haunt be ours."

Cleopatra now wants to follow her Antony. "Noblest of men, woo't die? / Hast thou no care of me? Shall I abide / In this dull world, which in thy absence is / No better than a sty? . . . / The soldier's pole is fallen . . . / And there is nothing left remarkable / Beneath the visiting moon."

This love would be sublime if it were anything but a delusion by way of punishment according to Swedenborg's concept. These two lovers do not like each other, because their most honest feeling is contempt. It seems as if their love were something outside themselves, in which they have no part; for their own feelings are a mixture of will to power, hate, contempt, cruel sensual pleasure, the need to debase [each other], faithlessness, in a word — enmity; and in the midst of the hatred both of them are whipped by the demon fear-of-losing (jealousy). Antony senses this for one waking moment (Act III, scene 13), senses that they are the prey of a delusion that is forced upon them. "But when we in our viciousness grow hard—/ O misery on't!—the wise gods seal our eyes;/ In our own filth drop our clear judgments; make us / Adore our errors; laugh at's, while we strut / To our confusion."

They long for each other, but when they meet they argue, are dejected, defile each other, and Cleopatra always suffers from a mania for committing suicide, which her very presence transfers to Antony.

This is what Swedenborg calls infernal or hellish love, which borrows forms of heavenly love but is its direct opposite.

Cleopatra's role is not easy. In the first acts she is unattractive in her jealousy and her raging; afterward, when she becomes gentle, she gets out of her role, gets to be a listener and becomes secondary; is somewhat neglected, one could say. In the last acts she raises herself, arouses sympathy even when she lies, and cheats Caesar out of the booty. In the death scene she is moving. "Peace, peace! / Dost thou not see my baby at my breast, / That sucks the nurse asleep?" (The serpent.) — "Downy windows close." (Her eyelashes.) — "Your crown's awry; / I'll mend it, and then play." (These are her last words.)

Caesar's funeral oration is diplomatic, but humane. "High events as these / Strike those that make them: and their story is / No less in pity than his glory which / Brought them to be lamented."

The composition is simple, clear; a straight line with flourishes; no *qui pro quo*, no sources of confusion or clash of tones. In its time it was not too circumstantial, but it is for us. There are many unfinished intentions: Antony's decision to desert Octavia, which is postponed; his decision to kill Cleopatra after her betrayal [of him]; the postponement of Cleopatra's suicide to the last moment possible; her postponed betrayal; and the eternal reunions. Antony's little victory *after* Actium retards the action, too, but provides retrospects with good effect, in which Antony may appear once more in all his glory before he falls.

Aside from the lovers the most interesting character is Enobarbus. His enlightened skepticism is good for the audience, but this addiction to doubt causes his desertion to the enemy; faithful by nature, he cannot bear his new role of traitor and goes under because of his inner disharmony. But there is a Christian quality in Enobarbus when he alone sees through and disapproves of the immorality practiced. It is, you see, the last act of heathendom which is being played; Herod's name is mentioned three times, and it was during the reign of Emperor Augustus that Christ was born. The pagan gods are suspect and are openly maligned. Cleopatra says that

> . . . I hear him mock
> The luck of Caesar, which the gods give men
> To excuse their after wrath. . . .

And in another place:

> . . . It were for me
> To throw my sceptre at the injurious gods. . . .

Everything in the drama concerns ambition, the desire for power, faithlessness, deception, all of which everyone but Enobarbus finds natural. He is the one who scourges [the rest] and plays the enlightened fool who says what is true.

When he has fled from Antony and the latter sends him his belongings (which can be irony, however), Enobarbus is so overcome by the noble act he is ashamed to the point of death!

Octavia also belongs to a school of philosophy different from the pagan. She prays to the gods for her unfaithful husband. And, whenever Antony comes into her presence, he becomes a better human being. Does he love her? Yes, he loves both [women]; the text says so.

Shakespeare won't do for reading; one cannot "read" him with pleasure, but has to work hard with him. The slightest lack of close attention, and one loses everything. So many people find him dull, because he requires effort, as a novel* does not. *Antony and Cleopatra* is heavy, because one has to know thirty-four characters and their family trees. But it is not tiresome to the point of giving one a headache as the comedies with their complications, disguises, and errors are.

Richard II

Shakespeare won't do for reading, and one has to plod through the first acts of *Richard II* as if one were preparing for an examination. One has to know a lot ahead of time to follow the action, and one has to memorize the many names of the same character. When, for example, on page 1 Hagberg says *Bol.*, this first means Bolingbroke, then Henry, later Hereford; but one ought to know, too, that Bolingbroke belongs to the House of Lancaster, that he is the son of Gaunt, who is Richard II's paternal uncle. But one should also have clearly in mind that *Bol.* later becomes Henry IV, whose son is Henry V, Falstaff's boon companion in taverns and on highways; and a Swedish reader can take pleasure in recalling that Engelbrekt's Queen Philippa is the daughter of *Bol.* or Henry IV.†

Richard II can hardly interest Swedish readers really, for

---

* I except by way of example, however, Jean Paul's *Titan*, which requires taking notes, mostly because the author gives so many names to the same character. [A.S.]

†When the play opens Philippa is five years old (born, 1393 [?]) and was married to Erik XIII in 1406 (at the age of 13?). Gloucester and Bedford in *Henry V* are Philippa's brothers. [A.S.]

there is too much English history in it, and the purely human elements in it are too detailed for us; there is too much talking about characters instead of revealing them in action; and I suspect the play has to be seen, but only after a thorough reading.

Richard is somewhat like Hamlet, weak and strong, frivolous and emotional, occasionally sentimental; but the year before he had overthrown the regents and made himself absolute monarch, and probably had murdered Gloucester. (Bolingbroke does insist that Mowbray did that, however.)

Goethe's Faust

When I use the word *Faust* I mean both the first and second parts. As a Teuton the first part appeals to me most, like the cathedral of Cologne; the second part is [like] the Madeleine Church or a Greek temple, not unpleasant for me but somewhat cold and foreign. But both make up *one* work. They are sixty years of Goethe's eighty-year span of life: his autobiography, his daybook, transformed into an artistic form.

About 1770 Goethe saw a marionette play in Strasbourg about the Faust legend,* and that was the seed from which grew man's greatest poem. He began writing in 1774; the *Faust* fragments were printed in 1790; in 1797 appeared *Zueignung: Ihr naht Euch wieder schwankende Gestalten*, as well as the Prologue in Heaven; the first part was printed in 1806. But "Helena" of Part II had been written in 1780 and was printed in 1827. The

---

* Faint traces of this puppet show are traceable in [the show] at the Casper Theater at Djurgården [Stockholm] as late as the 1870's. (See my *Gamla Stockholm*.) [A.S.]

second part was completed in 1831, but first appeared in print after Goethe's death (1832).

Anyone who wants to get to know *Faust* has to make a special effort. If he does not know the German language, he will have to learn it, but *Faust* was studied at Klara School [in Stockholm] in the 1860's, from which fact I conclude that the text is known to everyone, particularly since it is not so difficult as people have imagined. The best and least expensive edition is Hempel's (*Klassiker-Bibliothek*), 1 mark and 75 pfennigs for the whole work, with excellent footnotes on every page, clarifying every difficulty and even pointing out the places where Goethe has learned from our Swedenborg. Besides, the edition has two long introductions presenting the background and history, an explanation of the idea of the poem, contemporary judgments, and the like. Anyone who wants to know more can read Boyesen's *Kommentar* [6] (Reclams Universalbibliotek 1521, 1522; 80 pfennigs).

Goethe's *Faust* cannot be translated, should not be translated, because Goethe was extremely musical, and his German language has never been so beautiful in its melody except in Heine (and perhaps Rückert). Any translation [of *Faust*] is destructive when it is not undertaken by a poet with song in his heart and an ear for melody. For example, when one has learned these melodies in childhood:

> *Ihr naht Euch wieder schwankende Gestalten,*
> *die früh sich einst dem trüben Blick gezeigt.*
> *Versuch ich wohl Euch diesmal festanhalten?*
> *Fühl ich mein Herz noch jenem Wahn geneigt?*

and then reads Andersson's [7] [Swedish] translation, it seems like a travesty:

> *Nu nalkas åter, lätta bilders skara!*
> *Som tidigt svävat för min dunkla syn.*

Ej denna gång jag låter eder fara,
I tan mitt hjärta med er när I flyn!

In the first place it seems like a violation of the text to hear words other than precisely *"Ihr naht Euch wieder"*; in the second place the rhythm is distorted by the many two-syllable words: *nalkas, lätta, bilders, skara, tidigt, svävat, dunkla, denna, låter, eder, fara, hjärta.* All these trochees do not belong in the ottava rima which is iambic! In the third place, the very beginning *"Nu nalkas"* is ugly with its two *n*'s. Goethe has the trisyllabic *schwankende* and *Gestalten* and the four-syllable *festanhalten.* Furthermore: *"Ej denna gång jag låter eder fara"* is an empty, hollow, and flat verse.

Rydberg,[8] who lacks Andersson's ability to take over Goethe's realistic everyday speech, is still worse. Rydberg is affected, labored, prosaic, academic—where he wants to elevate and improve Goethe's simple easy style, and he [Rydberg] lacks all sense of melody. In the first stanza he has this line (which a secondary-school pupil would have corrected):

Och för den trollfläkt, som omkring er svävar. . . .

"Som omkring" is certainly an unforgivable novice's error. The second stanza in which he was going to operate with alliteration is also a failure:

Se, glada dagars bilder med er draga.

"Glada, dagar, draga!" Why, it's horrible.

Min levnads labyrintiskt vilsna lopp
is heavy!

Bland dem jag fordom sjöng för, ack! hur mången,

"Sjöng för" is low! without being easy.

Den krets, som vänskap slog om sången, sprängd.
Nu gör mig även bifall rädd, när sången. . . .

Is it a slip of the pen that *sången* appears twice, the one right after the other without rhyming as *Orientaler,* as Goethe and Rückert have fun doing?

> *Nu griper mig en länge fjärmad trånad.* . . .

"*En fjärmad trånad*"! What's that? Or in Part II this (miserable) verse! Listen!

> *När sig över alla sänker*

(Why, the man doesn't have the slightest sense for song!)

> *När sig över alla sänker*
> *vårligt regn av doft och blom,*
> *när för varje dödlig blänker*
> *fältets gröna rikedom;*
> *då har alven brått, den lille,*
> *stor i andens kraft och mod,*
> *var han kan, han hjälpa ville*
> *ömmande för ond och god.*

"*När sig över alla*" is terrible! "*Stor i andens kraft och mod*" is *loci communes,* an empty phrase." "*Var han kan, han . . .*" is miserable, ugly, flat, ignorant!

Listen to Goethe's music, with which Ariel opens Part II:

> *Wenn der Blüthen Frühlingsregen*
> *ueber alle schwebend sinkt,*
> *wenn der Felder grüner Segen*
> *allen Erdgebornen blinkt:*
> *Kleiner Elfen Geistergrösse*
> *eilet, wo sie helfen kann;*
> *ob er heilig, ob er böse*
> *jammert sie der Unglücksmann.*

H. H. Melin's translation [9] is much better than Rydberg's.

> *När om våren blomregn flöda*
> *över allas huvud ner,*
> *när de rika fältens gröda*

emot jordebarnen ler,
älvor små, högsinnad skara,
skynda dit, där hjälpas kan,
helig eller ond — må vara!
Ont dem gör om olycksman.

That is much better than Rydberg's! But there are educated
Swedes who *believe* that Rydberg has translated the second
part of *Faust*; the other day I listened to a cultivated theater
director who believed that. And just the same the late-lamented
great man [Rydberg] has translated only 23 of the 244 pages
of Part II (Hempel's edition). On the other hand, a great director did not know that H. M. Melin has translated all of Part
II into Swedish, and done a much better job than Rydberg. The
quotations cited above (*"När sig över alla sänker"* and *"Var
han kan, han"*) demonstrate Melin's superiority plainly.

But the one is taken up, the other is left behind. When the
whole *Faust* had already been translated into Swedish and the
translation printed (Part I, 1853; Part II, 1872), one wonders
what Rydberg intended with his? When Andersson's translation was reviewed in its day, it was judged good, very. I have
not compared it with the original, but it flows and is musical;
there is Goethe in it — in a word *song*. Rydberg's, on the other
hand, is plodding, dull, abstract as an isolated philosopher, in-
tangible, unsingable — in a word, bad.

I have pointed out two merits in Andersson's translation: I
believe it is impossible to find a perfect translation. Nor is Andersson's perfect, but compared to Rydberg's it's good.

The famous lines from the Prologue at the Theater which
can be read on the [façade of] Neues Theater in Berlin, resound
like this in German so that one never forgets them:

Wie machen wir's, das alles frisch und neu
und mit Bedeutung auch gefällig sei.

Now listen how the great V. R. [Rydberg] has mutilated our language:

> *Hur laga då, att allt är nytt och kan*
> *på samma gång ha värde och slå an?*

Eight monosyllabic words in a row, and then using the auxiliary verb *kan* as rhyme (*kunna* is here the auxiliary verb for *ha värde* and *slå an!*).

Or:

> *"Es war ein König in Thule"*
> *Det var i Thule en konung*

(Better: *Det var en konung i Thule.*)

> *så trogen till sin grav:*
> *Hans döende käresta honom* (*honom!*)
> *en gyllne bägare gav.*
> *Han skattar ej något däröver* (terrible!)
>
> . . . .
>
> *Så voro hans år förrunna:*
> *Sitt rike med städers tal* (affected!)

Or Margaret by the jewel case:

> *Hur kom det vackra skrinet hit? Ja hur?*
> *Mitt skåp var läst (låst) och nyckeln därutur* (*var ur*)
> *så underligt!* (Flat!)
>
> . . . .
>
> *Såg du väl nånsin maken, då?* (Low!)

Or Margaret:

> *Är varken fröken eller skön.*
> *Hem kan jag oledsagad gå!* (Heavy!)

When one turns to *Faust* to enjoy it, one should do so with good will, come with open arms to receive something good, and not with a critical and negative attitude, because then one will get nothing. And, as evidence for how skepticism can distort one's vision, I want to cite this. Even learned people used to talk about the formlessness of Part II compared to that of Part I, which is supposed to be more unified and better composed. Actually, the opposite is the truth. Part I has no division into acts, but the play runs on without apology through twenty-six scenes. Part II, on the other hand, is divided into five acts and has in all only eighteen scenes. So the criticism is unjustified.

I assume Part I is well known, but how anyone can be satisfied with Part I alone as a work complete in itself I cannot understand. If Part I were to be judged from the point of view of our time as a complete play, the summary would be like this. The philosopher Faust has wasted his life speculating and is now an old man. The devil appears and shows Faust that all learning and philosophy are nonsense! A pact is made; Faust regains his youth, falls in love with a girl, seduces and then deserts her; he kills her brother. By mistake the girl kills her mother by means of a sleeping potion and in despair drowns her child; she is imprisoned and condemned to death. With the help of the Devil, Faust wants to free her from prison, but the unfortunate woman prefers to attain reconciliation [forgiveness] through punishment. She stays; Faust leaves with the Devil. End!

From a vulgar point of view, this is a robber story, a picaresque tale, and the Faust legend ends in a criminal trial without development, without conclusion.

For that reason we shall look through Part II briefly and see if it is so incomprehensible.

After a restful sleep out of doors Faust is brought to the emperor's court. That means he is now to be tempted by Power and Riches, for the whole thing is a test as stated in the Prologue in Heaven, where Faust almost becomes a Job, where even the setting comes from the Book of Job. After dearly bought experi-

ences at court among statesmen and fools, Faust is returned to
Wagner's laboratory where a Homunculus is prepared, an abstraction of man, about whose significance one can read in the
footnotes and commentary. Then follows the classic Walpurgis
Night. In Act III Helena appears, and she and Faust become
parents of the child Euphorion. This signifies that Faust's spirit
through union with the classical period has "won the power of
viewing in pure beauty, the result of which is that thereafter
he is able to lift himself above the commonplace." In the fourth
act Faust finally goes out into practical life, and Mephistopheles,
who in Part I was a witty commentator, has become the tempter
and the powerful representative of Evil. He tempts Faust with
power over a great and glorious city. But Faust does not yield:
he wants to perform great and useful deeds; and he then plans
to drain a country threatened by encroachment of the sea. He
is to get the shores from the emperor if he helps the latter in a
war. He succeeds very well in this, too.

In Act V Faust is in his new home on the new land, and his
ships are busy carrying on commerce with foreign nations.

But there is a little area he does not own; and, since Faust can
never be satisfied, he is gripped by an impure desire for the little
spot of land where old Philemon and Baucis live. Mephistopheles, who can read people's thoughts and desires, arrives and
sets fire to the old people's hut. By way of punishment Faust
becomes blind but continues his work. One marsh remains to
be drained, and the creatures (Lemurs) procured by Mephistopheles come to dig. But it is Faust's grave they are really dig-
ging. Through his tireless and useful striving for humanity he
has been reconciled with life; he now must leave it; and he dies.
Evil and good powers struggle for his earthly body and then
for his soul, which the victorious angels carry away after
Gretchen has made her plea.

All this is not incomprehensible, of course, and in a footnote on the [appropriate] page one finds out the significance of the many allegorical figures. There are not any enigmatic profundities either, for with a little effort one discovers reflections from the dominant and successive views of the world through which Goethe had wandered: Rousseau's religion of nature, Spinoza's pantheism, Kant's critique; and in Mephistopheles one detects the grin of the Voltaire ape.

So *Faust* is both Part I and Part II, and playing Part I only is to mutilate the play. But Part I has also become so well known and vulgarized through Gounod's opera that it does not attract one to the theater when one knows everything ahead of time.

I have seen Josephson's production of Part I at the Swedish Theater. We sat there from seven until twelve (as I remember it). It was interesting to see it once, but I don't want to see *Faust* again.

All this philosophy of the whole world, which rushes by one's ear without getting time to penetrate and be understood made me weary and intellectually uncomfortable; besides, Faust did not become Faust, and Mephistopheles was not what he should have been. Briefly put: I wondered if this play could be produced and if it should be. When one has sacrificed five hours and does not get beyond the Gretchen episode, one begins to doubt the possibility of seeing all of *Faust*. In his *Mephistopheles*, Boïto[10] has settled the matter by courageously cutting the whole of Faust; and the continuation with the classical Walpurgis Night, Helena, and the Reconciliation has a soothing effect.

Both parts have been played in Germany — as festival productions, however, on two consecutive days. The first day Part I was given twice, 3–6 and 8–11 o'clock; the second day Part II twice, 3–6 and 8–11. But Karl Weiser did cut Part II so that only 111 of the 244 octavo pages remained. Weingarten[11] had composed music [for the occasion], and the productions seemed something like an opera with its ballet and choruses and luxurious scenery, it is said.

Two years ago Director Ranft asked me to try to adapt both parts of *Faust* for a two-evening production. But after two days' mutilation of the text I gave up the project feeling quite ashamed of myself. It was as if I had wanted to restore the cathedral of Cologne. What I had cut was just as interesting and important as what I had not cut.

After Goethe had had to listen to and read stupid critics' comments on his *Faust*, he was ultimately persuaded it was a failure, and he called it a torso.

Fine! A torso, then, that would not gain by being produced, that was never intended to be produced, and that, if produced should have the effect of completion. But what is complete is final; the incomplete seems unfinished, since it leaves one's imagination still active.

A work of art such as *Faust* should be accepted as a fact, as it is, or as a product of nature. Here is an oak forest; the trees are not rooted properly! Fine! So much the better! A branch is missing here! So much the more beautiful! The top is broken off there! So much the more picturesque! The forester would have much to criticize, but that does not concern us; the man who marks the trees would no doubt find the wood deficient, but that is not our point of view.

When one has — as I have — rushed back and forth (with a blue pencil in hand) in the primeval forest called *Faust*, he will not want to touch it [that is, cut it], but would rather leave it unproduced. Here are scenes, but no theater; and I go so far as to assert that producing it would be desecration.

I advised Director Ranft not to produce it, particularly when I heard that the Royal Theater was considering doing so.

If one should consider the production of *Faust* as part of the education of the young people, and be forced to give it, one would first have to plan to save as much of the text as possible. This can be done only by limiting the scenery, because every change of set represents a cut.

Years ago (1840?) there was a way in which all of *Faust* was produced; I think it was Devrients.'* His point of departure was based on the assumption that audiences wanted to see Faust's study, Margaret's room, the well, Blocksberg, etc., but in order to save the text he hit upon scenery that would not be changed but would be used for all scenes. For that reason he constructed on the stage floor a tabernacle resembling a triptych (in French *retable*), which with its three levels imitated the medieval mystery stage: Heaven, Earth, Hell (*das Loch*). Thus he could present the prologue in Heaven on the highest level. In the wings of the triptych he had Faust's study and Margaret's room; in the middle was a frame called the Bridge; the Blocksberg was shown figuratively, etc. Thereby he had gained: a medieval mood, tranquility on the stage, and, above all, had saved the text; but delighted the eye as well.

That is the Easter setting in the Oberammergau play, against which nothing can be said! So: it does go.

Twenty years ago (in the Preface to *Lady Julie*) naturalistic taste, adapted to the materialistic objectives of the time, strove for realistic accuracy. The German theater carried the matter furthest by means of the *Drehbühne*, the stage set up like a windmill, on which in three rotating parts the scenery was successively presented so that intermissions would not infringe on the text. But at the end of the century the public taste changed; the imaginative became active, the material gave way to the imma-

---

*I may be wrong as I am writing from memory since I lost my notes during the latest "earthquake." [A.S.]

terial, the spoken word became the major thing on the stage, and after the Kleines Theater in Berlin had taken the edge off the movement, the *Drehbühne* disappeared as it had come. At the same time something new appeared, but this time in France, where Josephin Péladan's tragedies began to be presented in old Roman amphitheaters in the open air, without scenery. This idea of the open-air theater adopted in Germany (Darmstadt, Harz) and England was the stimulus for the simplification of staging which we now have among us.

The Shakespeare stage in Munich had prepared the matter, but came too early and went under in the naturalistic wave; the revival of Oberammergau helped bring simplified staging into being. Now during a period of artificiality people had the right to get back simplification. The open-air theater demonstrated that plays could be produced without scenery.

I admit that even in the theater it is fun to look at pictures, to have one's eye refreshed with a new background every time the curtain goes up; but that sort of thing is not always suitable, and, if pleasure is to be provided at the expense of the drama, then let scenery go.

When until 1880 they played with open wings, changing scenery was quite easy. But when people began "to build" on the stage, then they had the carpenter's shop on stage, and the long intermissions between acts became a damnable nuisance, which frightened the public away from the theaters. These intermissions, however, got into an intimate connection with arrangements for selling liquor. A practical age had discovered that the restaurant keeper could pay the whole rent for the theater if he were only guaranteed that the intermissions would be long enough. The director managed these "punch" or liquid-refreshment interludes; and, when there were no intermissions provided for in the drama, he simply inserted them. It went so far that plays were amputated, and certain plays were more readily accepted. Yes, people began to detect a new style for theatrical pieces, and there was talk about a new dramatic form, called refreshment drama. The strong temperance movement made its silent counterattack, and those who did not want to imbibe but had to wait while the others did stayed away from the theaters. (In that you can find one contributing cause of our theater crisis!)

Even if it is fun to see beautiful scenery, it represents wasted effort considering the short while it is seen, and listening to what is said and observing the play of the actors' features is so taxing that one does not get time to look at pictures. For example: I happened not to see the production of my *The Crown Bride*. I asked several people who had attended the première and later performances as well: Did the church rise from the lake? — The answer: from all of them: I didn't see that! — I should say that I had expected a beautiful effect at the end of the play from the rising of the church out of the lake on Easter morning with its gilded church rooster appearing first. And no one had noticed it! In Helsingfors the stage machinery failed to work, and the church did not appear, but no one missed it, although the play had been published and read. When a person is to see on the actors' faces what they are expressing, there is really not time to look at the scenery. They say the public wants it and will not come if it does not get it. People demand scenery in an opera or an operetta, but they do not insist on it in a stage play. We have given [my] *Easter* over two hundred times, in a miserable room that reveals its shabbiness and that I am not happy about; but I do not believe we would have had more performances if we had had curtains, door hangings, and a Brussels carpet.

Another proof that a careful, detailed stage design can be

wasted effort is that sometimes a theater is praised because of junk, and sometimes even the best staging is criticized. When Ludvig Josephson staged [my] *Lucky Peter's Journey* at the Swedish Theater about 1882, he got so much praise he was ashamed. He smiled in his black beard when I came home [from abroad] and admitted that most of it was merely patched-up old stuff "But that's how it is," he added; "sometimes one gets scolded when it's really good!" I saw his staging later, and it was not anything to cheer about.

Molander was always praised, and he did create excellent mood effects when he could construct on stage; but he had to have unrestricted power to buy [what he needed]. Director Ranft feared him because he had to spend money freely and requisitioned as if he were a secretary of defense levying forced contributions in wartime. The Hanseatic office and the Blue Dove in *Gustav Vasa* were real museum sets, probably à la Düsseldorf. They were beautiful, but they would not have had to be so expensive to go.

Grandinson's sets for *To Damascus* were beautiful. The play could never have been given if we had not gone in for simplification. Composed in strict contrapuntal form, the first part [of the trilogy], the one that was produced, consists of seventeen tableaux. But allegorizing the pilgrimage the drama marches on until the ninth tableau — the Asylum scene; then the exiled couple turns back and has to return wearily, so the scenery is reversed to make the drama end at the street corner, where it started. In order to do this quickly, a smaller stage was constructed on stage, contained in an unusually attractive arch painted by Grabow.[12] Sides were needed, but we played against backgrounds which, hung up one behind the other, were raised by a silent pulley. Instead of unnecessary lowerings of the curtain the stage was darked out. I believe the innovation, somewhat varied, was used in the production of *King Lear*.

About Falck's still more radical attempt with the use of the drapery stage I have written earlier, and I just want to add that I have not found any reason to change my mind since I said that the attempt was absolutely successful.

Falck is now preparing the production of *A Dream Play* with the same drapery arrangement, which gives me a reason for expanding on that a little and to prepare for the revival.

When Director Castegren [13] had succeeded in getting the play accepted at the Swedish Theater, we began to discuss means of transforming the dream into visual representations without materializing it too much. The sciopticon was first used. We had already tried that in the production of *To Damascus* at the Royal Theater. Sven Scholander [14] actually projected a backdrop sufficiently large and clear, but, since it had to be kept dark in front of the backdrop so that it would show up, the actors could be seen less clearly. Another disadvantage was that the electric light showed through the fabric, but this could be improved by placing the lights below the level of the stage floor. That was too low, and we wearied. But I think, on the basis of my own experiments, that if one uses different types of lighting the sciopticon backdrop can be used. For example, if one has violet in the lamp behind the drop, and illuminates the figures in front of it by means of the red light of the incandescent lamp or the white of the Auerburner, it should be possible to illuminate the figures while the drop is visible.

In the text I stated about *A Dream Play* that it should be played with standing sides of "stylized wall paintings that would at the same time serve for room architecture and landscape." I assumed: changing of the backdrop as needed. Castegren went to Dresden where they had previously used the sciopticon for *Faust*. There he bought the apparatus, but in the tests here at home (which I never got to see, however) it did not measure up to what had been promised. When Director Ranft did not want to use the *Damascus* system of arch and backdrops, the only thing left to do was to "go to Grabow."

Castegren, who had ruined himself in Göteborg because of his good taste and excellent repertory, now applied his whole gift for inventiveness and energy to get *A Dream Play* produced, in opposition to various currents [of opinion] that are against everything new. I have thanked him, but I have also told him that the staging was not successful since it was too material for the dream. Grabow has not strained himself but has been careless. A certain justified fear of getting the same lighting effects "as used in variety shows" kept the director from using exactly those resources we needed. So when I got to see the prologue but could not tell one actor from the other in the relative darkness, I asked for lighting from above, because I had to see to understand. I was told: "That's vaudeville." As I had not seen variety shows for thirty-five years, I did not understand the danger. And when I objected: "Try it; I can learn anywhere at all; I first learned at a circus what an unexpected effect one can get by painting the scenery on transparent fabric." This destroyed the effect of my prologue, however! The construction on stage disturbed the actors' dedication of spirit and called for endless intermissions; besides, the whole performance became "a materialization phenomenon" instead of the intended dematerialization. Now we intend to make a new attempt with *A Dream Play* at the Intimate Theater, and we are going the whole way. But instead of painted sets, which in *this case* cannot reproduce unfixed and moving mirages or illusions, we intend to seek only the effect of colors. We have, you see, discovered that red plush drapes can take on all the nuances of color, from azure blue through molten metals to purple, simply by applying varied lights. And we have decided, instead of using the colorless costumes of our time, to introduce colorful costumes from all ages, just so they are beautiful, because here in the dream there is no question of reality, so we are fully justified in preferring Beauty over Truth. On the railing we have borrowed from the Molière stage, we had intended to set up allegorical properties, indicating in a visual image the locale in which the scene could be thought to take place. For example: a couple of large seashells will indicate the nearness of the sea; a couple of cypresses will take us to Italy; two signal flags in red and blue will mean Skamsund (Foulstrand); a part of statuettes is Fagervik (Fairhaven); a bulletin board with numbers (psalms) is the church; and the laurel wreaths will mean the commencement, a blackboard and an eraser will be the school, etc.

The costumes are from all ages, which is perfectly suitable for a dream, in which time and space have ceased to exist. I have presented these comments ahead of time so that the public will not think we have used just any old thing because of lack of scenery.

*

There is a whole literature about the revival of the theater, and from it I want to single out Gordon Craig's attractive periodical *The Mask* first of all. Craig has some peculiar ideas about the theater. He wants to have everything presented through the eye, so that the text is to be subordinated. He paints costumes and stylizes them, works with lighting effects and even with masks.

Georg Fuchs has published *Die Schaubühne der Zukunft* (*Das Theater*, Volume XV). He is strongest in what he says negatively and can therefore be read, but his positive proposals are vague. His stage is very small, lacks depth, since he finds perspective unreasonable, etc. He seems to want a return to antiquity, and to believe that the theater is not to be permanent but is to play only festival plays on exceptional occasions.

One can read a lot about theater, too, in *Die Fackel*, published by Karl Krause in Vienna.

*

Since the beginning of the Intimate Theater can be said to be Falck's successful production of *Lady Julie* (at the Folk Theater) three years ago, it is understandable that the young director feels he has been influenced by the Preface, which recommended that one try to achieve reality. But I wrote that twenty years ago, and, if I do not exactly need to attack myself on that point, [I may say] that all that scribbling about stage properties was unnecessary. The play itself, which in its day was received as an act of a villain in Sweden, has now had time to be accepted, and August Palme,[15] who resurrected it, noticed that it was a *Figaro* which contained more than an unusual seduction story. In it are the struggle between races and classes, the renewal of society from the roots up, the patrician and the plebeian, woman's foolish attempt to free herself from nature, the whole raging modern revolt against tradition, customs, and common sense.

Falck, faithful to the program, had [as his set] a kitchen complete in all details, which I got to see later on for the first time, however. And everything was as it should be!

The first production I saw at the Intimate Theater was that of *The Pelican*. I was amazed by a room in *l'art nouveau* style, with furniture in keeping. That was both proper and beautiful, but there was something else in that room; there was atmosphere, a white fragrance of sickroom and nursery, with something green on a bureau as if placed there by an invisible hand. "I'd like to live in that room," I said, though one sensed the tragedy that would play its last act with classic tragedy's most horrible motif: innocently suffering children, and the humbug mother Medea.

It was a beautiful production in which modern art was brought on stage, and it has probably been criticized severely by enlightened critics.

Afterward I saw *The Burned House*. The stylized apple tree screamed against the utterly realistic wooden house, and some stage properties opposed the attempt to modernize in the style of *Studio*. But there was atmosphere, too.

Then came *Storm!* For the first time the Intimate Theater's stage showed itself inadequate for construction on stage. I warned Falck, but he tried, and did not succeed in Acts I and III, but in Act II he had created a room in which one could live and enjoy living; there was a home that was more comfortably homelike than any I had ever seen on stage before. Ordinary rooms are most often unsuccessful; that is mainly because of the impossibility of including windows and tile stoves. Falck had eliminated both windows and tile stove, and had produced something finished, enclosed, which gave the effect of tranquillity and comfort. No false (warped) window arches with fly nets in them, no leaning tile stoves with dark cracks between the tiles! Only a buffet, a piano, and a dining table, but so [arranged] that one did not miss the rest, which often clutter and become clothes trees. It was successful in its simple beauty, and with it we had left the Preface and *Lady Julie*. I discovered, too, that Falck *was* a director, had the gift of inventiveness, was a painter, had taste, and could produce on stage what one seldom gets: atmosphere. That is a synonym for poetry! The first and last acts were not unsuccessful for any reason other than lack of space; but we ought to have simplified, cut, and not let ourselves in for construction on stage.

The Ghost Sonata immediately revealed itself as impossible to stage as it was. Falck, however, liked difficulties, but did not overcome them, because they could not be overcome. The play belonged to our theater, though, and we'll try again but in simplified form.

Falck created a masterpiece in producing *Lord Bengt's Wife*. His Hall of Knights would have honored a large theater: simple and beautiful, the costumes tasteful in beautiful soft colors that harmonized.

Then came the miracle: *Queen Christina,* accompanied by the discovery that scenery can be dispensed with without making the production either monotonous or shabby. With that we had searched our way through our apprenticeship year, and now we are going to use what we have learned!

*

Since I wrote the above, Falck has made a new attempt at simplifying the scenery and has succeeded. That was with *There Are Crimes and Crimes.* The sides painted as columns in neutral tints and unknown style remained throughout the whole play, and he used backdrops, little furniture and properties, as well as lighting. I attended a private performance for artists. After the play was over, I asked if the columns had disturbed the general impression. Several people did not understand what I meant, because they had not noticed the novelty. And I could not say if the columns were still there in the night café or if the room was closed. That is how little scenery signifies in a play where the content can capture the attention of the audience completely.

Falck has made yet another successful attempt at simplification — with the abstract plush draperies in *Swanwhite*, not using the available newly painted scenery. An effect that I thought was wonderful was achieved by means of only lights and a simple color tone.

The Concept of Stylizing etc.

I know what is meant by stylizing on the stage, but I cannot put it into words until I have thought it over a little.

The term became known after Maeterlinck's first splendid dramas (not after *Monna Vanna* when he had deteriorated).

Maeterlinck's secret is this. His characters are active on a plane other than the one on which we live; he is in communication with a higher world; his spiritual powers are so refined that he senses (his fate), prophesies his fall (his deterioration). "It was destined." By means of writing he tries to get away from what must happen, but that does not help; he prays in [the spirit of] the sweat and blood of Gethsemane. Let this cup be taken from me! But it did not help; he had to be crucified. — I have not understood why innocent little children are tortured in his dramas; perhaps they represent the innocent sufferers.

When Maeterlinck appeared, about 1890, in the last days of naturalism, I read a review of one of his plays. We know, of course, that when a stupid ass reviews the content of a clever play even the cleverest elements sound stupid! The review struck me as satire or pure rubbish. Afterward in Paris when I read Maeterlinck, he was like a closed book for me — I was so

thoroughly immersed in materialism. But I felt a certain uneasiness and a regret about not being able to grasp what he had
to say, the beauty and profundity of which I sensed and longed
for as one of the damned longs for the company of good people.

Only after I had passed through my Inferno years (1896–99)
did I get hold of Maeterlinck again, and then he came like a
newly discovered country and a new time.

He called his finest plays marionette plays and considered
them unproducible on the stage. By marionettes he does not
mean what we call *kasper* but figures of real proportions manip-
ulated by means of wires, which make possible such scenes as
the black dog's or the little lamb's, and even leads to an angu-
larity of movement that seems conventional.

This fact made people feel that they had to have a type of
performance different from the usual when they put on Maeterlinck's plays in the theater. It was not enough to depart from
reality; they had to do something else, too. That became something of the abstract gestures of opera or those of the old tragedies as they still survived at Théâtre Français.

I cannot get anything else out of the new concept, "stylizing,"
than what we offer in a high or exalted style. And that was
appropriate here.

But those who are led astray by every "new direction" to want
to discard what is justified in other directions make a mistake.
For a naturalistic play can be presented only naturalistically.
With increasing restraint, however, as good taste turns against
the tasteless.

I believe, however, that Maeterlinck is best unperformed. His
Inferno world is in the spirit of Swedenborg, but there is light
in the darkness, beauty in the suffering, and sympathy with
everything that lives. But it is [a world of] despair, disaster,
heaviness.

If one already has Materlinck as part of the repertory, one should preferably forget the term, "stylizing," and instead ask the actors to try to gain entrance into this poet's marvelous world, where everything has proportions, tones, and light other than we have in this world. If the actor can do this, he will have succeeded; otherwise, he will remain outside, the world [of Maeterlinck] closed to him. It cannot be learned, it can perhaps be acquired, but as part of the price: a wandering through Inferno.

The term, "stylizing," may as well disappear; we have the older concepts "high style" and "exalted style," and we understand those well.

*

History and the folk ballads have always and rightly been considered common property, which the writer has had the right to use and exploit. Fryxell, Afzelius, and Starbäck have been used for the purpose most advantageously since they have included more little human details than the dry chronicles and official histories. Fryxell narrates in a lively fashion with a flowing style, but rather colorlessly. Starbäck (and Bäckström) have amassed an amazing amount of material, badly worked up and not well arranged, so that one has to go at it with a drill and pickax to get at its jewels.

So: Starbäck's (and Bäckström's) *Stories Out of Swedish History*, which are not stories but make up a rather dry history of Sweden, is common property, and from it I have taken most of the raw material for my historical dramas. But now there are enlightened critics who have never seen Starbäck's *History* and who believe it is a matter of his novels and *novelle*.

If a person takes someone else's novel or *novella* and dramatizes it, his doing so is no longer considered theft exactly but a secondary adaptation, and can lead to legal action as when Verga sued the person who dramatized *Cavalleria Rusticana*.

In Charlotte Birch-Pfeiffer's[16] time this procedure was approved. She took the still living Victor Hugo's *The Hunchback of Notre-Dame*, George Sand's *Syrsan*, Currer Bell's *Jane Eyre*, and many more, close to a hundred, without being criticized so far as I know but with great profit.

Nowadays this practice of taking someone else's artistically developed plot is considered at least petty larceny, because the perpetrator takes over action, characters, and scenes, quite often the dialogue itself.

Some years ago an Italian comedy by a Swede was presented at the Royal Theater. In the printed text it was stated which story had been adapted, but I do not remember if it was stated on the playbill.

August Blanche[17] usually took foreign plays and adapted them in Swedish. In Klemming's *Sveriges Dramatiska Litteratur* (*Sweden's Dramatic Literature*) are listed the originals of most of Blanche's plays, and to start with Blanche used to insert, "based on a foreign idea," or something like that, but in the course of the years the acknowledgment of source disappeared and the plays were simply labeled Blanche's. Such a procedure is no longer approved but is labled literary theft. Hedberg[18] and Jolin,[19] too, used this method occasionally, and after Nestroy's *Lumpacius Vagabundus* had been rechristened Andersson, etc., we got the expression "destroying a foreign original for our stage."

The concept of literary rights has developed somewhat since then but not so much the people cannot take a Hans Christian Andersen story and "destroy" it for the stage, spiced with a little cancan, [Ibsen's] *Peer Gynt*, and [my] *The Keys to Heaven*, and still get praise from enlightened critics.

The other day I had a visitor who said this about the fool in

Earl Birger of Bjälbo: "You should have let him sit quietly on a stone just moving his tongue as Wamba does in *Ivanhoe*."

I wondered what the man meant: if he wanted me to copy Wamba, he was admitting I had *not* copied him. But he wanted to insinuate I had.

When I wrote *Earl Birger of Bjälbo*, I proceeded as usual. I read Starbäck's history, because I don't know that he has written a novel about Earl Birger. I made the major characters live by taking blood and nerves out of my own life, so that they became mine and are my own property. But in order to "capture a mood and atmosphere" and to move back into a remote time, I did as I usually do in my historical dramas: I read Walter Scott. There was no Earl Birger [in Scott], but there were ingredients, decorations, and stage properties for the Middle Ages, tournaments and inspection of weapons, because Walter Scott was a great antiquarian, and *Ivanhoe* is particularly rich in antiquities. But there is also the fool Wamba, about whom I do not remember anything more than his losing his collar. I read [the novel] last fall, but ten years earlier I had intended to include the voluntary slaves in *The Saga of the Folkungs*, and I imply in that play that Birgitta's brother was a hostage who had given himself away as security for a major loan, but I didn't get room in the play for that character but let King Magnus summarily set free a host of slaves. When *Earl Birger of Bjälbo* was taking shape I was weary of exalted rhetoric on stage, and in my plan the idea was that the fool should at the conventional court say what the others did not dare to say. But my fool — unlike other fools (Shakespeare used the term clown) — got a past, a characterization as a representative of the voluntary slaves, and became a living representative of Earl Birger's achievements in law, corresponding to the abolition of imprisonment for debt. The first sketch of my fool I had made thirty years before in *The Secret of the Guild*; there, too, the fool has a past and is not simply a

clown. Now when I ran across Wamba's collar, I found it picturesque and borrowed that detail, with an author's right, because I could show what otherwise would have to be declaimed.
The fool in *Earl Birger of Bjälbo* is my property, sketched in
1880 in *The Secret of the Guild*, and anyone who wants to rob
me of my property I'll call bluntly: *Thief!*

The earl is mine, too. He is no instructor in declamation but
a politician and an intrigant as he was in life.

In *Gamla svenska öden* (ca. 1880) I considered the celibate
priests thoroughly, and, if I borrow from myself, I am not taking anything from anyone else.

I have not taken any character from Walter Scott or any other
writer: I have had enough living models about me.

I have borrowed a collar, that's all, and I can return that on
demand without my drama's losing anything because of that
bagatelle! And it is a loan!

On the other hand the following is theft! I publish a play; it
is not performed, but the director commissions a similar one
arranged as "a street ballad" [i.e., popularized or vulgarized],
and that is performed. When my original is ultimately performed, I suspect it will be "advertised" as a copy of the copy.

This is petty larceny: I let the members of a literary circle
read a play of mine that has been rejected, a play with new,
strong motifs, a play which later proves very effective. A year
afterward I read a novel with the same motifs, but distorted, of
course.

Or: I read a play, the basis of which is my artistic concept in
There Are Crimes and Crimes, and in which the dialogue is
like that in Sudermann's *Sodoms Ende*, and in which I find
speeches out of my latest *Blue Book*. When neither threats nor
promises can persuade me to admire this "masterpiece," people
call me envious and I have to be liquidated.

Or this: I'm careless enough to relate the idea of a play I'm thinking of writing — to another writer. He goes home and writes the play, gets it performed of course, since it is weak, and he invites me to the opening performance!

*

I mentioned the folk ballads (anonymous) as being common property.

For a long time I had thought of skimming our most beautiful ballads about knights (not the ugly ones which are sung at Skansen[20] and Hasselbacken[21]) and use them in plays. Then Maeterlinck got in my way, and under the influence of his marvelous marionette plays, which were not intended for the stage, I wrote my Swedish stage play: *Swanwhite*. One can neither steal nor borrow from Maeterlinck; one can hardly become his disciple (before *Monna Vanna*), because there is no free admission into his world of beauty; but one can be inspired to hunt for gold in one's own refuse heaps, and in that I admit my ties with the master.

Under Maeterlinck's influence then, and borrowing his divining rod, I searched in such sources as Geijer,[22] Afzelius, and Dybeck's *Runa*.[23]

There were princes and princesses to excess. I had already discovered the stepmother motif as a constant (in twenty-six Swedish folktales); awakening from death was there (and is found in Queen Dagmar's story, too). So I put everything into the separator with maidens and the Green Gardener and the young king, and so the cream was tossed out, and in this way it has become mine!

But it's mine, too, because I've lived that tale in my fantasy! One spring, during the winter!

NOTES

FIRST LETTER

1. Martin Lamm (1880–1950), professor at the University of Stockholm (1919–45), set such a pattern of Strindberg research in Sweden through the major works, *Strindbergs dramer* (2 vols.; 1924, 1926); *Strindberg och makterna* (1936); and *August Strindberg* (2 vols.; 1940, 1942; 2nd ed., 1948). Lamm's *Det moderna dramat* (1948), one chapter of which is devoted to Strindberg, was translated as *The Modern Drama* (1953).

2. See Harry Jacobsen's *Digteren og Fantasten* (1945) and *Strindberg og hans første Hustru* (1946).

3. See August Falck's *Fem år med Strindberg* (1935).

4. See Stellan Ahlström's *Strindbergs erövring av Paris* (1956).

5. Carl Kylberg, Swedish artist and friend of Strindberg, provided two copies of Arnold Böcklin's famous painting. See also the end of *The Ghost Sonata* for further evidence of Strindberg's fascination with this particular painting by the Swiss artist (1827–1901).

6. Falck, *Fem år med Strindberg*, p. 22.

7. *Strindberg och teater: Bref till medlemmar af gamla Intima teatern från August Strindberg* (1918) contains a substantial number of such Strindberg letters to actors at the Intimate Theater. The introduction and the commentaries in the volume were written by August Falck.

8. Falck, *Fem år med Strindberg*, pp. 358–59.

9. *Strindberg och teater.*

10. Although Strindberg was proposed as a candidate for the Nobel Prize in literature, he had no chance of getting it. One of his

most violent enemies, Carl David af Wirsén, was secretary of the Swedish Academy, which awards the prize. Admirers throughout Sweden made a collection which got the appropriate title, the Anti-Nobel Prize.

11. *Strindberg och teater.*

12. Björnstjerne Björnson (1832–1910), Norwegian leader as well as dramatist, poet, writer of prose fiction, and winner of the Nobel Prize in literature in 1903, influenced Strindberg as he admits through such historical dramas as *Mellem slagene* (*Between the Blows*, 1857) and at least indirectly through such realistic dramas as *Redaktören* (*The Editor*, 1875). See any biography of Strindberg for an account of the relationship between the two.

13. André Antoine (1858–1943) founded the experimental Théâtre Libre in Paris in 1887; among the plays he presented as examples of realism-naturalism were Strindberg's *The Father*, *Lady Julie*, and *Creditors*.

14. In 1889 Strindberg tried to start a Scandinavian experimental theater; unfortunately, the attempt lasted only through two performances, one in Copenhagen, the other in Malmö. The importance of the attempt is probably two-fold: Strindberg's intensified interest in getting a theater in which his plays could be performed, and the three one-act plays he wrote for the theater: *Pariah*, *The Stronger*, and *Samum*. See note 2.

15. Aurelien Lugné-Poe (1869–1940) founded his Théâtre de l'Oeuvre in Paris in 1893. See Stellan Ahlström's *Strindbergs eröv-ring av Paris* (1956) for detailed information about the production of Strindberg plays both at this theater and at the Théâtre Libre.

16. Otto Brahm (1856–1912) founded his Freie Bühne in Berlin on the model of the Théâtre Libre in 1889; from 1894 to 1904 he headed the Deutsches Theater.

17. Max Reinhardt (1873–1943), the proprietor and director of the Deutsches Theater (1905–20 and 1924–32), was important to Strindberg's dramaturgy not only because of his little theater (Kleines Theater, 1902–4) but also because of guest performances of Strindberg plays in 1915, 1917, and 1920. See Gunnar Ollén's *Strindbergs dramatik* (1962) for detailed information.

18. Reinhardt's *Kammerspiel-Haus* opened in 1906; he was in charge of the theater until 1924.

19. The Hebbel Theater in Berlin.

20. Rachel (Elisa Felix, 1820–58) was probably the outstanding French actress of her day. In addition to creating roles at the Comedie Française, she toured Europe and the United States.

21. What Strindberg had in mind was the tendency on the part of many Stockholmers and some other Swedes to use extremely easy colloquial pronunciation, one practical effect of which was to make the words less distinct.

22. The old or so-called Gustav III's Opera House was used from 1782 to 1891 for both opera and drama. The present Royal Opera House opened in 1898.

23. Strindberg's *A Blue Book* (4 vols.; 1907–12) is an astonishing and fascinating four-volume set of relatively brief commentaries on all sorts of matters that interested him in his final years, including drama, religion, science, philology, and himself.

24. Johanne Luise Heiberg (1812–90) was probably the greatest Danish actress of her time.

25. Adam Oehlenschläger (1779–1850) was the leading Danish romantic poet and dramatist. While Strindberg was a student at Uppsala he wrote an essay on Oehlenschläger, and some of his earliest plays were influenced by the Dane's works.

26. Ludvig Holberg (1684–1754), the Danish-Norwegian author, is nowadays particularly appreciated for his fine comedies. He was also a historian, a satirist, and a poet. The four plays Strindberg mentions are among Holberg's best comedies.

SECOND LETTER

1. Georg Brandes' *William Shakespeare* was published in 1895–96. The Brandes book that had the greatest influence on Strindberg's interpretation of Shakespeare was *Kritiker og Portraiter* (1870), in which Brandes stressed Shakespeare's realism.

2. Karl Bleibtreu (1859–1928), German dramatist, novelist, and literary historian and critic, was among the key figures in charge of the Deutsche Bühne, Berlin, in 1890–91. His works, *Der wahre*

Shakespeare and *Die Lösung der Shakespeare-frage,* were published in 1905 and 1907, respectively.

3. Friedrich Christian Diez (1794–1876), the German authority on Romance philology, was primarily responsible for the idea that the study of language should be comparative and historical.

4. During his stay in Lund late in 1898 and well on into 1899, Strindberg resumed his private study not only of Shakespeare but of Swedish history.

5. Goethe's *Wilhelm Meister* (*Wilhelm Meisters Lehrjahre,* 1795–96; *Wilhelm Meisters Wanderjahre,* 1821–33).

6. Lorentz Dietrichson (1834–1917), Norwegian teacher, lecturer, author, and scholar, was a highly influential docent in literature at the University of Uppsala from 1860 on and was a member of the staffs at other Swedish institutions. In 1875 he became a professor at the university in (then Christiania) Oslo. His popular history of art, *Det skönas värld* (*The World of Beauty*) appeared in 1872–79 (two volumes).

7. See Amundsen's *Die neue Shakespearebühne des Müncher Hoftheaters* (1911).

8. For the story of David, Uriah, and Bathsheba, see II Sam. 11.

9. See the list of productions of Strindberg plays at the Intimate Theater, pp. 12–13.

10. Israel Gollancz (1864–1930), professor at the University of London, prepared the Temple edition of Shakespeare's works.

11. Mr. S. is Emil Schering, Strindberg's German translator.

12. For detailed information about all these matters, see *The Vasa Trilogy: Master Olof, Gustav Vasa, Erik XIV* (1959).

13. *Hávamál,* one of the major poems in the Old Icelandic *Poetic Edda,* contains epigrammatic and proverblike statements about the art of living, stressing, among other things, the values of hospitality, knowledge, alertness, and moderation.

14. See note 23, chap. i.

15. The influence on Strindberg of the German philosophers Arthur Schopenhauer (1788–1860) and Eduard von Hartmann (1842–1906) has been considered by Martin Lamm and other Strindberg scholars.

16. Giordano Bruno (1548–1600), the Italian ex-monk and philosopher who was burned at the stake as a heretic.

17. Strindberg disliked the great eighteenth-century Swedish poet Carl Michael Bellman (1740–95). The Bellman poem he refers to here is "Fredmans Epistel n:o 23" ("Ach du min moder!"); in the song, the drunken Fredman lies in the gutter speculating about how much better it would have been if he had never been conceived.

18. *Fliegende Blätter*, the German humorous weekly published in Munich from 1845 on, used the services of prominent cartoonists and other artists.

19. Strindberg may be referring to Sarah Bernhardt (1844–1923), who was in Sweden in 1883 and 1902.

20. Isaac D'Israeli (1766–1848), scholar and writer, published collections of literary and cultural studies in *Curiosities of Literature* (6 vols.; 1791–1823).

21. Anna Flygare, Manda Björling, and Helge Wahlgren were members of the original company of thirteen actors of the Intimate Theater.

THIRD LETTER

1. The translation of the sonnets by Professor Carl Rupert Nyblom (1832–1907) of the University of Uppsala appeared as *William Shaksperes sonetter* in 1871.

2. Ludvig Josephson (1832–99) was manager of the New (or Swedish) Theater in Stockholm from 1879 to 1887. See my *Strindberg and the Historical Drama* (Seattle, Wash., 1963), p. 53.

3. Harald Molander (1858–1900) was a director of the Swedish Theater in Helsingfors (1886–93) and of the Swedish Theater in Stockholm (1898–1900).

4. Emil Grandinson (1863–1915), a writer and director, served as a director at the Dramatic Theater (1900–10).

5. Gustaf Fredrikson (1832–1921) was director of the Royal Dramatic Theater (1888–98 and 1904–7). Fredrikson's tastes in theater were largely those of contemporary French drama (Sardou, for example).

6. In 1873–74, Strindberg while on the staff of *Dagens Nyheter* reviewed the production of plays at Stockholm theaters.

7. Fritz von Uhde (1848–1911) was a German painter whose paintings with Biblical motifs became widely known.

8. Adam Oehlenschläger's tragedy inspired by the Scandinavian ballad, "Axel and Valborg," which concerns two lovers. Because they were christened at the same time, they were prevented from marrying by the church.

9. Strindberg's role as director apparently was never clearly defined. Even in the productions of *The Father* and *Swanwhite*, Falck took the final responsibility.

10. The theater opened under the name Nya teatern (The New Theater) in 1875; its name was changed to Svenska teatern (The Swedish Theater) in 1888.

11. In 1888 Parliament (Riksdagen) withdrew its financial support and, as Strindberg says, rented its theater to Gustaf Fredrikson (see note 5 above) and Nils Personne (1850–1928), actor, theater manager, and theater historian.

12. Albert Ranft (1858-1938), frequently called "Stockholm's theater king," owned the Swedish Theater in Stockholm from 1898 to 1925 and Stora teatern in Göteborg from 1899 to 1917. In addition to these he controlled Djurgårds teater (1892–1917), the Vasa Theater (1895–1928), Södra teatern (1900–26), Oscar's Theater (1906–26), and the Royal Theater (1908–10). He also organized tours of the provinces.

13. Oscar's Theater (Oscarsteatern) opened in 1906. Its theater fare has consisted mainly of operettas and musicals.

14. In 1901 Parliament authorized a lottery, the proceeds of which were to be used primarily for the construction of a new royal theater building. When the theater (the present Dramaten) was completed, it was dedicated on February 19, 1908, with the production of Strindberg's verse *Master Olof* (published, 1877).

15. No other Swedish king has done so much for the theater as Gustaf III (reigned, 1771–92). Largely because of his support, the Royal Swedish Opera could move into its own house in 1782. In 1788, the opera and the theater together got the name Royal Swedish Theater (Kungliga svenska dramatiska teatern).

16. In 1907, Gustaf Birger Anders Holm (1845–1910) became vice-

chairman of the board of the corporation building the new Dramatic Theater.

17. Knut Michaelson (1841–1915), playwright, businessman, and director, was manager of the Dramatic Theater from 1907 to 1910.

18. Henning Berger's *Syndafloden* (1908) is a three-act play with its setting in a large city on the Mississippi. The title of the play may be translated *The River of Sin*.

19. The Östermalm Theater (Östermalmsteatern) was open from 1888 to 1913; it was used mainly for the production of operettas.

20. The Vasa Theater, which opened in 1886, has been used mainly for the production of comedies.

21. The People's House (Folkets hus teater, opened in 1902, concentrated mainly on the production of folk comedies and revues.

22. Under construction from 1891 on, the new Royal Opera House opened in 1898.

23. Otto Hack Roland Printzsköld (1846–1930), courtier and government official, became chairman of the board of the royal theaters in 1898 and chairman of the board of Dramaten in 1909.

24. Erik Vilhelm af Edholm (1817–97) was the managing director of the royal theaters from 1866 to 1881.

25. The Royal Dramatic Theater (popularly called Dramaten) has a façade of light marble.

FOURTH LETTER

1. Carl Jonas Love Almqvist (1793–1866), one of Sweden's greatest and most revolutionary poets and writers of prose fiction, produced *Törnrosens bok* (*The Book of the Wild Rose*) in several volumes between 1833 and 1851. What Strindberg probably had in mind were such matters as Almqvist's attacks on the church and conventional morality.

2. Emil Schering.

3. Hagberg in his notes on *Macbeth* quotes J. Hunter (1783–1861), the English antiquary who wrote works on Shakespeare in 1839 ("A Study of *The Tempest*") and 1845 (*New Illustrations of Shakespeare*).

4. Richard Bergström, Strindberg's friend and colleague at the Royal Library, translated and adapted Eduard Hülsmann's German

work on Shakespeare as *Shakspeare och hans dramatiska arbeten: En ledtråd till orientering* (Stockholm, 1865).

5. Hagberg says: "Malone criticizes the author because he just had the maid say it's almost twelve o'clock, but now lets it strike three. The criticism is unfair; time goes faster in a play than on the face of a clock. I say this because inexperienced dramatists not infrequently commit the mistake of dealing with drama time as if it were ordinary time."

6. August Lindberg (1846–1916), one of Sweden's greatest actors of all time, toured Sweden giving readings of *The Tempest* in the early years of this century. Lindberg and Strindberg were friends.

7. Henrik Schück (1855–1947), professor first at Lund and then at Uppsala, was one of Sweden's most productive scholars. His *William Shakspere: Hans lif och värksamhet* appeared in 1883–84 and his *Shakspere och hans tid* in 1916.

8. Cesare Lombroso (1836–1909), the Italian psychiatrist, whose *L'uomo delinquente* (1876) was important in the development of modern criminal psychology. Sir William Crookes (1832–1919), aside from his achievements as a physicist and chemist, tried to study scientifically the "phenomena of spiritualism."

9. *When We Dead Awaken* (*Når vi døde vågner: En dramatisk epilog*, 1899).

10. *Näcken* or *strömkarlen,* who frequently appears in Swedish literature, is thought of as an old, bearded river sprite and master fiddler who sings about his longing for salvation. See *The Crown Bride* for Strindberg's use of this figure out of folklore.

11. L. Edman was Strindberg's instructor (*adjunkt*) in English at the University of Uppsala.

12. Georg Gervinus (1805–71), German politician, historian, and scholar, published his four-volume study, *Shakespeare*, in 1849–50.

13. Otto Lindblad (1809–64), composer and choir director.

14. Jakob Böhme (1575–1624), the German philosopher and shoemaker who believed that everything positive must have its negative opposite in order to be revealed.

15. Felix Mendelssohn-Bartholdy (1809–47) composed his overture to *A Midsummer-Night's Dream* in 1826 and then in 1843 sup-

plemented that with several other compositions, including the famous wedding march.

16. Gertrud Eysoldt was an actress at the Deutschen Theater from 1905 on.

17. Emanuel Swedenborg (1688–1772), scientist, mystic, and religious leader, influenced not only Strindberg and many other Swedish writers but such foreign authors as Goethe, Balzac, Coleridge, Carlyle, the Brownings, and Emerson.

18. The Swedish Academy, founded in 1786 by King Gustav III, controls not only the award of the Nobel Prize in literature but a great many other less well-known prizes. Strindberg's relationship with the academy was, to say the least, hardly cordial.

19. Karl Vilhelm August Strandberg (1818–77), poet and critic, translated several of Lord Byron's works, including *Don Juan* (1857–65).

20. "Joachim uti Babylon," one of Bellman's most popular songs, is a Biblical travesty based on the apocryphal Book of Susanna. "November den femtonde" is a Bellman drinking song ("Fredmens sång n:o 48: om handlingarne rörande Bacchi konkurs").

21. Par Bricole is a Stockholm club, originally organized as an order designed for bacchanalian entertainment and pleasure. Bellman composed songs about an imaginary order of Bacchus. Gustav III was one of Bellman's patrons.

FIFTH LETTER

1. For further information, see my *Strindberg and the Historical Drama* (Seattle, Wash., 1963).

2. Since the Church of Sweden is a state church, pupils in the Swedish schools receive instruction in Christianity. The pupils study the catechism and, at least in Strindberg's day, memorized large portions of it, including the Ten Commandments. The Swedish version of "Thou shalt not commit adultery" is *"Du skall icke göra hor."* *Hor* is the cognate of "whore."

3. See *Strindberg and the Historical Drama*, p. 190, for a brief account of the reception of *Engelbrekt* in 1901. Strindberg was justified in saying that the critics murdered his play.

4. For a discussion of this, see *Strindberg and the Historical*

Drama and the introduction to my translation of *Earl Birger of Bjälbo* (Seattle, Wash., 1956).

5. Bernhard Severin Ingemann (1789–1862), Danish poet, dramatist, and author of historical novels, was an instructor at Sorö Academy, one of Denmark's most respected educational institutions.

6. Hjalmar Hjorth Boyesen's *Goethe and Schiller: Their Lives and Works, Including a Commentary on Goethe's Faust* (New York, 1911).

7. Johan Andersson (1820–94) published his translation of Part I of *Faust* in 1853.

8. Viktor Rydberg (1828–95), one of Sweden's greatest poets and novelists, translated the first part of *Faust* (1876).

9. H. M. Melin (1805–77) translated the second part of *Faust*; it was published in 1872.

10. Arrigo Boïto (1842–1918), Italian composer whose opera *Mephistopheles* appeared in 1868 (revised, 1875).

11. Felix Weingartner (1863–1942), Austrian opera director, composer, and writer.

12. Karl Ludvig Grabow (1847–1922), stage designer at the Royal Dramatic and other Stockholm theaters.

13. Adolf Victor Castegren (1861–1914), actor and director, was a director at the Swedish Theater when Strindberg wrote these letters.

14. Sven Scholander (1860–1936), popular singer of ballads and songs, composed music to many of the songs he had on his programs in Stockholm, in the provinces, and throughout Europe. He was also a photographer and an instructor in drawing.

15. August Palme (1856–1924), actor at the Dramatic Theater from 1885 to 1921, appeared in several Strindberg plays, including *Lady Julie.*

16. Charlotte Birch-Pfeiffer (1800–68), German actress and writer, dramatized a great many works of prose fiction. See Hes's *Charlotte Birch-Pfeiffer als Dramatikerin* (1914).

17. August Blanche (1811–68), one of the most popular Swedish writers of his time, wrote a great many plays, most of which, as Strindberg says, were adaptations of foreign dramas.

18. Frans Hedberg (1828–1908), wrote both comedies and histori-

cal dramas. Many of his comedies were mere adaptations of foreign originals, but one of his historical plays, *Bröllopet på Ulfåsa* (*The Wedding at Ulfåsa*, 1865), is one of the few really good non-Strindbergian plays based on Swedish history. During Hedberg's ten years as director of the Royal Theater (1871–81), Strindberg had good reason to be aware of him. See *Strindberg and the Historical Drama*, chap. iv.

19. Johan Jolin (1818–84) adapted a number of foreign plays and wrote some that were essentially original.

20. Skansen, the famous open-air museum founded in 1891 by A. Hazelius, was designed to present representative exhibits of Swedish culture throughout the centuries. Folk singing and folk dancing are parts of Skansen's program.

21. Hasselbacken is a popular summer restaurant near Skansen.

22. Erik Gustaf Geijer (1783–1847), poet, historian, politician, and professor of history at Uppsala, collaborated with Arvid August Afzelius (1785–1871), popular historian, pastor, and folklorist, in producing the collection of Swedish folk ballads, *Svenska folkvisor från forntiden* (3 vols.; 1814–16).

23. Richard Dybeck (1811–77), folklorist and poet, published the journal *Runa* (1842–50, 1865–76), which was devoted to Swedish folklore. Dybeck was the author of the Swedish national anthem, "Du gamla, du fria."

INDEX